Uniform System of Accounts for the Lodging Industry

Uniform System of Accounts for the Lodging Industry

Tenth Revised Edition

Hotel Association of New York City
New York, New York

Hospitality Financial and Technology Professionals
Austin, Texas

American Hotel & Lodging Association
Washington, D.C.

Disclaimer

This publication is designed to provide accurate and authoritative information in regard to the subject matter covered. It is sold with the understanding that the publisher is not engaged in rendering legal, accounting, or other professional service. If legal advice or other expert assistance is required, the services of a competent professional person should be sought.

—From the Declaration of Principles jointly adopted by the American Bar Association and a Committee of Publishers and Associations.

Nothing contained in this publication shall constitute an endorsement by the American Hotel & Lodging Educational Institute (the Institute), the American Hotel & Lodging Association (AH&LA), Hospitality Financial and Technology Professionals (HFTP).or the Hotel Association of New York City (HANYC) of any information, opinion, procedure, or product mentioned, and the Institute, AH&LA, HFTP, and HANYC disclaim any liability with respect to the use of such information, procedure, or product, or reliance thereon.

©2006
By the HOTEL ASSOCIATION of NEW YORK CITY, INC.
320 Park Avenue, 22nd Floor
New York, New York 10022

Published by the
AMERICAN HOTEL & LODGING EDUCATIONAL INSTITUTE
2113 N. High Street
Lansing, Michigan 48906

With support from
HOSPITALITY FINANCIAL and TECHNOLOGY PROFESSIONALS
11709 Boulder Lane, Suite110
Austin, Texas 78726

Printed in the United States of America
    7 8 9 10 11 12 13 16 15 14 13 12

ISBN: 978-0-86612-282-5

Hospitality
Financial and
Technology
Professionals

A few words from the sponsor of this edition of the *Uniform System of Accounts for the Lodging Industry*

Hospitality Financial and Technology Professionals is the international society for financial and technology professionals in the hospitality industry. Serving the industry since 1953, HFTP provides outstanding educational programs, networking opportunities, and information resources to hospitality professionals around the world. HFTP also awards the Certified Hospitality Accountant Executive (CHAE) and Certified Hospitality Technology Professional (CHTP) designations.

The goal of HFTP is to be recognized by the global business community as the authoritative information source on finance and technology for the hospitality industry. We are reaching that goal through the following.

Invaluable Resources

- *www.hftp.org.* The HFTP Web site provides members with convenient access to industry checklists, forms, and tips; streaming video and audio educational sessions; CHAE and CHTP reviews; online meeting registration; publication archives; Job Mart; membership directory and ability for members to update their profiles; and resources for chapter leaders.

- *The Bottomline.* Produced eight times a year, HFTP's professional journal provides members with industry news covering everything from taxes and technology to HR and accounting issues.

- *Infoline.* HFTP's bimonthly newsletter notifies members of association activities on both the local and international levels, providing well-deserved recognition to chapters and individual members for their contributions to the hospitality industry.

- *Industry Partnerships.* We pride ourselves on enhancing the image of financial and technology professionals through increased visibility, support, and networking in the hospitality industry. HFTP represents members at industry meetings and associations, and has collaborated with other organizations to conduct industry research in the areas of hospitality salaries, technology, capital, and e-business.

Education and Technology

- *HITEC (Hospitality Industry Technology Exposition and Conference): www. hitec.org.* Internationally known, this conference offers industry professionals the largest, most comprehensive coverage of hospitality technology of its kind in the world. HITEC offers live demonstrations of the latest in hospitality technology, equipment, products and services, first-rate educational programs, and networking.

- *Annual Convention & Tradeshow.* More than 600 members attend the Annual Convention & Tradeshow each year to participate in information-sharing, educational sessions, and fun-filled entertainment.

- *Professional Development Seminars.* Each year, a series of specialized educational opportunities are offered to various segments of the hospitality industry, including the Club Controllers Conference, Hotel Controllers Conference, and Casino Controllers Conference.

- *Online Master's Program.* HFTP has collaborated with the University of Nevada, Las Vegas to provide an online master's degree in hospitality administration (finance or technology concentration). HFTP members are eligible for tuition discounts.

Professional Opportunities

- *Certification.* The Certified Hospitality Accountant Executive (CHAE) designation is recognized worldwide as a symbol of achievement and competence. The Certified Hospitality Technology Professional (CHTP) designation— co-sponsored with the Educational Institute—symbolizes a high level of competency and professionalism in hospitality technology. Individuals who earn these designations are respected by employers and colleagues for their high level of commitment and dedication.

- *Networking.* The Colleague Advisory Network connects members who have expressed experience on particular subjects with members who have questions in that area. In addition, local chapters around the world provide members with leadership opportunities, discussion forums, and social activities.

For more information, contact HFTP at 11709 Boulder Lane, Ste. 110, Austin, TX 78726, membership@hftp.org, 800-646-4387, fax: 512-249-1533, or visit www.hftp.org and www.hitec.org.

Contents

Preface

The first edition of the *Uniform System of Accounts for Hotels* was published in 1926 by the Hotel Association of New York City. It represented the first successful organized effort to establish a uniform responsibility accounting system for the lodging industry and one of the first such efforts in any industry.

All members of the original committees, appointed by the Hotel Association of New York City to prepare a uniform system of accounts for hotels, deserve commendation for their untiring devotion to the completion of this task. The personnel of these committees were as follows:

Proprietor's Committee

E. M. Statler, Chairman—Hotel Pennsylvania

L. M. Boomer—The Waldorf-Astoria	Julius Manger—Hotel Times Square
I. Fluegelman—12 East 86th Street	Fred A. Muschenheim—Hotel Astor
David H. Knott—Hotel Albert	Charles G. Stamm—Hotel Willard
Arthur L. Lee—Hotel McAlpin	George W. Sweeney—Hotel Commodore

Accountants' Committee

William J. Forster, CPA, Chairman

R. H. Browne	Hotel McAlpin
W. E. Dodd	Hotel San Remo
R. E. Frederickson	Hotel Astor
C. W. Kramer	Hotel Pennsylvania
E. E. Lightburne	The Waldorf-Astoria
H. M. Phelps	The Waldorf-Astoria
W. M. Ross, CPA	The Biltmore
Thomas E. Ross, CPA	The Biltmore
R. Schickler	The Plaza
F. W. Squires, CPA	Hotel Astor
C. B. Stoner	Hotels Statler Company Inc.

Accounting Societies

Chester P. Child, CPA, representing N.Y. State Society of CPAs
W. D. Cranstoun, CPA, representing American Institute of Accountants

One of the important results of the work of the Accountants' Committee was the organization of the Hotel Accountants Association of New York City. After the printing of the first edition of the manual, a Manual Committee of the Association was formed, which has been the medium through which the work of the original group has been continued. The Hotel Accountants Association of New York City became the founding chapter of the organization now known as the Hospitality Financial and Technology Professionals. The names of those who worked on previous revisions of the uniform systems can be found in each of those revisions.

In 1961, to meet the needs of its members, the American Hotel & Lodging Association appointed the National Association of Accountants to develop a uniform system of accounts for small hotels and motels. In 1979 and again in 1986, members of the Committee on Financial Management of the American Hotel & Lodging Association revised the original uniform system of accounts for small hotels to reflect the changes in terminology used in the lodging industry. The names of the committee members involved in these publications can be found in the respective editions.

In 1996, a decision was made to combine the two uniform system books into one publication, called the *Uniform System of Accounts for the Lodging Industry*. A subcommittee of the Committee on Financial Management of the American Hotel & Lodging Association, with representation from the Hotel Association of New York City and Hospitality Financial and Technology Professionals, worked to produce the new guide. The names of those involved in the publication can be found in that book.

This publication is also the result of a joint effort of the Committee on Financial Management of the American Hotel & Lodging Association and Hospitality Financial and Technology Professionals. The committee members responsible for this edition are:

W. Peter Temling, CPA, Chairman—Continental Hospitality Holdings, LLC, Inc.

Kapila K. Anand, CPA . . . . KPMG, LLP
Daniel Araujo[*] . . . . Fairmont Hotels & Resorts Inc.
John Baldante, CPA . . . . PKF, CPAs, PC
James Barnish, CHTP . . . . Gulfeagle Supply, Inc.
William J. Baumann . . . . Carlson Hotels Worldwide
Jeffrey Carter . . . . Carter Hospitality Advisors
George R. Conrade, CHA, CHE, CHTP . . . . University of Delaware
Michael K. Craft, CPA, CHAE, CHTP . . . . Peabody Hotel Group
Clyde Cruise (retired) . . . . Starwood Hotels and Resorts Worldwide
Carlos Garcia . . . . Hilton Hotels Corporation
Rachelle Johnston . . . . Smith Travel Research
Robert Kalchik . . . . Marriott International, Inc.
Francis Kwansa, Ph.D. . . . . University of Delaware
Robert Mandelbaum . . . . PKF Consulting
Bernard P. Morgan, CPA . . . . PricewaterhouseCoopers, LLP
Timothy Morrey . . . . LXR Luxury Resorts
Louis Petruzzelli, CHAE . . . . Mohonk Mountain House
Gordon Potter, Ph.D., CPA . . . . Cornell University
Neale Redington, ACA, CPA . . . . Deloitte & Touche, LLP
Randa Saleh . . . . Hyatt Hotels Corporation
Donald Walton, CHAE, CHTP (retired) . . . . Grove Park Inn and Resort, Inc.

Charles Warczak, Jr. CPA, CHA, CHTP . . . . Sunburst Hospitality Corporation
Henry A. "Buddy" Weeks, CHAE . . . . The Homestead
Melvyn M. Wilinsky, CPA . . . . Outrigger Enterprises, Inc.

*deceased

This publication is the result of cooperation between the Hotel Association of New York City, which owns the copyright to the publication, the Educational Institute of the America Hotel & Lodging Association, which has agreed to publish and distribute the work, and the Hospitality Financial and Technology Professionals.

Changes from the Ninth Revised Edition

This Tenth Revised Edition of the *Uniform System of Accounts for the Lodging Industry* contains a number of significant changes from the prior edition. These changes include some basic philosophical changes as well as content and format modifications to both the financial and operating statements.

Philosophical Changes

There are a number of fundamental philosophical changes in this Tenth Revised Edition. The first is the decision that this edition would focus on only the basic financial statements and the operating statements. As a result, Part I covers the basic financial statements, including the Balance Sheet, the Statement of Income, the Statement of Owners' Equity, and the Statement of Cash Flows. All of these statements are designed for external reporting purposes and must be prepared in accordance with generally accepted accounting principles (GAAP). Part II presents the departmental statements, which serve as the underlying basis for a new Summary Operating Statement. Part III continues the tradition of including information about ratio analysis and statistics. Deleted from this edition are sections on alternative financial statement formats, breakeven analysis, budgeting and control, guidelines for allocating expenses, and the sample chart of accounts. Sections on gaming operations and management companies have also been deleted. Part IV contains the Expense Dictionary in both alphabetical and departmental formats.

A second decision was to disallow, for external reporting purposes, alternative formats of the Summary Operating Statement, the departmental schedule presentations, and the accounts or line items shown on the Summary Operating Statement or supporting departmental schedules. Consequently, the Summary Operating Statement and each departmental schedule included in Part II designate the specific revenue and expense accounts that are approved as line items for reporting in conformity with the *Uniform System*, but the terms used may not be in accordance with GAAP. Individual properties may delete irrelevant line items, but the Tenth Revised Edition does not provide for the addition or substitution of other revenue or expense line items. Rather, properties will now have to develop a sub-account/sub-schedule to provide more detail related to a particular revenue or expense item. This sub-account/sub-schedule is then to be rolled into the appropriate line item on either the departmental schedule or the Summary Operating Statement. This method of presentation will permit external users of financial statements to compare the financial position and operational performance of a particular property with similar types of properties in the lodging industry.

Financial Statements

There are only a few changes to the Balance Sheet and no significant changes to any of the other statements in Part I. These changes reflect changes in GAAP since the

Ninth Revised Edition. Lodging-specific changes include accounting for operating equipment and reporting amounts due to or from owners, management companies, or other related entities.

Operating equipment includes china, glassware, silver, linen, and uniforms. Operating equipment that is determined to have a period of consumption of one year or less is recorded as a current asset. Operating equipment with a period of consumption of more than one year is recorded under Other Assets. Operating equipment is expensed ratably to the appropriate department expense account over its estimated useful life. On the effective date of the implementation of this edition of the *Uniform System*, a property should expense, in accordance with this Tenth Revised Edition, the balance of any remaining linen, china, glassware, silver, or uniforms on its books.

The Tenth Revised Edition requires the separation of amounts due to or from the owner, a management company, or other related entities for loans, advances for capital improvements, management fees, and other expenses or advances provided to a property. The accounts are classified as current or long term based on their payment terms, and amounts are not offset against each other unless there is a legal right to offset them.

Operating Statements

There are numerous significant changes to the format and content of the departmental statements. The overall statement, now titled the Summary Operating Statement, differs from the previous edition's Summary Statement of Income in several ways.

First, account titles have been altered to reflect typical lodging terminology, such as replacing the term "income after undistributed operating expenses" with "gross operating profit" and the term "income before interest, depreciation and amortization, and income taxes (EBITDA)" with "net operating income."

Second, the Summary Operating Statement does not link to net income, as it deducts from net operating income the property's replacement reserves to obtain adjusted net operating income. The revision committee believes that this approach is more informative for the owner or manager who is focused on "operating cash flows."

Third, the Summary Operating Statement is prepared for analytical purposes and is not in accordance with generally accepted accounting principles. It allows for only four sources of revenue: rooms, food and beverage, other operated departments, and rentals and other income. Because of problems allocating resources between food and beverage departments, a property may present the results of its food and beverage operations as a single department on a combined food and beverage schedule. Those properties desiring to continue to show food and beverage as separate departments with separate food and beverage schedules may do so, but for the Summary Operating Statement, they must combine the results into a single food and beverage schedule. The Summary Operating Statement also requires that a property combine all operated departments other than rooms and food and beverage into a single revenue line item and a single expense line item. This means that Telecommunications is no longer shown as a separate department, but is now one of the Other Operated Departments. Guidance is provided to distinguish when to present revenue and expenses on a gross basis (Other Operated Department) or net basis (Rentals and Other Income).

Finally, this Tenth Revised Edition requires that all undistributed operating expenses be classified into one of four categories: Administrative and General, Sales and Marketing, Property Operation and Maintenance, and Utilities. There is no longer an option to create separate schedules for Human Resources, Information Systems, and Security that existed in the Ninth Revised Edition; these expenses are now listed as line items under Administrative and General.

Room revenue is now divided into four parts: transient, group, contract, and other. Contract Rooms Revenue is derived from a contract with a third party for a consistent block of rooms for an extended period over 30 days. Other Rooms Revenue is defined to include no-show revenue, day use fees, late and early departure fees, and rentals of items such as rollaways and cribs. Group attrition and cancellation fees are included in Rentals and Other Income, not Other Room Revenue, and are therefore excluded from the computation of average daily rate.

The Tenth Revised Edition also develops more guidance concerning resort fees, wholesaler sales, and allowances. Resort fees and surcharges charged at either a flat amount or a percentage of the room rate are to be recorded as revenue. The revenue is allocated to all departments based on the relative value of the components included in the surcharge. Guestroom sales to wholesalers and other similar entities are recorded at the net rate received by the property for the room, exclusive of any taxes or other charges. Allowances includes only reductions in revenue due to a service problem, and not an error in posting. Errors in posting, such as posting an incorrect rate, are treated as an adjustment to revenue.

The Tenth Revised Edition also provides guidance for reporting operations derived from projects that include elements where ownership is held by a party other than the hotel owner. These projects could include timeshare, fractional, and whole ownership elements where the hotel operator may be providing hotel services for the element owners. The industry has also seen a new trend in hotel financing that has created another variant on the hotel structure. This new concept has become known as the condo hotel. Simply put, a condo hotel is a project wherein hotel developers finance new hotel projects and convert existing hotels by selling off elements of the hotel projects to third parties, while retaining key elements of the project for operational efficiency. Although the concept of a condominium project wherein owners of the individual units enter into a program for the purpose of retaining an operator to lease their units on a transient basis is not new, a purpose-built mixed-use building that combines elements of long-term ownership and transient rentals is becoming more commonplace. Another recent trend has seen developers purchasing existing hotels and then selling off the hotel units to individuals, who in turn retain the services of a hotel operator to market their units for transient rental. Regardless of the circumstances that give rise to mixed ownership of a hotel, the operator of the hotel is faced with the same issue: how to report hotel revenues and expenses and how to report rate and occupancy statistics. The Tenth Revised Edition does not deal with the timeshare and its "cousin," fractional ownership, which is covered by another publication. The

Tenth Revised Edition does, however, provide direction for reporting when a mixed-ownership project exists and operators find themselves managing certain of the units for third parties for a fee. Under generally accepted accounting principles, the revenues derived from such activities are for the account of the owner and therefore are reported on *Rentals and Other Income—Schedule 4.* The criteria for reporting rentals and other income are set forth in the discussion of Schedule 4. On the other hand, if the facts and circumstances of the relationship between the operator and the third-party owner of the unit are such that under generally accepted accounting principles the services performed for these owners result in a situation wherein the operator is required to report the revenues from the mixed ownership unit(s), that activity is properly reported in the Rooms schedule. The operating results from mixed-ownership projects should be reported in Other Operated Departments if the activity meets the criteria for reporting revenues and expenses as set forth in the discussion of *Other Operated Departments—Schedule 3* and the activity is expected to last less than one year.

Changes in the food and beverage department include the classification of food and beverage revenue sources and the format of the schedule. Food and beverage revenues are identified as coming from outlet, in room dining, banquet/catering, mini-bar, and other. Other Revenue includes audiovisual, public room rentals, cover and service charges, and miscellaneous. Total net revenue is now defined as the sum of food and beverage sales and other revenue less their respective allowances. Only one gross profit number is provided that is net of both cost of food and beverage sales and cost of other revenue.

All of the department schedules in the Tenth Revised Edition provide much more detail on expenses. Labor expenses are reported as Salaries and Wages and Bonuses and Incentives. In addition, more information is provided on payroll-related expenses. There are also more Other Expenses categories that are consistent across departments. Finally, a new schedule has been created—Employee Cafeteria.

Ratios and Statistics

The ratio and statistics section has been expanded to include added commentary regarding the use of ratios and statistics, along with a number of new ratios related to overall performance. These include ratios based on gross operating profit, income before fixed charges, and net operating income. Rooms available is defined as total rooms inventory less rooms not available for rent. Rooms not available for rent includes seasonally closed rooms, extended closed rooms, and rooms for permanent house use. Also, the calculation of occupied rooms has changed to provide consistency across measures. The numerator for the occupancy rate calculation, as well as the denominator for the average daily rate calculation, is rooms occupied. Complimentary rooms are not considered occupied rooms and thus do not affect the average daily rate and occupancy calculations.

As described under the previous heading, GAAP will dictate whether mixed-ownership activity is reported as an Other Operated Department or as Rental and Other Income. Less defined is how to deal with the operating statistics (rate and occupancy) for these types of projects. Until now, hotels have reported operating statistics for the rooms division in conformity with the criteria set forth in the statistics section of the *Uniform System of Accounts*. However, in this Tenth Revised Edition, the reporting required for mixed-ownership projects requires that supplemental statistics be developed. Accordingly, the Tenth Revised Edition provides guidance on computing rate occupancy and RevPAR statistics that takes into account the operating statistics of the hotel as well as the results from mixed-ownership units of the hotel. Further, the Tenth Revised Edition requires that the hotel project report its statistics to reporting agencies based upon the alternative statistical computation, which takes into account the totality of the hotel's operating results.

The ratios and statistics section also provides guidance for mixed condo hotel projects where it is not clear whether the entirety of the project qualifies as a hotel for statistical reporting purposes. Thus, while there is currently *no* consensus as to what constitutes a hotel, generally speaking industry analysts have suggested that if a project places at least 30 percent of its rooms in a transient hotel program and the project has the elements of a hotel in its structure, such as a hotel lobby and a front desk, the project qualifies as a "hotel" for purposes of reporting rooms statistics. In such circumstances, the guidelines set forth in Part III: Ratios and Statistics should be followed for these projects as well.

Expense Dictionary

The Expense Dictionary has been totally overhauled. The dictionary now includes two ways of looking for expense items. The first section of the Expense Dictionary shows the expense items alphabetically, followed by the department or departments to which the expense is charged and then the specific line item or account name. The second section is organized alphabetically by department and then secondly by expenses appropriate to that department. In both sections of the Expense Dictionary, many items are repeated under different names so that users can more easily find an expense item based on what they perceive the correct item name to be.

Introduction

A uniform system of accounts establishes standardized formats and account classifications to guide individuals in the preparation and presentation of financial statements. The information set forth in this uniform system is based on a consensus of senior lodging industry financial executives, public accounting authorities, representatives from industry benchmarking companies, and leading academic experts, and is intended to be consistent with GAAP. The resulting standardization established by the uniform system of accounts permits internal and external users of financial statements to compare the financial position and operational performance of a particular property with similar types of properties in the lodging industry.

Uniform System of Accounts for the Lodging Industry, Tenth Revised Edition, is divided into four parts. Part I presents the formats and explains the line items appearing on the basic financial statements produced for external users, such as lenders and stockholders. The statements include:

* Balance Sheet

* Statement of Income

* Statement of Owners' Equity

* Statement of Cash Flows

The format and level of detail for these basic financial statements should be developed to meet an owner's financial statement needs, while remaining consistent with GAAP.

Part II details the financial reports related to the operational activities of a lodging property, as shown in the Summary Operating Statement and its supporting schedules. It details the required format and explains the line items for departmental statements essential in the reporting and analyzing of operating results.

The Summary Operating Statement is not a GAAP financial statement, but rather a statement that displays operating results, including property taxes, insurance costs, and replacement reserves. Terms such as Gross Operating Profit, Net Operating Income, and Adjusted Net Operating Income, which are used in the Summary Operating Statement, are not GAAP terms, but are widely used within the hospitality industry.

The statements provided were developed with full-service lodging properties operating food and beverage outlets in mind, but can be easily adapted to other types of properties. For example, limited-service properties would delete those schedules that do not apply to their business, such as the food and beverage schedule.

Likewise, individual properties may delete irrelevant line items, but the *Uniform System* does not provide for the addition or substitution of other revenue and expense line items. Rather, if a property determines that more detailed information is required, sub-accounts/sub-schedules may be prepared. These sub-accounts/sub-schedules are then to be rolled into the appropriate line items detailed in the *Uniform System.*

Since the *Uniform System of Accounts for the Lodging Industry* is used by lending institutions and specifically cited in many management contracts, those preparing both the financial statements and the Summary Operating Statement and its supporting schedules must adhere to the prescribed statement formats and the classification of revenue and expense items if the financial statements are to be "in conformity with the *Uniform System.*"

Part III deals with financial analysis and statistics and presents a series of ratios and other information useful in analyzing the financial and operating statements in both Part I and Part II. Part IV contains the Expense Dictionary.

Format of Accounts Outside the United States

The examples and formats used throughout this book follow U.S. accounting standards for the presentation of financial statements. Users of the book outside the United States should be aware that the accounting requirements of their own jurisdictions will not necessarily follow those of the United States. The laws of other jurisdictions and the application of accounting standards may significantly affect the format and presentation of financial statements.

Part I
Financial Statements

A complete set of financial statements includes a Balance Sheet, a Statement of Income, a Statement of Owners' Equity, a Statement of Cash Flows, and Notes to the Financial Statements that amplify the information presented in the basic statements. The Balance Sheet reflects the financial position of the business by detailing the assets, liabilities, and owners' equity as of a given date. The Statement of Income presents revenues and expenses associated with operations over a given period. The Statement of Owners' Equity summarizes transactions affecting equity over a given period. The Statement of Cash Flows presents information about the operating, investing, and financing activities that affected cash over a given period.

It should be noted that the financial statements discussed in Part I and the examples presented have been developed following generally accepted accounting principles (GAAP) in the United States. There are comprehensive bases of accounting other than GAAP under which financial statements can be prepared, principally the cash basis and the income tax basis. While the usefulness of such statements is recognized, the principles and practices relating to the preparation of financial statements under these other bases of accounting are beyond the scope of this book. Should a question arise related to financial statement presentation, the principles of GAAP prevail.

Section 1
Balance Sheet

The Balance Sheet presents a listing of a business's assets and the claims to those assets, called liabilities and owners' equity, as of a given date. Assets represent those items owned by the business; liabilities represent the claims to the assets by outsiders, and owners' equity represents the claims of the owners to the assets.

The accounts appearing on the Balance Sheet may be arranged in either an account format or a report format. The account format of the Balance Sheet lists the asset accounts on the left side of the page and the liability and the owners' equity accounts on the right side of the page. The report format of the Balance Sheet lists assets, liabilities, and owners' equity in a single column. These arrangements allow the form of the Balance Sheet to reflect that either assets equal liabilities plus owners' equity or that assets minus liabilities equal owners' equity.

An illustration of the account format of the Balance Sheet follows. This illustration includes accounts applicable to many types of lodging properties. Each line item appearing on the Balance Sheet is explained in the pages that follow.

The number and types of accounts that appear on the Balance Sheet will vary according to the needs and requirements of the business. Accordingly, appropriate modification should be made to the suggested format to accommodate the individual requirements of the business, while remaining consistent with GAAP. It is important to remember, however, that similar items should be appropriately grouped and that all significant items should be reflected separately. Significant items are those that are considered material for financial statement purposes.

BALANCE SHEET

Assets

	Current Year	Prior Year
CURRENT ASSETS		
Cash		
House Banks	$	$
Demand Deposits		
Temporary Cash Investments		
Total Cash		
Restricted Cash		
Short-Term Investments		
Receivables		
Accounts Receivable		
Notes Receivable		
Current Maturities of Non-current Receivables		
Other		
Total Receivables		
Less Allowance for Doubtful Accounts		
Net Receivables		
Due To/From Owner, Management Company, or Related Party		
Inventories		
Operating Equipment		
Prepaid Expenses		
Deferred Income Taxes—Current		
Other		
Total Current Assets		
NON-CURRENT RECEIVABLES, Net of Current Maturities		
INVESTMENTS		
PROPERTY AND EQUIPMENT		
Land		
Buildings		
Leaseholds and Leasehold Improvements		
Furnishings and Equipment		
Construction in Progress		
Total Property and Equipment		
Less Accumulated Depreciation and Amortization		
Net Property and Equipment		
OTHER ASSETS		
Intangible Assets		
Cash Surrender Value of Life Insurance		
Deferred Charges		
Deferred Income Taxes—Non-current		
Operating Equipment		
Restricted Cash		
Other		
Total Other Assets		
TOTAL ASSETS	$	$

BALANCE SHEET

Liabilities and Owners' Equity

	Current Year	Prior Year
CURRENT LIABILITIES		
Notes Payable		
Banks	$	$
Others		
Total Notes Payable		
Due To/From Owner, Management Company		
or Related Party		
Accounts Payable		
Accrued Expenses		
Advance Deposits		
Income Taxes Payable		
Deferred Income Taxes—Current		
Current Maturities of Long-Term Debt		
Other		
Total Current Liabilities		
LONG-TERM DEBT, Net of Current Maturities		
Mortgage Notes, other notes, and similar liabilities		
Obligations Under Capital Leases		
Total Long-Term Debt		
OTHER LONG-TERM LIABILITIES		
DEFERRED INCOME TAXES—Non-current		
COMMITMENTS AND CONTINGENCIES		
OWNERS' EQUITY—one of the formats found on the next page		
TOTAL LIABILITIES AND OWNERS' EQUITY	$	$

Alternative Owners' Equity Presentations in the Balance Sheet

CORPORATION
Stockholders' Equity

	Current Year	Prior Year
____% Cumulative Preferred Stock, $ ____ par value, authorized ____ shares; issued and outstanding ____ shares	$	$
Common Stock, $____ par value, authorized ____ shares; issued and outstanding ____ shares		
Additional Paid-In Capital		
Retained Earnings		
Accumulated Other Comprehensive Income (Loss), Net of Income Tax		
Less: Treasury Stock, ____ shares of Common Stock, at cost		
Total Stockholders' Equity	$	$

PARTNERSHIP
Partners' Equity

	Current Year	Prior Year
General Partners	$	$
Limited Partners		
Accumulated Other Comprehensive Income (Loss), Net of Income Tax		
Total Partners' Equity	$	$

LIMITED LIABILITY COMPANY

	Current Year	Prior Year
Members' Equity	$	$
Accumulated Other Comprehensive Income (Loss), Net of Income Tax		
Total Members' Equity	$	$

SOLE PROPRIETORSHIP

	Current Year	Prior Year
Owner's Equity	$	$
Accumulated Other Comprehensive Income (Loss), Net of Income Tax		
Total Owner's Equity	$	$

ASSETS

Current Assets

This section of the Balance Sheet includes accounts that are to be converted to cash or used in operations within 12 months of the Balance Sheet date. Non-current assets (such as Non-current Receivables, Property and Equipment, and Other Assets) refer to accounts that are not expected to be converted to cash or used in operations within 12 months of the Balance Sheet date. The accounts appearing under the Current Assets section of the Balance Sheet are commonly listed in the order of their liquidity.

Cash

Cash includes Cash on Hand (House Banks), Demand Deposits, and Temporary Cash Investments. Temporary Cash Investments are those investments of a demand nature or that have maturities within 90 days at the time of purchase.

Restricted Cash

Cash that is restricted should be separately classified as current or non-current based on the purpose of the restriction. If the purpose of the restriction is to pay for capital improvements, furniture and fixtures, or portions of the debt that would be classified as long term, the cash should be classified as long term. If the cash is restricted to pay portions of the debt that are classified as current or for current expenses such as real estate taxes, the cash should be classified as current.

Short-Term Investments

Short-Term Investments are not Temporary Cash Investments, but are intended to be converted to cash or cash equivalents within a year. Short-Term Investments are, essentially, trading securities and are reflected at market value with the unrealized gain or loss recognized in the Statement of Income. The basis for valuation of such securities is disclosed in Notes to the Financial Statements.

Receivables

This line item groups Accounts Receivable and Notes Receivable. Based on the needs of the property, a supporting schedule may accompany the Balance Sheet, detailing significant items included within current receivables.

Accounts Receivable. Consists of the total amount due to the property from accounts carried in the guest and city ledgers. Accounts not expected to be collected within the next 12 months are included under Non-current Receivables. Significant credit balances are included in current liabilities under Advance Deposits or Other Liabilities, depending on the nature of the credit balance.

Notes Receivable. Includes notes that are expected to be collected within the next 12 months. Notes that are not expected to be collected within the next 12 months are included under Non-current Receivables.

Current Maturities of Non-current Receivables. Includes amounts that are expected to be collected within the next 12 months. Amounts that are not expected to be collected within the next 12 months are included under Non-current Receivables.

Other. Includes those receivables that are not either Accounts or Notes Receivable, such as Accrued Interest Receivables.

Allowance for Doubtful Accounts. Represents an allowance for the portion of current accounts and notes receivable estimated to be uncollectible. The allowance is based on historical experience, specific appraisal of individual accounts, or other accepted methods. Accounts that become uncollectible are charged to this account and recoveries of accounts previously written off are credited to it. The balance at the end of any period, however, represents the best estimate of the portion of accounts and notes receivable that will not be collected.

Due To/From Owner, Management Company, or Related Party

Due to/from accounts contain the balances due to or from the owner, a management company, or other related entities for loans, advances for capital improvements, management fees, and other expenses or advances provided to a property. The accounts are classified as current or long term based on their payment terms. For example, if a management company has made advances for capital improvements that are being repaid over a period of years or are offset against future distributions, these amounts are reflected as long term. The various due to/ from accounts are not offset against each other unless there is a legal right to offset them.

Inventories

Inventories includes the cost of merchandise held for sale and the cost of supplies used in operating the property. The cost of merchandise held for sale includes such items as food, beverages, gift merchandise, and significant tobacco products. The cost of supplies used in operating the property includes such items as cleaning supplies and guest supplies. The basis for valuing inventory is disclosed in the Notes to the Financial Statements and, if individual inventory categories are significant, they are separately stated.

Operating Equipment

Operating equipment includes linen, china, glassware, silver, and uniforms. When a property purchases operating equipment items, it must determine the period of consumption and expense the purchase over that time period. If the estimated usage of the equipment is less than one year, the item is considered a current asset and expensed ratably to the appropriate department expense account over its estimated period of consumption, not to exceed 12 months. Operating equipment items with useful lives of more than one year are treated as long-term assets and recorded under Other Assets.

Prepaid Expenses

Prepaid Expenses generally represents payments for items that will benefit future operating periods. Normally, the amounts are charged to operations based upon when the benefits are received. Examples include insurance, property taxes, rent, interest, maintenance, the unused net benefit under barter contracts, and other similar items.

Deferred Income Taxes—Current

Deferred Income Taxes—Current represents the tax effects of temporary differences between the bases of current assets and current liabilities for financial and income tax reporting purposes. For example, only the direct write-off of a bad debt is deductible for tax purposes; therefore, a provision for an Allowance for Doubtful Accounts will result in a current deferred tax asset. Deferred Income Taxes—Current is presented as net current assets or net current liabilities as circumstances dictate. The deferred tax asset must be evaluated for realization and a valuation allowance established for any portion that is not to be realized.

Other

Other current assets include items not shown elsewhere that are reasonably expected to be realized in cash or otherwise in the next 12 months. The category is normally used to capture minor items that are not separately disclosed.

Non-current Receivables

Non-current Receivables represents accounts and notes that are not expected to be collected during the next 12 months. Amounts due from owners, officers, employees, and affiliated entities are shown separately, unless insignificant. If any Non-current Receivables are estimated to be uncollectible, an Allowance for Doubtful Non-current Receivables is established using procedures similar to those described under the caption Allowance for Doubtful Accounts.

Investments

Investments generally includes debt or equity securities, whether or not they are traded in recognized markets, and ownership interests that are expected to be held on a long-term basis. Investments in marketable equity securities and debt securities, where there is not the intent and ability to hold such securities to maturity, are considered "available for sale" and are reflected at market value with unrealized gains and losses being shown, net of tax effects, as a separate component of equity. Investment in debt securities where there is the intent and ability to hold such securities to maturity are considered "held to maturity" and reflected at amortized cost. Investments in affiliated entities are shown separately, unless insignificant. Investments in entities over which the reporting entity has the ability to exercise significant influence (generally by ownership of more than 20 percent) are recorded using the equity method. The equity method requires the recording of the investor's share of the investee's operations in the income statement and an adjustment in the carrying value of the investment. The method of accounting for and the basis for valuing investments is dictated by GAAP and disclosed in the Notes to the Financial Statements.

Property and Equipment

This grouping of accounts includes owned Land; Buildings; Furnishings and Equipment; the cost of Leaseholds and Leasehold Improvements; and construction in progress. It also includes similar assets held under capital leases. If material, assets held under capital leases are separately presented on the Balance Sheet or in the Notes to the Financial Statements.

Depreciation is a method of allocating the net cost (after reduction for expected salvage value) of the individual assets or classes of assets to operations over their anticipated useful lives. There are several different methods used for depreciation, including straight-line, declining balance, and other variants. Under GAAP, the straight-line method of depreciation is preferred. Declining balance is a method of depreciation usually used for tax depreciation. The number of years chosen for the life of an asset or class of assets also varies somewhat in practice for similar items; however, the methods and the lives used should result in a reasonable allocation of the cost of the assets to operations over their useful lives.

Amorization is a method of ratably charging off to income intangible assets with a life greater than one year.

The total Accumulated Depreciation and Amortization should appear as a separate line item. This amount is subtracted from the Total Property and Equipment line to arrive at the Net Property and Equipment line. The methods of depreciation and amortization used are identified in the Notes to the Financial Statements.

GAAP requires that a long-lived asset (group) be tested for impairment whenever events or changes in circumstances indicate that its carrying amount may not be recoverable. The recoverability test is based on the estimated future cash flows that are directly associated with, and that are expected to arise as a direct result of the use and eventual disposition of, the long-lived asset (group) that is being tested. GAAP pronouncements describe how the test is to be performed. An impairment loss is recognized only if the carrying amount of a long-lived asset (group) is not recoverable and is reflected as a loss on impairment (difference between the value and the cost) in the Income Statement. The carrying amount of the asset (group) is generally not recoverable when the sum of the cash flows expected to be generated from the use of a long-lived asset (group) and its value upon disposition (undiscounted and without interest charges) is less than the carrying amount of the asset (group). If the test is not met, impairment does not exist and, therefore, no loss is recognized, even if the net book value of the asset (group) exceeds its fair value.

If a lodging operation has property and equipment held for sale, the classification of the assets and the related operations should be reflected in accordance with GAAP.

Other Assets

Intangible Assets

Intangible assets are assets that lack physical substance. Many intangible assets are readily identifiable, such as patents, trademarks, customer lists, etc. Goodwill is an unidentifiable intangible asset.

Goodwill represents the excess of the purchase price over the fair value of the net assets acquired in the purchase of a business. Goodwill is evaluated periodically for impairment and an impairment loss recognized, if necessary, based on such evaluation.

Current GAAP literature provides guidelines on the amortization of all other intangible assets.

Cash Surrender Value of Life Insurance

Some organizations purchase life insurance on the lives of key individuals. Many of these policies have a cash surrender value that is recorded as an asset. Changes in the amount of the Cash Surrender Value are reflected as adjustments to Insurance Expense.

Deferred Charges

Deferred Charges typically relates to financing activities and represents direct costs of obtaining financing such as loan fees and bond issuance costs. Such costs are usually amortized over the life of the related financing. The method and period of amortization is disclosed in the Notes to the Financial Statements.

Deferred Income Taxes—Non-current

Deferred Income Taxes—Non-current represents the tax effects of temporary differences between the bases of non-current assets and non-current liabilities for financial and income tax reporting purposes. For example, if a liability is accrued that will not be paid for an extended period and the expense is deductible only when paid for tax purposes, the accrual will result in a non-current deferred income tax asset. Deferred Income Taxes—Non-current is presented as net non-current assets or net non-current liabilities as circumstances dictate. The deferred tax asset must be evaluated for realization and a valuation allowance established for any portion that is more likely than not to be realized.

Operating Equipment

Operating equipment includes linen, china, glassware, silver, and uniforms. When a property purchases operating equipment items, it must establish the period of consumption. If the period of consumption of the operating equipment items is expected to be less than one year, the items are classified as current assets. Whether the items are categorized as current or long-term assets, operating equipment items are not depreciated, but are expensed to the appropriate department expense account. Most purchases of operating equipment are expected to be consumed within a period of one year or less. However, if a property makes a bulk purchase of china, for example, and the expected usage period is greater than one year, the usage period is appropriately stated at the longer time period.

Restricted Cash

Cash that is restricted should be separately classified as current or non-current based on the nature of the restriction. For example, if the restriction is to pay for capital improvements, furniture and fixtures, or portions of the debt that would be classified as long term, the cash should be classified as long term.

Other

Non-current items that cannot be included under other groupings, such as security deposits, initial franchise costs, and other miscellaneous or individually immaterial assets, are included under this caption. Restricted cash balances that are restricted to, for example, the acquisition of property and equipment (e.g., FF&E reserves) could also be included in this classification when such amounts are not material. The nature of these items, if material, is to be clearly indicated on the Balance Sheet or in the Notes to the Financial Statements. Amortization policies are also disclosed in the Notes to the Financial Statements.

LIABILITIES
Current Liabilities

Notes Payable

Notes Payable includes short-term notes that are payable within the next 12 months, classified on the Balance Sheet as notes due to banks and notes due to other creditors.

Due To/From Owner, Management Company, or Related Party

Due to/from accounts contain the balances due to or from the owner, a management company, or other related entities for loans, advances for capital improvements, management fees, and other expenses or advances provided to a property. The accounts are classified as current or long term based on their payment terms. For example, if a management company has made advances for capital improvements that are being repaid over a period of years or are offset against future distributions, these amounts are reflected as long term. The various due to/from accounts are not offset against each other unless there is a legal right to offset them.

Accounts Payable

Accounts Payable represents amounts due to vendors. Amounts due to concessionaires for guest charges collected by the property may be included with Accounts Payable or shown separately.

Accrued Expenses

Accrued Expenses represents expenses incurred, but not payable until after the Balance Sheet date. Each item of Accrued Expense, if material, is listed separately, either on the Balance Sheet or in the Notes to the Financial Statements. Examples include salaries and wages and related benefits, vacation pay, interest, management fees, rent, taxes other than on income, and utilities.

Advance Deposits

Advance Deposits represents amounts received that are to be applied as part of the payment for future sales of rooms, food and beverage, or other goods and services.

Income Taxes Payable

Income Taxes Payable represents the estimated obligations for income taxes.

Deferred Income Taxes—Current

Deferred Income Taxes—Current represents the tax effects of temporary differences between the bases of current assets and current liabilities for financial and income tax reporting purposes. For example, revenue recognized in the financial statements before it is taxable will result in Deferred Income Taxes—Current if it will be taxable in the next year. Deferred Income Taxes—Current is presented as net current assets or net current liabilities as circumstances dictate.

Current Maturities of Long-Term Debt

Current Maturities of Long-Term Debt includes the principal payments of mortgage notes, other notes, and similar liabilities, and the installments on capital leases due within the next 12 months.

Other

Current liabilities not included under other captions are shown here. The category is normally used to capture minor items that are not separately disclosed. Examples include the unearned portion of amounts received or charged to non-guests for the use of recreational facilities, unredeemed gift certificate sales, unclaimed wages, and the net liability under barter contracts.

Long-Term Debt

This category includes mortgage notes, other notes, and similar liabilities and obligations under capital leases that are not payable during the next 12 months.

Mortgage Notes, Other Notes, and Similar Liabilities

For this caption, the following information is disclosed either on the Balance Sheet or in the Notes to the Financial Statements:

- Interest rates
- Payment or sinking fund requirements
- Maturity dates
- Collateralization and assets pledged
- Financial restrictive covenants
- Payment and sinking fund payments required for each of the five years subsequent to the Balance Sheet date

Obligations Under Capital Leases

For Obligations Under Capital Leases, disclosure is made with regard to the future minimum lease payments for each of the five years subsequent to the Balance Sheet date and the total future minimum lease obligations, with a deduction for the imputed interest necessary to reduce the net minimum lease payments to present value.

Other Long-Term Liabilities

Long-term liabilities that do not require satisfaction within a year and are not included under other captions are included here. Examples include deferred compensation, deferred management fees, tenants' lease deposits, and accrued obligations for pension and other post-employment benefits. The nature of these items, if material, should be clearly indicated on the Balance Sheet or in the Notes to the Financial Statements.

Deferred Income Taxes—Non-current

Deferred Income Taxes—Non-current represents the tax effects of temporary differences between the bases of non-current assets and non-current liabilities for financial and income tax reporting purposes. For example, the use of accelerated depreciation for tax purposes and straight-line depreciation for financial reporting purposes will result in non-current deferred income taxes. Deferred Income Taxes—Non-current is presented as net non-current assets or net non-current liabilities as circumstances dictate.

Commitments and Contingencies

The Commitments and Contingencies caption is indicated on the Balance Sheet only to bring the reader's attention to such items. No dollar amounts are shown on the Balance Sheet. Adequate disclosure of all significant commitments and contingencies is made in the Notes to the Financial Statements. Examples include commitments for purchase contracts, employment contracts, long-term leases, management agreements, contingencies for pending or threatened litigation, and certain guarantees of indebtedness of others.

OWNERS' EQUITY

The Owners' Equity section of the Balance Sheet is presented differently for corporations, partnerships, limited liability companies, and sole proprietorships, depending upon the type of equity ownership. Balance Sheet presentation formats are shown on page 6. Examples of detailed presentations of Statements of Owners' Equity are shown in Section 3.

Corporation

Stockholders' Equity

Capital Stock. Capital Stock denotes the shares of ownership of a corporation that have been authorized by its articles of incorporation. The most prevalent classes of Capital Stock are Preferred and Common Stock. The par or stated value and the number of shares authorized and issued for each class of stock is presented on the Balance Sheet. Changes during the period should be shown in the Statement of Stockholders' Equity.

Additional Paid-In Capital. Additional Paid-In Capital includes cash, property, and other capital contributed to a corporation by its shareholders in excess of the stated or par value of Capital Stock. Changes during the period are shown in the Statement of Stockholders' Equity.

Retained Earnings. Retained Earnings represents the accumulated Net Income not distributed as dividends but retained in the business. Changes during the period are shown in the Statement of Stockholders' Equity. Negative retained earnings are generally referred to as deficits.

Treasury Stock. Treasury Stock represents the cost of the company's stock acquired by the company and not retired, and is reflected as a reduction in total Stockholders' Equity. Changes during the period are shown in the Statement of Stockholders' Equity.

Partnership

Partners' Equity

Partners' Equity represents the net equity of the partners in the partnership and is classified where appropriate as general and limited partners' equity. Changes during the period are shown in the Statement of Partners' Equity.

Contributions. Contributions include the amount of any additional assets that are invested in the business by the partners during the period just ended.

Withdrawals. Withdrawals include the amount of any assets that are taken out of the business and distributed to the partners during the period just ended.

Limited Liability Company

Members' Equity

Members' Equity represents the net equity of the members in the limited liability company and is classified where appropriate as general and limited partners' equity. Changes during the period are shown in the Statement of Members' Equity.

Contributions. Contributions include the amount of any additional assets that are invested in the business by the partners during the period just ended.

Withdrawals. Withdrawals include the amount of any assets that are taken out of the business and distributed to the partners during the period just ended.

Sole Proprietorship

Owner's Equity

The Owner's Equity of a sole proprietorship is similar to the equity of a partnership except that it represents the interest of one individual as opposed to a number of partners. Changes during the period should be shown in the Statement of Owner's Equity.

Contributions. Contributions include the amount of any additional assets that are invested in the business by the owner during the period just ended.

Withdrawals. Withdrawals include the amount of any assets that are taken out of the business and distributed to the owner during the period just ended.

Comprehensive Income (Loss)

Comprehensive Income refers to net income plus "other comprehensive income," which includes certain revenues, expenses, gains, and losses that are reported as separate components of equity instead of net income. Other comprehensive income currently includes:

- Unrealized gains and losses on available-for-sale marketable securities.

- Unrealized gains and losses that result from a transfer of a debt security to the available-for-sale category from the held-to-maturity category.

- Foreign currency translation adjustments.

- Gains and losses on foreign currency transactions that are designed and are effective as economic hedges on a net investment in a foreign entity.

- A change in the fair value of a derivative instrument that qualifies as the hedging instrument in a cash flow derivative.

- Gains and losses on inter-company foreign currency transactions that are of a long-term investment nature when the entities to the transaction are consolidated, combined, or accounted for under the equity method.

- Minimum pension liability adjustments.

Section 2
Statement of Income

The Statement of Income reflects the results of operations for a period of time. The time covered by this statement usually ends at the Balance Sheet date. When the statement reflects a net loss, the title is generally changed to a Statement of Operations.

Hospitality organizations prepare income statements for both external users (e.g., potential investors, creditors, and owners not active in managing the business) and internal users (i.e., managers of the business). These statements differ in the amount of information presented. The statement presented to external users is typically relatively brief, providing only summary detail about the results of operations.

A sample GAAP income statement for external users follows. The degree of detail presented in the statement is somewhat discretionary, although captions for revenue, expenses, interest, depreciation, and income taxes are included unless the amounts are insignificant. To the extent that any individual revenue or expense item is significant, separate disclosures are made. A format useful for analytical users such as managers operating the property, asset managers, and similarly involved parties is discussed in Part II.

STATEMENT OF INCOME

	Period	
	Current Year	**Prior Year**
REVENUE		
Rooms	$	$
Food and Beverage		
Other Operated Departments		
Rentals and Other Income		
Total Revenue		
EXPENSES		
Rooms		
Food and Beverage		
Other Operated Departments		
Administrative and General		
Sales and Marketing		
Property Operation and Maintenance		
Utilities		
Management Fees		
Rent, Property Taxes, and Insurance		
Interest Expense		
Depreciation and Amortization		
Loss or (Gain) on the Disposition of Assets		
Total Expenses		
INCOME BEFORE INCOME TAXES		
INCOME TAXES		
Current		
Deferred		
Total Income Taxes		
NET INCOME	$	$

Section 3
Statement of Owners' Equity

A separate Statement of Owners' Equity should be presented if there is significant activity in the accounts during the period. If net income or loss is the only change to the equity accounts in the period, it is permissible to reconcile the change in retained earnings at the bottom of the Statement of Income and exclude presentation of the separate owners' equity statement. The format of the owners' equity statement will depend on the type of entity. The following pages show examples of the type of presentation for corporations, partnerships, limited liability companies, and sole proprietorships.

STATEMENT OF STOCKHOLDERS' EQUITY

	Preferred Stock		Common Stock			Retained Earnings	Treasury Stock		Accumulated Other Comprehensive Income (Loss), Net of Income Taxes	Total Stockholders' Equity
	Number of Shares Outstanding	Amount	Number of Shares Outstanding	Amount	Additional Paid-in Capital		Number of Shares	Amount		
BALANCE AT BEGINNING OF PRIOR YEAR		$		$	$	$		$	$	$
Add (Deduct)										
Net Income										
Dividends Declared										
Change in Unrealized Gains (Losses)										
Net Proceeds from Sale of Stock										
Treasury Stock Acquired										
Other										
BALANCE AT END OF PRIOR YEAR		$		$	$	$		$	$	$
Add (Deduct)										
Net Income										
Dividends Declared										
Change in Unrealized Gains (Losses)										
Net Proceeds from Sale of Stock										
Treasury Stock Acquired										
Other										
BALANCE AT END OF CURRENT YEAR		$		$	$	$		$	$	$

Cumulative foreign currency translation adjustments should also be reflected in this statement.

STATEMENT OF PARTNERS' EQUITY

	General Partners	Limited Partners	Accumulated Other Comprehensive Income (Loss), Net of Income Taxes	Total
BALANCE AT BEGINNING OF PRIOR YEAR	$	$	$	$
Add (Deduct)				
Net Income				
Contributions				
Change in Unrealized Gains (Losses)				
Withdrawals				
Other				
BALANCE AT END OF PRIOR YEAR	$	$	$	$
Add (Deduct)				
Net Income				
Contributions				
Change in Unrealized Gains (Losses)				
Withdrawals				
Other				
BALANCE AT END OF CURRENT YEAR	$	$	$	$

Cumulative foreign currency translation adjustments should also be reflected in this statement.

STATEMENT OF MEMBERS' EQUITY

	Members	Accumulated Other Comprehensive Income (Loss), Net of Income Taxes	Total
BALANCE AT BEGINNING OF PRIOR YEAR	$	$	$
Add (Deduct)			
Net Income			
Contributions			
Change in Unrealized Gains (Losses)			
Withdrawals			
Other			
BALANCE AT END OF PRIOR YEAR	$	$	$
Add (Deduct)			
Net Income			
Contributions			
Change in Unrealized Gains (Losses)			
Withdrawals			
Other			
BALANCE AT END OF CURRENT YEAR	$	$	$

Cumulative foreign currency translation adjustments should also be reflected in this statement.

STATEMENT OF OWNER'S EQUITY

	Owner	Accumulated Other Comprehensive Income (Loss), Net of Income Taxes	Total
BALANCE AT BEGINNING OF PRIOR YEAR	$	$	$
Add (Deduct)			
Net Income			
Contributions			
Change in Unrealized Gains (Losses)			
Withdrawals			
Other			
BALANCE AT END OF PRIOR YEAR	$	$	$
Add (Deduct)			
Net Income			
Contributions			
Change in Unrealized Gains (Losses)			
Withdrawals			
Other			
BALANCE AT END OF CURRENT YEAR	$	$	$

Cumulative foreign currency translation adjustments should also be reflected in this statement.

Section 4
Statement of Cash Flows

The Statement of Cash Flows summarizes the change in Cash and Temporary Cash Investments over the same period of time as that covered by the Statement of Income. Temporary Cash Investments are readily convertible investments with a maturity of less than three months at the time of purchase. The change in Cash and Temporary Cash Investments is classified as being derived from three activities: operating, investing, and financing.

Cash flows from operating activities represent the amount of cash generated by property operations. Operating activities include transactions involving acquiring, selling, and delivering goods for sale, as well as providing services. Cash flows from operating activities for a property include cash collected from customers, cash paid to employees and other suppliers, interest paid and received, taxes paid, and other operating payments and receipts. Cash from operating activities measures the amount that net income would have been if the cash method were used for measuring revenues and expenses.

Cash flows from investing activities represent changes in cash arising from transactions related to asset accounts that do not affect operations. Transactions include acquisition and disposal of property and facilities as well as the purchase and sale of investments, whether they are current or noncurrent.

Cash flows from financing activities represent cash changes related to liability and equity accounts that do not affect operations. These include obtaining and repaying debt (whether current or noncurrent), issuing and repurchasing stock, and dividend payments.

Cash flows from operating activities can be computed using either the direct or indirect approach. The direct method identifies the operating cash receipts and cash disbursements. The indirect approach determines the cash from operations by adjusting net income for noncash items. The indirect approach is useful for identifying why net income differs from cash from operating activities. The direct approach is easier to interpret, as it specifically identifies the cash inflows and outflows from operations.

If the direct method of presentation is used, a summarized reconciliation of the significant items comprising the difference between net income and cash flows from operating activities should also be presented.

While the Statement of Cash Flows summarizes all significant sources and uses of cash, there is also a requirement to disclose significant non-cash investing and financing activities. This information is generally presented in narrative form immediately below the Statement. Items that should be disclosed include the purchase of capital assets by incurring debt or through capital lease transactions. Transactions involving the sale of assets where the seller provides financing is another example requiring disclosure.

Direct Method

Statement of Cash Flows

	Period	
	Current Year	Prior Year
CASH FLOWS FROM OPERATING ACTIVITIES		
Guest Receipts	$	$
Other Receipts		
Payroll Disbursements		
Other Operating Disbursements		
Interest Paid		
Income Taxes Paid		
Net Cash Provided By (Used In) Operating Activities		
CASH FLOWS FROM INVESTING ACTIVITIES		
Capital Expenditures		
Decrease (Increase) in Restricted Cash		
Proceeds from Asset Dispositions		
Proceeds from Sale of Investments		
Purchases of Investments		
Net Cash Provided By (Used In) Investing Activities		
CASH FLOWS FROM FINANCING ACTIVITIES		
Proceeds from Debt or Equity Financing		
Debt Repayments		
Dividends Paid		
Distribution to Owners/Partners		
Net Cash Provided By (Used In) Financing Activities		
INCREASE (DECREASE) IN CASH AND TEMPORARY CASH INVESTMENTS		
CASH AND TEMPORARY CASH INVESTMENTS, BEGINNING OF PERIOD		
CASH AND TEMPORARY CASH INVESTMENTS, END OF PERIOD	$	$

SUPPLEMENTAL INFORMATION RELATED TO NONCASH INVESTING AND FINANCING ACTIVITIES (DISCLOSE SIGNIFICANT ITEMS SEPARATELY.)

Indirect Method

Statement of Cash Flows

	Period	
	Current Year	Prior Year
CASH FLOWS FROM OPERATING ACTIVITIES		
Net Income	$	$
Adjustments to Reconcile Net Income		
To Cash Provided By (Used In) Operating Activities:		
Depreciation and Amortization		
Loss (Gain) on Sale of Property and Equipment		
Deferred Taxes		
Decrease (Increase) in Accounts Receivable		
Decrease (Increase) in Inventory		
Decrease (Increase) in Prepaids		
Increase (Decrease) in Payables		
Increase (Decrease) in Accruals		
Net Cash Provided By (Used In) Operating Activities		
CASH FLOWS FROM INVESTING ACTIVITIES		
Capital Expenditures		
Decrease (Increase) in Restricted Cash		
Proceeds from Asset Dispositions		
Proceeds from Sale of Investments		
Purchases of Investments		
Net Cash Provided By (Used In) Investing Activities		
CASH FLOWS FROM FINANCING ACTIVITIES		
Proceeds from Debt or Equity Financing		
Debt Repayments		
Dividends Paid		
Distribution to Owners/Partners		
Net Cash Provided By (Used In) Financing Activities		
INCREASE (DECREASE) IN CASH AND TEMPORARY CASH INVESTMENTS		
CASH AND TEMPORARY CASH INVESTMENTS, BEGINNING OF PERIOD		
CASH AND TEMPORARY CASH INVESTMENTS, END OF PERIOD	$	$
CASH PAID FOR INTEREST		
CASH PAID FOR INCOME TAXES		
SUPPLEMENTAL INFORMATION RELATED TO NONCASH INVESTING AND FINANCING ACTIVITIES (DISCLOSE SIGNIFICANT ITEMS SEPARATELY)		

Cash Flows from Operating Activities

Guest Receipts

Guest Receipts includes all receipts from guest-related activities including those applicable to unearned income.

Other Receipts

Other Receipts includes proceeds from transactions other than with guests; for example, from casual sales of furnishings, salvage, interest and dividends received, and other activities.

Payroll Disbursements

Payroll Disbursements includes salary and wage payments as well as related payments for employee benefits.

Other Operating Disbursements

Other Operating Disbursements includes payments for food and beverage, other merchandise and supplies, energy, rent, taxes other than income, franchise and other management fees, and other expenditures incurred by operations.

Interest Paid

Interest Paid includes cash payments to lenders and other creditors for interest. The amount should be shown net of interest capitalized.

Income Taxes Paid

Income Taxes Paid includes all payments for taxes based on income. It does not include amounts paid for sales or occupancy taxes.

Cash Flows from Investing Activities

Capital Expenditures

Capital Expenditures represents payments to purchase property, buildings, equipment, and other productive assets. These payments include interest payments capitalized as part of the cost of those assets. A separate disclosure may be appropriate for the portion of the capital expenditures that results in an increase in the revenue-generating capacity of the lodging property. Separating cash payments that represent an increase in revenue-generating capacity from cash payments that are required to maintain operating capacity is helpful in enabling users to determine whether the lodging property is investing adequately in the maintenance of its operating capacity.

Decrease (Increase) in Restricted Cash

The change in the noncurrent restricted cash is included in this item. The change represents the difference between the additional cash set aside or restricted and the use of those funds for the restricted purpose.

Proceeds from Asset Dispositions

The Proceeds from Asset Dispositions, reduced by selling cost payments, are included in this item. This item should not include any amount of the sales consideration that has been financed by the seller.

Proceeds from Sale of Investments

The net Proceeds from the Sale of Investments, after deduction of selling expenses, should be included in this item.

Purchases of Investments

The purchase price paid for investments, including the transaction costs paid, should be included in this item.

Cash Flows from Financing Activities

Proceeds from Debt or Equity Financing

The net proceeds after deduction of transaction costs should be included in this item. Separate captions are shown if amounts are significant. This item includes long- and short-term financing.

Debt Repayments

Aggregate principal repayments on indebtedness should be included in this item.

Dividends and Distributions Paid

The amount of Dividends Paid to owners should be included. Other distributions to owners should be included, with appropriate modification of the caption, if the entity is not a corporation.

Section 5
Notes to the Financial Statements

In order for a financial presentation to be complete, the financial statements are accompanied by explanatory notes. The notes should describe all significant accounting policies followed by the organization. Commonly required disclosures include, but are not limited to, policies regarding the following:

- Description of business
- Earnings per share
- Stock-based compensation
- Basis of consolidation
- Use of estimates
- Cash and temporary cash investments
- Inventory methods and valuation
- Accounting for investments, including the valuation of marketable securities
- Property, plant, and equipment
- Depreciation and amortization policies
- Intangibles—Goodwill
- Accounting for deferred charges
- Advertising costs
- Accounting for pensions
- Revenue recognition
- Accounting for income taxes
- Fair value of financial instruments
- Capitalization
- Lease disclosure
- Computation of net income (loss) per share (only public companies)
- Foreign currency translation
- Concentration of credit risk

Disclosure of accounting policy-related footnotes should be followed by such additional notes as are necessary to provide for full disclosure of all significant events or conditions reflected in the financial statements, or as otherwise required by the rules of professional accounting or regulatory organizations. Typical events and conditions which are disclosed in the notes accompanying financial statements include the following:

- Changes in accounting methods
- Long-term debt agreements
- Pension and/or profit–sharing plans
- Other post–retirement and post–employment benefits
- Income taxes
- Long-term contracts
- Extraordinary items of income or expense
- Significant long–term commitments, including leases
- Foreign operations
- Related party transactions
- Contingent liabilities, including pending litigation
- Subsequent events
- Stockholders' equity transactions
- Financial instruments (including derivatives)
- Impairment or disposal of long–lived assets
- Restructuring costs
- Extinguishment of debt
- Discontinued operations
- Business combinations
- Accumulated other comprehensive income (loss)
- Business segment information (public companies only)
- Quarterly financial information (public companies only)
- Organization (geographic and nature of business)
- Subsequent events
- Major customers

Part II
Operating Statements

The Operating Statements consist of a Summary Operating Statement and its supporting schedules. Together, they reflect the results of operations for a given period. While the terminology may not follow exact GAAP wording, the format and the methodology used in preparing the statements are, at the time of printing, generally consistent with GAAP.

The Summary Operating Statement is designed to serve three major purposes: (1) to provide management information regarding the results of operations; (2) to facilitate the comparison of results between different lodging properties; and (3) to enable comparison to a standard consisting of combined data from multiple properties. As a result, the Summary Operating Statement presentation is detailed through what is referred to as Adjusted Net Operating Income and does not include such items as Interest, Depreciation, Amortization, and Income Taxes. These items, normally found on a Statement of Income, vary based on ownership needs and decisions, and are not usually under the control of the management company.

The proper format for the Summary Operating Statement is shown on the next page. While properties may choose to delete some of the columns or to show them in a different order, the revenue and expenses lines, unless they are irrelevant, are to be included exactly as presented if the Summary Operating Statement is to be "in conformity with the *Uniform System*."

Summary Operating Statement[1]

| | CURRENT PERIOD | | | | | | YEAR-TO-DATE | | | | | |
| | ACTUAL | | FORECAST | | PRIOR YEAR | | ACTUAL | | FORECAST | | PRIOR YEAR | |
	$	%	$	%	$	%	$	%	$	%	$	%
REVENUE[2]												
Rooms												
Food and Beverage												
Other Operated Departments												
Rentals and Other Income												
Total Revenue												
DEPARTMENTAL EXPENSES[3]												
Rooms												
Food and Beverage												
Other Operated Departments												
Total Departmental Expenses												
TOTAL DEPARTMENTAL INCOME												
UNDISTRIBUTED OPERATING EXPENSES												
Administrative and General												
Sales and Marketing												
Property Operation & Maint.												
Utilities												
Total Undistributed Expenses												
GROSS OPERATING PROFIT												
MANAGEMENT FEES												
INCOME BEFORE FIXED CHARGES												
FIXED CHARGES												
Rent												
Property and Other Taxes												
Insurance												
Total Fixed Charges												
NET OPERATING INCOME												
LESS: REPLACEMENT RESERVES												
ADJUSTED NET OPERATING INCOME												

[1] For a complete Statement of Income, refer to page 18.
[2] Departmental Revenue is shown as a percentage of Total Revenue.
[3] Departmental Expenses is the sum of Cost of Sales (when applicable) and Total Expenses. Departmental Expenses are shown as a percentage of their respective department revenue.

As shown on the previous page, the Summary Operating Statement is divided into six sections: Revenue, Departmental Expenses, Undistributed Operating Expenses, Management Fees, Fixed Charges, and Replacement Reserves. The following describes the content of each of these sections.

Revenue

The *Uniform System* includes only four revenue categories. The first two categories, Rooms and Food and Beverage, report the results of those departments. Revenue from any other department included in property operations—for example, telecommunications, a golf course, spa, or parking garage—is included in Other Operated Departments. The fourth revenue category is Rentals and Other Income, which includes items such as space rental, commissions, and interest income.

Total Revenue is determined by adding the amounts for all four categories of revenue. The Total Revenue line is considered to be 100 percent, and the percentage for each revenue category is determined by dividing the dollar amount for that revenue category by Total Revenue.

Departmental Expenses

There are three categories of departmental expenses, each of which relates to an operated department revenue category. In the schedules that accompany the Summary Operating Statement, departmental expenses are separated into four groups: cost of sales, cost of other revenue, payroll and related expenses, and other expenses. The total of these four groups of expenses for each category of revenue is the amount reported on the respective line of the Summary Operating Statement.

The percentage for each departmental expense is calculated by dividing the dollar amount of the expense by the corresponding revenue dollar amount.

Total Departmental Expenses is the sum of the amounts for all three categories of departmental expenses. The percentage for Total Departmental Expenses is calculated by dividing Total Departmental Expenses by Total Revenue.

Total Departmental Income is calculated by subtracting Total Departmental Expenses from Total Revenue. The Total Departmental Income percentage is calculated by dividing the dollar amount of Total Departmental Income by Total Revenue.

Undistributed Operating Expenses

The Undistributed Operating Expenses section reports expenses that are considered applicable to the entire property. In order to achieve uniformity, it is not appropriate to allocate these types of expenses to specific departments. The Undistributed Operating Expenses are separated into four categories: Administrative and General, Sales and Marketing, Property Operation and Maintenance, and Utilities.

The percentage for each Undistributed Operating Expense is calculated by dividing the dollar amount of the expense by Total Revenue.

Total Undistributed Expenses is the sum of the amounts for all four categories of Undistributed Operating Expenses. The percentage for Total Undistributed

Expenses is calculated by dividing Total Undistributed Expenses by Total Revenue.

Gross Operating Profit is calculated by subtracting Total Undistributed Expenses from Total Departmental Income. The Gross Operating Profit percentage is calculated by dividing the dollar amount of Gross Operating Profit by Total Revenue.

Management Fees

Management Fees represents the cost for management services performed by a management company to operate the property as a whole. If a management fee is paid for the oversight of a department other than Rooms within the property, such as Food and Beverage, that fee is charged to the specific department for which the fee is incurred. The percentage for the Management Fees line is determined by dividing the dollar amount of Management Fees by Total Revenue.

Income Before Fixed Charges is calculated by subtracting Management Fees from Gross Operating Profit. The percentage for Income Before Fixed Charges is calculated by dividing the dollar amount of Income Before Fixed Charges by Total Revenue.

Fixed Charges

The items included under Fixed Charges include Rent, Property and Other Taxes, and Insurance. The percentage for each of these expenses is calculated by dividing the dollar amount of the expense by Total Revenue.

Total Fixed Charges is the sum of the amounts shown for Rent, Property and Other Taxes, and Insurance. The Total Fixed Charges percentage is calculated by dividing the dollar amount for Total Fixed Charges by Total Revenue.

Net Operating Income is determined by subtracting the Total Fixed Charges from Income Before Fixed Charges. The Net Operating Income percentage is calculated by dividing the dollar amount for Net Operating Income by Total Revenue.

Replacement Reserves

Many management contracts, loan agreements, and owners/operators specify the establishment of a reserve to accumulate the funds required for future replacements of furniture, fixtures, and equipment. These funds may also provide for certain capital improvements and the replacement of existing assets such as the major building systems. Replacement Reserves indicates the amount set aside for the period covered by the Summary Operating Statement, whether or not the reserve is actually funded. The percentage for Replacement Reserves is calculated by dividing the dollar amount of the reserve by Total Revenue.

Adjusted Net Operating Income

Adjusted Net Operating Income is determined by subtracting Replacement Reserves from Net Operating Income. The Adjusted Net Operating Income percentage is calculated by dividing the dollar amount for Adjusted Net Operating Income by Total Revenue.

ROOMS—SCHEDULE 1

	CURRENT MONTH			YEAR-TO-DATE		
	ACTUAL	FORECAST	PRIOR YEAR	ACTUAL	FORECAST	PRIOR YEAR
	$ %	$ %	$ %	$ %	$ %	$ %
REVENUE						
Transient Rooms Revenue						
Group Rooms Revenue						
Contract Rooms Revenue						
Other Rooms Revenue						
Less: Allowances						
Total Rooms Revenue						
EXPENSES						
Payroll and Related Expenses						
Salaries, Wages, and Bonuses						
Salaries and Wages						
Bonuses and Incentives						
Total Salaries, Wages, and Bonuses						
Payroll-Related Expenses						
Payroll Taxes						
Supplemental Pay						
Employee Benefits						
Total Payroll-Related Expenses						
Total Payroll and Related Expenses						
Other Expenses						
Cable/Satellite Television						
Cleaning Supplies						
Commissions						
Commissions and Rebates—Group						
Complimentary Services and Gifts						
Contract Services						
Corporate Office Reimbursables						
Decorations						
Dues and Subscriptions						
Equipment Rental						
Guest Relocation						
Guest Supplies						
Guest Transportation						
Laundry and Dry Cleaning						
Licenses and Permits						
Linen						
Miscellaneous						
Operating Supplies						
Printing and Stationery						
Reservations						
Royalty Fees						
Telecommunications						
Training						
Travel—Meals and Entertainment						
Travel—Other						
Uniform Laundry						
Uniforms						
Total Other Expenses						
TOTAL EXPENSES						
DEPARTMENTAL INCOME (LOSS)						

Rooms—Schedule 1 illustrates the proper format for reporting the Revenue, Payroll and Related Expenses, Other Expenses, and Income (Loss) amounts for the Rooms department. Individual properties may delete irrelevant line items, but the *Uniform System* does not provide for the addition or substitution of other revenue or expense line items. Rather, properties may choose to develop a sub-account/sub-schedule to provide more detail related to a particular revenue or expense item such as in the case of a mixed-ownership project where ownership of some of the hotel units rests with third parties, but revenues and expenses are properly reported in the operating results of the hotel. This sub-account/sub-schedule is then to be rolled into the appropriate line item. Additionally, properties may choose to delete some of the columns or to show them in a different order and remain "in conformity with the *Uniform System.*"

Revenue

The primary source of revenue for a lodging property generally arises from the rental of rooms and suites to guests. Rooms Department Revenue is divided into four parts: Transient Rooms Revenue, Group Rooms Revenue, Contract Rooms Revenue, and Other Rooms Revenue.

Transient Rooms Revenue

Transient Rooms Revenue commonly includes revenue derived from rental of rooms and suites by individuals or groups occupying less than 10 rooms per night. It also includes rooms leased to guests who have established permanent residence, with or without a contract. Transient stays typically include the following categories:

- Commercial/Corporate
- Leisure
- Government/Military
- Frequent Guest or Preferred
- Travel Packages, FIT
- Hotel Packages
- Internet

Group Rooms Revenue

Group Rooms Revenue includes revenue derived from renting blocks of 10 or more rooms or suites per night to a group. A group is defined as a number of individuals (typically 10 or more) collected or traveling together. Group Rooms Revenue is recorded net of discounts to wholesalers for selling large blocks of rooms. To facilitate effective sales and marketing efforts, Group Rooms Revenue is generally segregated by market segment. Market segments typically include the following categories:

- Corporate

- Association/Convention

- Government

- Tour group

- SMERF (Social, Military, Educational, Religious, Fraternal)

- Wholesalers, including Internet providers

Contract Rooms Revenue

Contract Rooms Revenue includes revenue derived from a contract with another entity for a consistent block of rooms for an extended period over 30 days. Contract Rooms Revenue is recorded net of discounts. Examples include domiciled airline crews, ongoing corporate training seminars, and incentive-based benefit programs.

Other Rooms Revenue

Other Rooms Revenue is miscellaneous revenue associated with an occupied room. This revenue is included in determining Total Rooms Revenue and is used in the calculation of Average Daily Rate (ADR). Items associated with Other Rooms Revenue include:

- *No-shows.* This is revenue derived from a transient or group guest who has individually guaranteed payment to reserve a room, but has failed either to occupy the room or to cancel the reservation within the prescribed timeframe. No-show revenue is to be included only when collection is reasonably assured. Group Attrition and Cancellation is included in Rentals and Other Income, not Other Rooms Revenue.

- *Day use.* This is revenue derived from sources such as rooms used for hospitality suites, dressing rooms, employment interviews, movie auditions, and wholesale distributors (for example, clothing, toys, other merchandise).

- *Early departure fees.*

- *Late check-out fees.*

- *Rental of rollaway beds and cribs.*

Items placed in the guestroom for sale to guests are not included in the calculation of Other Rooms Revenue. For example, bottled water or packaged food items that are charged to guests if consumed are considered Mini Bar Food Revenue. Non-food and beverage items sold in the room are credited to Miscellaneous Other Revenue in the Food department. Properties without food and beverage operations would show commission income in Rentals and Other Income. However, if the property earns revenue and incurs expenses, the gross amounts should be reported in Other Operated Departments.

Other Rooms Department Considerations

This section discusses other issues affecting the Rooms Department. These include package revenues, resort fees and surcharges, barter transactions, sales and excise taxes and transient occupancy taxes, frequent stay programs, and wholesaler revenues.

   Package Revenues. Package revenues are lodging accommodations sold in conjunction with other services provided by either the property or third parties as part of a single transaction with the customer. For example, a guest could obtain accommodations, meals, golf, spa treatment, and a rental vehicle for a single price. Care needs to be taken to ensure that revenues are appropriately allocated among departments and/or third-party vendors.

   When properties provide incidental (gratis) food and/or beverages to a guest, such as a free breakfast, or where the guest cannot opt out of the food program, or where meals are provided as part of a franchise company brand standard, the cost of the food and/or beverage item is charged to the Rooms department, and no allocation of revenues should be made to the Food and Beverage department. In all other situations, such as resorts, which market their room product on a Modified American Plan basis, it is appropriate to allocate the food and/or beverage revenue to the Food and Beverage department.

   In the case where interdepartmental allocations are necessary (for example, where revenues have to be allocated between rooms and food and beverage or other departments), the allocation is made based on the theoretical "market" values for the separate services. The "market" values represent average realized amounts achieved by the property for similar services. The packaged revenue is then allocated based on the ratio among these market values. The ratio should be used on a consistent basis and modified only when the theoretical values are estimated to have changed materially.

   As an example, consider the following spa package consisting of a guestroom for one night, four meals, and the use of the property's spa facilities at an inclusive price of $240, not including taxes, gratuities, or service charges. Despite the fact that the fair market value of the package is $320, only the $240 total amount will show on the guest account plus sales, excise, and transient taxes as applicable to each category of revenue. Special attention must be taken to ensure that the taxes charged meet the requirements of the taxing authorities. The property computes the departmental allocations of the $240 sales price as follows:

Department	Market Value	Ratio	Package Allocations
Rooms	$160	50%	$120
Food	112	35%	84
Spa	48	15%	36
Total	$320	100%	$240

In the case of packages that include a third-party vendor, the rate for the provision of the third-party service will likely be established by contractual arrangement. The third-party portion of a package is deducted from the price of the package before the allocation. Amounts to be paid to a third party are recorded to a liability account until paid and are not considered revenue.

Resort Fees and Surcharges. Resort fees and surcharges are mandatory fees charged at either a flat amount or a percentage of the room rate. They are charged per room night rather than per person and allow the guest to use services such as fitness facilities, spa, pool, local phone calls, Internet access, airport transportation, golf driving range, and other recreational facilities. These fees may also include gratuities. Resort fees and mandatory surcharges include any charges to offset expenses, such as an energy surcharge.

Resort fees and surcharges are recorded as revenue. Resort fees are allocated to other departments based on the relative value of the components normally supplied by those departments. If the surcharge cannot be allocated to a revenue-producing department, it is included in Other Rooms Revenue. If the surcharge to be allocated is related to an item normally recorded as revenue by the Rooms department, for example, a rollaway, the amount is recorded as Other Rooms Revenue.

Barter Transactions. Lodging properties often enter into barter transactions. Typically, these arrangements require the property to provide accommodations and possibly food, beverages, golf packages, and other services in exchange for other services, such as advertising. These are non-monetary transactions that are settled through the provision of goods and services. While the form and details of barter transactions vary, they typically occur during periods of low occupancy.

Generally accepted accounting principles require that revenue and expenses associated with barter transactions be recognized. Typically, this means that Prepaid Expenses will be charged with the value of the services to be received by the property and Other Liabilities will be credited with the value of the services to be provided by the property. As the property receives the services agreed to in the barter transaction, it expenses the value of those services, leaving in Prepaid Expenses only the unused value of the barter transaction. Likewise as the property provides the services agreed to in the barter transaction, it recognizes the revenue by writing down the liability, leaving only the unredeemed value of the services in Other Liabilities. The value assigned within the barter agreement to the services received should, accordingly, be a conservative average of the market rate for similar accommodations or services at the property. When rooms are part of a barter transaction, they are counted as occupied rooms and the corresponding statistics included.

Sales and Excise Taxes and Transient Occupancy Taxes. Most jurisdictions levy sales or excise taxes on revenues. In addition, many jurisdictions assess a transient occupancy, value added, accommodations or resort tax on certain lodging revenues. In these cases, the property merely acts as a conduit in the collection of taxes for the taxing authority. The property is required to pay the taxes to the taxing authority regardless of whether the tax is charged to the guest. No revenue is recognized. Special attention must be taken with regard to the treatment of complimentary rooms by the taxing authorities.

Frequent Stay Programs. In an attempt to build customer loyalty and repeat business, some properties and chains have implemented frequent stay programs where low priced or free accommodations or services are provided to frequent guests based on points earned at various levels of patronage. The value of the frequent stay points is charged as a marketing expense when the points are issued with a corresponding credit to a liability account. When a guest redeems the points, the value of the points is credited to Rooms Revenue and debited to the liability account if the frequent stay program is solely at the property level, or to a receivable account if the program is operated at a chain level. In the latter case, the cost is passed on to the chain to reimburse the property. Special attention must be paid so that the value assigned to points issued covers the liability associated with the estimated redemption of points. When rooms are part of a Frequent Stay Program, they are counted as occupied rooms and included in the corresponding statistics.

Wholesaler Revenues. Many lodging properties use the services of a wholesaler in connection with the sale and distribution of guestrooms. In turn, wholesalers generally market the rooms on behalf of the properties to retail travel agents. To entice wholesalers to perform the marketing function, they are offered a block or a set number of rooms at a discounted price. The rate offered to the wholesaler is typically a discount off of the rack or posted room rate for the rooms in the block. The block is typically non-binding, which means that the wholesaler is not obligated to purchase any of the allotted rooms in the block. The marketing and packaging efforts carried out by wholesalers are at no direct cost to the property. From the property's perspective, the marketing efficiency that a wholesaler represents justifies the lower rate charged to the wholesaler. The property does not exercise control over the pricing a wholesaler charges its customer.

With the growth in importance of the Internet as a marketing channel, a new breed of wholesaler has appeared on the scene. These new wholesalers focus not on travel agents, but rather on the end consumer whom they reach by marketing over the Internet. However, dot.com wholesalers are no different than traditional wholesalers, and therefore the accounting for a dot.com wholesaler is unchanged from the accounting treatment previously afforded to traditional wholesalers.

The fact that a wholesaler or a dot.com wholesaler resells a room product either in combination with other travel services or alone is irrelevant to the way a property records the revenue received from a wholesaler. Guestroom sales to wholesalers and other similar entities are recorded at the net rate received by the property for the room, exclusive of any taxes or other charges, such as porterage, which may be added to the sale. It is not appropriate for a property to record a sale to a wholesaler at rack rates, which would have the effect of overstating revenues, daily average rate, RevPAR, and expenses, by virtue of recording an artificial expense, or commission, which would be implicit if the sale were grossed up. From a property's perspective, the sale occurs not to the end user, the consumer, but to the wholesaler. It is at this point in the revenue cycle that the sale occurs, and it is with the wholesaler that the property bears the risk of collection. Hence, it is at this time that the sale is recorded on the books of the property, and at the contracted price with the wholesaler. What happens beyond that initial sale is not part of the revenue cycle for the property, and is therefore not reflected on the books of the property.

Commissions paid to travel agents and meeting planners are not synonymous with the marketing services performed by a wholesaler. Travel agents are not afforded special rates for individual bookings, as there is no marketing efficiency brought to the hotel by a travel agent, unlike a wholesaler. Accordingly, commissions are not treated as reductions in room rates, but are charged to the appropriate commissions account in the Rooms department.

Mixed-Ownership Lodging Facilities. Properties of all types and sizes are building or converting rooms into condominiums, creating "mixed-ownership" entities. These facilities may be timeshares, fractional use, or whole ownership. Merely operating these mixed-ownership projects as a lodging operation does not in and of itself qualify the revenue stream to be recorded in the Rooms department. Consideration must be given to the individual facts and circumstances of each project.

Generally, if the property has assumed the economic risk associated with operating the third-party-owned units pursuant to a contractual relationship that extends beyond one year, the associated revenue stream is recorded in the Rooms department within the Transient, Group, Contract, and Other revenue categories as described previously in this section. Alternately, a property could create a sub-schedule for "mixed ownership" revenue and roll up the individual revenues and expenses into the appropriate revenue and expense categories in the Rooms department.

Conversely, if the third-party owner of the unit shares in the risk associated with the operation of the unit, a management relationship exists. In such situations, revenues and expenses are not recorded in the Rooms department. In this circumstance, the revenues received directly by the property, and expenses paid directly by the property (if any), for the third-party-owned units are recorded in either Other Operated Departments or Rentals and Other Income. If the facts and circumstances of the relationship between a property and the third-party owners of the units dictate that the revenues and associated expenses of the condominium operation incurred directly by the property are to be recorded separately, then a Condominium Department is established within Other Operated Departments and the revenues and expenses are reported on a gross basis. (A discussion of gross and net basis reporting is presented under Schedule 3, beginning on page 77.) On the other hand, if the facts and circumstances of the relationship between a property and the third-party owners of the units dictate that the revenue received by the property is a fixed dollar amount, a percent of revenue, or net of expenses, then the revenue received by the property is recorded in Rentals and Other Income. Further discussion is contained under *Other Operated Departments— Schedule 3.*

Average rate and occupancy statistics are affected depending upon the facts and circumstances. If the relationship between property and owner qualifies for inclusion in the Rooms department, then it is appropriate to record the available and occupied third-party-owned units in the total rooms available and total occupied rooms statistics of the property. Failing to meet the criteria set forth with respect to inclusion of such rental revenue in the Rooms department warrants the exclusion of the third-party-owned units from the Rooms department operating statistics. Instead, such statistics are recorded on a supplemental basis as discussed in Part III.

Allowances

Allowances refers to a reduction in revenue due to a service problem, and not an error in posting. Errors in posting, such as posting an incorrect rate, are treated as an adjustment to revenue, regardless of the accounting period in which the error occurred.

Total Rooms Revenue

Total Rooms Revenue is calculated by adding together Transient Rooms Revenue, Group Rooms Revenue, Contract Rooms Revenue, and Other Rooms Revenue and subtracting Allowances. Total Rooms Revenue is the same amount that appears on the Summary Operating Statement under Revenue—Rooms.

   In completing the revenue section of Schedule 1, consider the Total Rooms Revenue line to be 100 percent. The percentage for each source of revenue is determined by dividing the dollar amount for that revenue source by Total Rooms Revenue.

Expenses

Rooms department expenses are separated into two major categories: Payroll and Related Expenses and Other Expenses.

Payroll and Related Expenses

Payroll and Related Expenses for the Rooms department comprises the expenses associated with Salaries, Wages, and Bonuses and Payroll-Related Expenses for employees of the Rooms department. A list of the positions typically included in the Rooms department is shown on page 174.

   Salaries, Wages, and Bonuses. This grouping includes (1) Salaries and Wages and (2) Bonuses and Incentives. Salaries and Wages includes only earnings paid to an employee for duties that relate to the operation of the property, such as regular pay, overtime pay, and shift differential pay. If an employee works in a department other than his or her regular home department, his or her earnings are charged as Salaries and Wages in that other department, regardless of the duties being performed. For example, if a Rooms department employee works as a server for an employee awards banquet, his or her earnings are charged to Salaries and Wages in Administrative and General, and not to this line item. Payroll-Related Expenses (described below) for the above example are treated similarly and charged as Payroll-Related Expenses in Administrative and General.

   Salaries and Wages also includes contract or leased labor. Contract or leased labor refers to those situations in which a property enters into an agreement with an outside service to provide employees to fill positions that would normally be held by individuals paid on the regular payroll. In these situations, the property usually supervises the individuals and records or tracks their hours worked and pays them on an hourly basis. A typical example is the use of individuals brought into the property to fill in for a shortage of housekeeping staff. This situation differs from a contract service in which a property has an agreement with an outside company to provide some type of service, such as cleaning public area space during the early morning hours. In this case, the contracted organization typically provides the supervision and ensures that the work is performed. The costs associated with this type of agreement are charged under Contract Services for the department receiving the service.

Bonuses and Incentives includes bonuses, incentive pay, and other types of performance pay designed to drive revenue through sales, profit, or guest satisfaction measures.

Total Salaries, Wages, and Bonuses. Calculated by adding together Salaries and Wages and Bonuses and Incentives.

Payroll-Related Expenses. Payroll-Related Expenses includes amounts paid for an employee for duties that relate to the operation of the property and amounts paid for an employee who works in a department other than his or her regular home department regardless of the duties being performed. Payroll-Related Expenses includes the following items:

- *Payroll Taxes.* Includes Federal Retirement and Medicare (FICA), Federal and State Unemployment Taxes (FUTA and SUTA), State Disability Insurance (SDI), and other mandated payroll-related taxes or social insurance items. (See *Payroll-Related Expenses—Schedule 13.*)

- *Supplemental Pay.* Includes personal days, vacation pay, sick pay, holiday pay, jury duty pay, relocation pay, paid time off, and severance pay. Supplemental Pay also includes bonuses and incentive payments that are discretionary and not determined by results from operations.

- *Employee Benefits.* Includes all other payroll-related expenses, such as employer-paid health insurance expenses, cost of meals furnished to employees, pension contributions, and union fees. (See *Payroll-Related Expenses—Schedule 13.*) The distribution of employee meal costs from *Employee Cafeteria—Schedule 12* is charged to this line.

Total Payroll-Related Expenses. Calculated by adding together Payroll Taxes, Supplemental Pay, and Employee Benefits.

Total Payroll and Related Expenses

Total Payroll and Related Expenses is calculated by adding together Total Salaries, Wages, and Bonuses and Total Payroll-Related Expenses. The percentage for each payroll and related expense line item as well as Total Payroll and Related Expenses is calculated by dividing the line item amount by Total Rooms Revenue.

Other Expenses

This expense grouping includes the significant Rooms department expenses approved as Other Expenses in the *Uniform System.* Individual properties may delete irrelevant line items, but the *Uniform System* does not provide for the addition or substitution of other expense line items. Rather, properties may choose to develop a sub-account/sub-schedule to provide more detail related to a particular expense item. This sub-account/sub-schedule is then to be rolled into the appropriate line item listed below.

Cable/Satellite Television. Includes the cost of providing cable, satellite video services, and other related services (DVD, VHS players etc.) to guestrooms. It does not include the cost associated with pay-per-view movies, which is charged to Other Operated Departments or netted against revenue in Rentals and Other Income, whichever is appropriate.

Cleaning Supplies. Includes the cost of products used in cleansing, sweeping, polishing, waxing, and disinfecting areas associated with the Rooms department.

Commissions. Includes the remuneration paid to authorized agents for securing rooms business for the property, such as travel agent commissions. Travel agent commissions are generally reflected as an expense of the Rooms department regardless of whether the commission relates to accommodations only or to other services as well. This practice is generally followed because allocations of these commissions to other departments would not be cost-effective.

In some properties, blocks of rooms are provided to travel agents, wholesalers, and consolidators at a negotiated rate. These rooms are subsequently remarketed to the eventual guest. Revenue from these transactions is to be recorded at the negotiated rate and no attempt made to record additional revenue based on a rack or normal rate with an offset to commission expense.

Commissions also includes remuneration paid to rental agents for permanent rooms business that may involve leases. In the case of leases, the remuneration is prorated over the term of the lease.

Commissions and Rebates—Group. Includes payments made to third-party meeting planners who act as a liaison between a hotel and a group in finding suitable meeting and accommodation space for the group. This line item also includes rebates or subsidies granted directly to the group or fees paid to third-party housing companies.

Complimentary Services and Gifts. Includes the cost of providing gift items used in gratis presentations for promotional purposes to guests and vendors of the Rooms department, such as the cost of newspapers provided to guests on a complimentary basis or a complimentary fruit basket sent to the room of a frequent guest. This line item also includes the cost of providing food and beverage items on a gratis basis, such as a breakfast or an evening reception. The costs of bottled water and coffee provided at no charge to the guest are included in Guest Supplies.

Contract Services. Includes expenses for activities performed for the Rooms department by outside companies rather than hotel employees. The costs of contracting outside companies to clean carpets and rugs or to disinfect areas associated with the Rooms department are typical examples. If supplies are purchased for contract companies to use, the supplies are charged to the appropriate supply account. The cost of contracts for Rooms department laundry and dry cleaning is charged to Laundry and Dry Cleaning.

Corporate Office Reimbursables. Includes the allocations of salaries and expenses of corporate or management company Rooms department personnel billed to the property by the regional or corporate office or by the management company. Travel expenses of corporate or management company Rooms department personnel that are incurred while visiting the property, including the costs of meals and other applicable services or amenities provided to corporate or management company staff while on business in the property for the benefit of the property, are also charged to this account.

Decorations. Includes the cost of decorative items used in Rooms department areas for holidays and special events. Decorations also includes the cost of fresh floral arrangements used in the public areas.

Dues and Subscriptions. Includes the cost of representation of the Rooms department, or of members of the staff when authorized to represent the Rooms department, in business or professional organizations. Dues and Subscriptions is also charged with the cost of subscriptions to newspapers, magazines, and books for use by the staff of the Rooms department.

Equipment Rental. Includes the cost of renting any type of equipment that may be used either sporadically in the Rooms department or as a replacement for equipment out of service on a temporary basis. Equipment that is rented on a continuous basis and, if purchased, would qualify as a capital purchase is charged to Other Property and Equipment under the Rent section of *Rent, Property and Other Taxes, and Insurance—Schedule 10.*

Guest Relocation. Includes the cost of renting accommodations in other properties when a decision is made to move a guest (usually on arrival) to another property because of a lack of available rooms. This item also includes any incidental costs, gratuities, or compensation paid in connection with these circumstances.

Guest Supplies. Includes the cost of consumable supplies and amenities provided for guests on a gratis basis in the guestroom, such as soaps, shampoos, lotions, toilet tissue, shoeshine mitts, shower caps, and writing materials. The costs of bottled water and coffee provided at no charge to the guest are also included in Guest Supplies.

Guest Transportation. Includes all costs associated with transporting guests to and from the property, such as fuel costs, costs of washing and cleaning vehicles, the occasional rental of vehicles for transporting large groups, or the costs of contracting guest transportation services. The costs of mechanical maintenance of vehicles used to transport guests are charged to Property Operation and Maintenance. If a vehicle used to transport guests is leased, the cost of the lease is charged to Rent under *Rent, Property and Other Taxes, and Insurance—Schedule 10.*

Laundry and Dry Cleaning. Includes the cost of laundry and dry cleaning services applicable to the Rooms department, whether the services are performed by an in-house facility or are contracted to an outside company. If the services are performed by an in-house laundry, an allocation from House Laundry is charged to Laundry and Dry Cleaning. If the services are performed by an outside company, the amount charged to Laundry and Dry Cleaning should be based on invoices sent by the outside laundry. The cost of cleaning employee uniforms is charged to the Uniform Laundry account.

Licenses and Permits. Includes the cost of federal, state, and local licenses, including costs of inspections needed for licensing, for all activities of the Rooms department.

Linen. Includes the cost, whether purchased or rented, of towels, face cloths, bath mats, blankets, guest robes, pillowcases, sheets, comforters, duvets, and bedspreads used by the Rooms department.

Miscellaneous. Includes any expenses of the Rooms department that do not apply to the other line items discussed in this section.

Operating Supplies. Includes the cost of items needed to operate the Rooms department that are not included in the descriptions of specific supply accounts such as Guest Supplies, Cleaning Supplies, and Printing and Stationery. Examples of items included in Operating Supplies are clock radios, irons, keycards, "Do-Not-Disturb" signs, ice buckets, drinking glasses, and all general office supplies. The cost of firewood for lobby and/or guestrooms is charged to this line item. The cost of consumable supplies and amenities provided in guestrooms is charged to Guest Supplies.

Printing and Stationery. Includes the cost of printed forms used in the Rooms department, whether they are purchased from an outside source or produced internally. The costs associated with providing a guestroom or service directory, including the binder and the contents pages, are included in Printing and Stationery. The cost of writing materials provided in guestrooms is charged to Guest Supplies.

Reservations. Includes the costs associated with participating in an internal or external central reservation system, such as any fees paid for chain reservation services. Reservations also includes the cost of any communication lines, including Internet site communications costs, that are dedicated to generating reservations.

Royalty Fees. Includes all costs associated with the right to use a brand name in connection with a Rooms department activity. The fees paid for the use of a hotel brand name are charged to Franchise Fees in *Sales and Marketing—Schedule 6.*

Telecommunications. Includes any telecommunications expenditures that can be directly related to the Rooms department, including the costs of local, long distance, and Internet communications. Telecommunications includes not only traditional telephone systems, but also the cost of cellular phones, including the equipment and periodic service charges, used in the Rooms department. Telecommunications charged to room guests is recorded in the Telecommunications department.

Training. Includes the cost, other than time, that can be directly attributed to the training of employees in the Rooms department. Examples include the costs of training materials, supplies, and instructor fees. The cost of employee wages incurred during training is charged to Salaries and Wages.

Travel—Meals and Entertainment. Includes the reimbursable cost of food and beverage expenditures for travel and entertainment by employees of the Rooms department traveling on property business.

Travel—Other. Includes the cost of travel and reimbursable expenditures, other than food, beverage, and entertainment, by employees of the Rooms department traveling on property business

Uniform Laundry. Includes the cost of cleaning uniforms for employees of the Rooms department whether performed by an in-hotel facility or contracted to an outside company.

Uniforms. Includes the cost of employee uniforms used in the Rooms department, whether purchased or rented. Repair costs are also included in this line item. The cost of cleaning uniforms is charged to the Uniform Laundry account.

Total Other Expenses

Total Other Expenses is calculated by adding all items listed under Other Expenses. The percentage for each line item expense as well as Total Other Expenses is calculated by dividing the line item amount by Total Rooms Revenue.

Total Expenses

Total Expenses is calculated by adding Total Payroll and Related Expenses to Total Other Expenses. Total Expenses is the same amount that appears on the Summary Operating Statement under Departmental Expenses—Rooms. The percentage for Total Expenses is calculated by dividing the dollar amount of Total Expenses by Total Rooms Revenue.

Departmental Income (Loss)

Departmental Income (Loss) is calculated by subtracting Total Expenses from Total Rooms Revenue. The percentage for Departmental Income (Loss) is calculated by dividing Departmental Income (Loss) by Total Rooms Revenue.

FOOD AND BEVERAGE—SCHEDULE 2

	CURRENT MONTH			YEAR-TO-DATE		
	ACTUAL	FORECAST	PRIOR YEAR	ACTUAL	FORECAST	PRIOR YEAR
	$ %	$ %	$ %	$ %	$ %	$ %
REVENUE						
Outlet Food Revenue						
Outlet Beverage Revenue						
In-Room Dining Food Revenue						
In-Room Dining Beverage Revenue						
Banquet/Catering Food Revenue						
Banquet/Catering Beverage Revenue						
Mini Bar Food Revenue						
Mini Bar Beverage Revenue						
Other Food Revenue						
Other Beverage Revenue						
Less: Allowances						
Total Food and Beverage Revenue						
OTHER REVENUE						
Audiovisual						
Public Room Rentals						
Cover Charges						
Service Charges						
Miscellaneous Other Revenue						
Less: Allowances						
Total Other Revenue						
TOTAL REVENUE						
COST OF FOOD AND BEVERAGE SALES						
Cost of Food Sales						
Cost of Beverage Sales						
Total Cost of Food and Beverage Sales						
COST OF OTHER REVENUE						
Audiovisual Cost						
Miscellaneous Cost						
Total Cost of Other Revenue						
TOTAL COST OF SALES AND OTHER REVENUE						
GROSS PROFIT (LOSS)						
EXPENSES						
Payroll and Related Expenses						
Salaries, Wages, and Bonuses						
Salaries and Wages						
Bonuses and Incentives						
Total Salaries, Wages, and Bonuses						
Payroll-Related Expenses						
Payroll Taxes						
Supplemental Pay						
Employee Benefits						
Total Payroll-Related Expenses						
Total Payroll and Related Expenses						

(continued)

FOOD AND BEVERAGE—SCHEDULE 2 *(continued)*

	CURRENT MONTH			YEAR-TO-DATE		
	ACTUAL	FORECAST	PRIOR YEAR	ACTUAL	FORECAST	PRIOR YEAR
	$ | %	$ | %	$ | %	$ | %	$ | %	$ | %
Other Expenses						
Banquet Expense						
China						
Cleaning Supplies						
Complimentary Services and Gifts						
Contract Services						
Corporate Office Reimbursables						
Decorations						
Dishwashing Supplies						
Dues and Subscriptions						
Equipment Rental						
Flatware						
Glassware						
Ice						
Kitchen Fuel						
Laundry and Dry Cleaning						
Licenses and Permits						
Linen						
Management Fees						
Menus and Beverage Lists						
Miscellaneous						
Music and Entertainment						
Operating Supplies						
Paper and Plastics						
Printing and Stationery						
Royalty Fees						
Telecommunications						
Training						
Travel—Meals and Entertainment						
Travel—Other						
Uniform Laundry						
Uniforms						
Utensils						
Total Other Expenses						
TOTAL EXPENSES						
DEPARTMENTAL INCOME (LOSS)						

The financial results of a property's food and beverage operations can be presented in two ways: (1) as a single department with a combined food and beverage schedule, or (2) as separate departments with separate food and beverage sub-schedules, which then must be combined into a single food and beverage schedule. The structures of the schedules are the same in either case, and the categories of revenues and expenses are common to both departments. *Food and Beverage—Schedule 2* reflects the proper format for a combined food and beverage department and designates the revenue and expense accounts that are approved as line items in the *Uniform System.* Individual properties may delete irrelevant line items, but the

Uniform System does not provide for the addition or substitution of other revenue or expense line items. Rather, properties may choose to develop a sub-account/sub-schedule to provide more detail related to a particular revenue or expense item. This sub-account/sub-schedule is then to be rolled into the appropriate line item. Additionally, properties may choose to delete some of the columns or to show them in a different order and remain "in conformity with the *Uniform System.*"

The line items for Food and Beverage—Schedule 2 are defined in the following discussions of the Food and Beverage Sub-schedules.

FOOD—SUB-SCHEDULE 2-1

	CURRENT MONTH			YEAR-TO-DATE		
	ACTUAL	FORECAST	PRIOR YEAR	ACTUAL	FORECAST	PRIOR YEAR
	$ %	$ %	$ %	$ %	$ %	$ %
REVENUE						
Outlet Food Revenue						
In-Room Dining Food Revenue						
Banquet/Catering Food Revenue						
Mini Bar Food Revenue						
Other Food Revenue						
Less: Allowances						
Total Food Revenue						
OTHER REVENUE						
Audiovisual						
Public Room Rentals						
Cover Charges						
Service Charges						
Miscellaneous Other Revenue						
Less: Allowances						
Total Other Revenue						
TOTAL REVENUE						
COST OF FOOD SALES						
COST OF OTHER REVENUE						
Audiovisual Cost						
Miscellaneous Cost						
Total Cost of Other Revenue						
TOTAL COST OF FOOD SALES AND OTHER REVENUE						
GROSS PROFIT (LOSS)						
EXPENSES						
Payroll and Related Expenses						
Salaries, Wages, and Bonuses						
Salaries and Wages						
Bonuses and Incentives						
Total Salaries, Wages, and Bonuses						
Payroll-Related Expenses						
Payroll Taxes						
Supplemental Pay						
Employee Benefits						
Total Payroll-Related Expenses						
Total Payroll and Related Expenses						
Other Expenses						
Banquet Expense						
China						
Cleaning Supplies						
Complimentary Services and Gifts						
Contract Services						
Corporate Office Reimbursables						
Decorations						
Dishwashing Supplies						

(continued)

FOOD—SUB-SCHEDULE 2-1 *(continued)*

	CURRENT MONTH			YEAR-TO-DATE		
	ACTUAL	FORECAST	PRIOR YEAR	ACTUAL	FORECAST	PRIOR YEAR
	$ %	$ %	$ %	$ %	$ %	$ %
Dues and Subscriptions						
Equipment Rental						
Flatware						
Glassware						
Ice						
Kitchen Fuel						
Laundry and Dry Cleaning						
Licenses and Permits						
Linen						
Management Fees						
Menus and Beverage Lists						
Miscellaneous						
Music and Entertainment						
Operating Supplies						
Paper and Plastics						
Printing and Stationery						
Royalty Fees						
Telecommunications						
Training						
Travel—Meals and Entertainment						
Travel—Other						
Uniform Laundry						
Uniforms						
Utensils						
Total Other Expenses						
TOTAL EXPENSES						
DEPARTMENTAL INCOME (LOSS)						

Food—Sub-schedule 2-1 presents the proper format for a separate Food department. When separate schedules for food and beverage are prepared, it must be noted that whether a sale is classified as food or beverage revenue is decided by definition of those revenues and is not dependent on the type of outlet in which the sale occurs or the department whose staff is performing service. Moreover, proper recording of payroll costs, other expenses, and other income must occur when Food and Beverage departments are separate in order to match revenues and expenses on departmental schedules.

Revenue

Food Revenue includes all sales of food and non-alcoholic beverages for consumption by customers. Non-alcoholic beverages are included in beverage revenue only when served in a "beverage only" outlet (bar or lounge) where no food is sold. Non-consumable items sold in the Food department are recorded as Other Income.

Outlet Food Revenue

Outlet Food Revenue includes sales of food in specific dining areas in the property. Examples of outlets are restaurants, lounges, delicatessens, bakeries, snack shops, and pool areas. Banquet rooms and guestrooms are not considered outlets.

In-Room Dining Food Revenue

In-Room Dining Food Revenue includes sales of food that require delivery to customers in their guestroom. In-Room Dining Food Revenue can also include sales that require delivery to other areas inside the hotel or outside as in the example of condominiums that may be located near a hotel. Group sales of food ordered from and serviced by the Banquet/Catering department and delivered to guestrooms/suites or outside locations are recorded as Banquet/Catering Food Revenue.

Banquet/Catering Food Revenue

Banquet/Catering Food Revenue includes sales of food in a property's banquet rooms and for group functions outside the property. The banquet designation is used for sales related to groups of customers occupying guestrooms, while catering sales are related to groups of customers who are not occupying guestrooms. Banquet/Catering Food Revenue also includes sales from food service performed by the Banquet/Catering department in a guestroom/suite.

Mini Bar Food Revenue

Mini Bar Food Revenue includes sales of packaged food—for example, candy, snacks, or soft drinks—placed in a guestroom. Revenue from the sale of bottled water in the guestroom is also credited to this account.

Other Food Revenue

Other Food Revenue includes sales of consumable food items not designated as Outlet, In-Room Dining, Banquet/Catering, or Mini Bar revenues. An example of Other Food Revenue is food sold at the property's front desk or on a golf course.

Allowances

Allowances refers to a reduction in revenue due to a service problem, and not an error in posting. Errors in posting, such as charging an incorrect amount on a guest check, are treated as an adjustment to revenue, regardless of the accounting period in which the error occurred.

Total Food Revenue

Total Food Revenue is calculated by adding together Outlet Food Revenue, In-Room Dining Food Revenue, Banquet/Catering Food Revenue, Mini Bar Food Revenue, and Other Food Revenue and subtracting Allowances.

Other Revenue

Other Revenue includes sales of services and all products that are not consumable food items.

Audiovisual

Audiovisual includes revenues and commissions derived from supplying audiovisual equipment and services to customers, whether the equipment is owned by the property or rented from a third party. If the services and equipment are obtained from an outside company, the costs incurred are charged to Audiovisual Cost.

Public Room Rentals

Public Room Rentals includes revenue derived from the rental of public meeting rooms to customers. If a guestroom/suite is used as a meeting room and Banquet/Catering Food Revenue occurs, the meeting room revenue is recorded as Public Room Rentals. If Banquet/Catering Food Revenue does not occur in the guestroom/suite, meeting room revenue is recorded as Other Rooms Revenue in the Rooms department.

Cover Charges

Cover Charges includes charges to customers for entrance to special events where food is sold.

Service Charges

Service Charges includes automatic charges added to any food sale to help cover the cost of staff service to the customer. Service Charges must be recorded as revenue and may not be credited to any expense account. Discretionary amounts added to a food sale as a gratuity to an employee by the customer are treated as tip income to the employee.

Miscellaneous Other Revenue

Miscellaneous Other Revenue includes all non-food items or services sold to customers in the Food department that are not included in Audiovisual, Public Room Rentals, Cover Charges, or Service Charges. Miscellaneous Other Revenue also includes any revenue generated by the sale of non-food items in the guestroom. Costs associated with providing these items and services are charged to Miscellaneous Cost. Temporary Internet connection service fees are included in the Telecommunications department.

Allowances

Allowances refers to a reduction in revenue due to a service problem, and not an error in posting. Errors in posting, such as charging an incorrect price, are treated as an adjustment to revenue, regardless of the accounting period in which the error occurred.

Total Other Revenue

Total Other Revenue is calculated by adding together Audiovisual, Public Room Rentals, Cover Charges, Service Charges, and Miscellaneous Other Revenue and subtracting Allowances.

Total Revenue

Total Revenue is the sum of Total Food Revenue and Total Other Revenue. The sum of Total Revenue from the Food department and Total Revenue from the Beverage department is amount that appears on the Summary Operating Statement under Revenue—Food and Beverage.

In completing the revenue section of Schedule 2 or Sub-schedule 2-1, the Total Revenue line is considered to be 100 percent, and the percentage for each source of revenue is determined by dividing the dollar amount for that revenue source by Total Revenue for the Food and Beverage department (on Schedule 2) or for the Food department (on Sub-schedule 2-1).

Cost of Food Sales

Cost of Food Sales includes the cost of food served to guests in all segments of food revenues. Cost of Food Sales also includes the cost of beverage items transferred from the beverage department and used in food preparation and service. Spoilage, waste, and spillage are included in Cost of Food Sales and are not charged to Other Expenses. Cost of Food Sales does not include costs of food items that have been transferred to other departments to be used in preparation or decoration in those departments (this includes the cost of non-alcoholic beverages such as soft drinks whose sales are included in the definition of beverage revenue). Such transfers are charged directly to the appropriate cost accounts in the departments receiving the items. If food items are sold at cost and revenue is not recorded (commissary and steward's sales), the sale is credited to the Cost of Food Sales. Cost of Food Sales does not include the cost of food used in preparation of meals provided for employees during the workday even if employees are charged for food consumed. The cost of Employee Meals and revenues collected from employees are both charged to the Employee Cafeteria for allocation to each department having employees. Cost of Food Sales does not include the cost associated with food inventory items used for gratis presentation to customers, vendors, and employees of all departments in a hotel. The cost of this complimentary food is charged as an expense to Complimentary Services and Gifts in the department that makes the gratis presentation. Finally, if a vendor provides a rebate on food purchased, it is subtracted from the Cost of Food Sales.

The percentage for Cost of Food Sales is calculated by dividing Cost of Food Sales by Total Food Revenue.

Cost of Other Revenue

Cost of Other Revenue includes the costs associated with the sales of services and all products that are not consumable food items. The percentage for each item under Cost of Other Revenue is calculated by dividing the dollar cost by its corresponding revenue amount.

Audiovisual Cost

Audiovisual Cost includes the cost associated with providing audiovisual services to customers in the Food department. The income received from charging customers for these services is recorded as Audiovisual revenue.

Miscellaneous Cost

Miscellaneous Cost includes the cost associated with providing non-food items and services other than audiovisual services to customers in the Food department. The income received from charging customers for these items and services is recorded as Miscellaneous Other Revenue. The cost of providing temporary Internet connections is reported in the Telecommunications department.

Total Cost of Other Revenue

Total Cost of Other Revenue is calculated by adding Audiovisual Cost and Miscellaneous Cost. The percentage for Total Cost of Other Revenue is calculated by dividing Total Cost of Other Revenue by Total Other Revenue.

Total Cost of Food Sales and Other Revenue

Total Cost of Food Sales and Other Revenue is the sum of Cost of Food Sales and Total Cost of Other Revenue. The percentage for Total Cost of Food Sales and Other Revenue is calculated by dividing the dollar amount of Total Cost of Food Sales and Other Revenue by Total Revenue for the Food department.

Gross Profit (Loss)

Gross Profit (Loss) is calculated by subtracting Total Cost of Sales and Other Revenue from Total Revenue for the Food department. The percentage for Gross Profit (Loss) is calculated by dividing the dollar amount of Gross Profit (Loss) by Total Revenue for the Food department.

Expenses

Food department expenses are separated into two major categories: Payroll and Related Expenses and Other Expenses.

Payroll and Related Expenses

Payroll and Related Expenses for the Food department comprises the expenses associated with Salaries, Wages, and Bonuses and Payroll-Related Expenses for employees of the Food department. A list of the positions typically included in the Food department is shown on page 175.

Salaries, Wages, and Bonuses. This grouping includes (1) Salaries and Wages and (2) Bonuses and Incentives. Salaries and Wages includes only earnings paid to an employee for duties that relate to the operation of the property, such as regular pay, overtime pay, and shift differential pay. If an employee works in a department other than his or her regular home department, his or her earnings must be charged as Salaries and Wages in that other department, regardless of the duties being performed. For example, if a Food department employee works as a server for an employee awards banquet, his or her earnings are charged to Salaries and Wages in Administrative and General, and not to this line item. Payroll-Related Expenses (described below) for the above example are treated similarly and charged as Payroll-Related Expenses in Administrative and General.

Salaries and Wages also includes contract or leased labor. Contract or leased labor refers to those situations in which a property enters into an agreement with an outside service to provide employees to fill positions that would normally be held by individuals paid on the regular payroll. In these situations, the property usually supervises the individuals and records or tracks their hours worked and pays them on an hourly basis. A typical example is the use of individuals brought into the property to fill in for a shortage of Food department staff. This situation differs from a contract service in which a property has an agreement with an outside company to provide some type of service, such as cleaning kitchen area space. In this case, the contracted organization typically provides the supervision and ensures that the work is performed. The costs associated with this type of agreement are charged under Contract Services for the department receiving the service.

Bonuses and Incentives includes bonuses, incentive pay, and other types of performance pay designed to drive revenue through sales, profit, or guest satisfaction measures.

Total Salaries, Wages, and Bonuses. Calculated by adding together Salaries and Wages and Bonuses and Incentives.

Payroll-Related Expenses. Payroll-Related Expenses includes amounts paid for an employee for duties that relate to the operation of the property and amounts paid for an employee who works in a department other than his or her regular home department regardless of the duties being performed. Payroll-Related Expenses includes the following items:

- *Payroll Taxes.* Includes Federal Retirement and Medicare (FICA), Federal and State Unemployment Taxes (FUTA and SUTA), State Disability Insurance (SDI), and other mandated payroll-related taxes or social insurance items. (See *Payroll-Related Expenses—Schedule 13.*)

- *Supplemental Pay.* Includes personal days, vacation pay, sick pay, holiday pay, jury duty pay, relocation pay, paid time off, and severance pay. Supplemental Pay also includes bonuses and incentive payments that are discretionary and not determined by results from operations.

- *Employee Benefits.* Includes all other payroll-related expenses, such as employer-paid health insurance expenses, cost of meals furnished to employees, pension contributions, and union fees. (See *Payroll-Related Expenses—Schedule 13.*) The distribution of employee meal costs from *Employee Cafeteria—Schedule 12* is charged to this line.

Total Payroll-Related Expenses. Calculated by adding together Payroll Taxes, Supplemental Pay, and Employee Benefits.

Total Payroll and Related Expenses

Total Payroll and Related Expenses is calculated by adding together Total Salaries, Wages, and Bonuses and Total Payroll-Related Expenses. The percentage for each payroll and related expense line item as well as Total Payroll and Related Expenses is calculated by dividing the line item amount by Total Revenue for the Food department.

Other Expenses

This expense grouping includes the significant Food department expenses approved as Other Expenses in the *Uniform System.* Individual properties may delete irrelevant line items, but the *Uniform System* does not provide for the addition or substitution of other expense line items. Rather, properties may choose to develop a sub-account/sub-schedule to provide more detail related to a particular expense item. This sub-account/sub-schedule is then to be rolled into the appropriate line item listed below.

Banquet Expense. Includes the cost of items used in providing banquet service for which matching Other Revenue and Cost of Other Revenue accounts cannot be identified. If expenses can be matched to specific other revenue accounts (audiovisual or miscellaneous), they are recorded as Cost of Other Revenue.

China. Includes the cost of purchased or rented plates, bowls, serving platters, etc., constructed from any material (ceramic, glass, metal, non-disposable plastic, etc.) and used in providing food service with the exception of non-alcoholic beverage items. The cost of containers for consumption of non-alcoholic beverages is charged to Glassware.

Cleaning Supplies. Includes the cost of products used in cleansing, sweeping, polishing, waxing, and disinfecting areas associated with the Food department. The cost of cleaning supplies used in dishwashing is charged to Dishwashing Supplies.

Complimentary Services and Gifts. Includes the cost of providing gift items used in gratis presentations for promotional purposes to guests and vendors of the Food department.

Contract Services. Includes expenses for activities performed for the Food department by outside companies rather than hotel employees. The cost of contracting an outside company to clean the ducts and other components of the kitchen ventilation system is an example. If supplies are purchased for contract companies to use, the supplies are charged to the appropriate supply account. The cost of contracts for Food department laundry and dry cleaning is charged to Laundry and Dry Cleaning.

Corporate Office Reimbursables. Includes the allocations of salaries and expenses of corporate or management company food personnel billed to the property by the regional or corporate office or by the management company. Travel expenses of corporate or management company food personnel that are incurred while visiting the property, including the costs of meals and other applicable services or amenities provided to corporate or management company staff while on business in the property for the benefit of the property, are also charged to this account.

Decorations. Includes the cost of decorative items used in Food department areas for holidays and special events that are not charged directly to banquet customers. (The cost of decorations charged to banquet customers is recorded as Cost of Other Revenue.) Decorations also includes the costs of ice blocks used in decorative carvings.

Dues and Subscriptions. Includes the cost of representation of the Food department, or of members of the staff when authorized to represent the Food department, in business or professional organizations. Dues and Subscriptions is also charged with the cost of subscriptions to newspapers, magazines, and books for use by the staff of the Food department.

Dishwashing Supplies. Includes the cost of cleaning, rinsing, and soaking agents used specifically in washing china, glassware, flatware, and utensils in the Food department.

Equipment Rental. Includes the cost of renting any type of equipment that may be used either sporadically in the Food department or as a replacement for equipment out of service on a temporary basis. Equipment that is rented on a continuous basis and, if purchased, would qualify as a capital purchase is charged to Other Property and Equipment under the Rent section of *Rent, Property and Other Taxes, and Insurance—Schedule 10*. The costs of equipment rental charged to banquet customers is recorded as Cost of Other Revenue.

Flatware. Includes the cost of all flatware and serving pieces (serving spoons, cake knives, ladles, etc.), either purchased or rented, used in providing food service.

Glassware. Includes the cost of purchased or rented containers constructed from any material (glass, ceramic, metal, non-disposable plastic, etc.) used in consumption of non-alcoholic beverages. Service items such as pitchers and tea sets are charged to China, along with the costs of cups and mugs used for coffee service.

Ice. Includes the cost of ice used in food service, storage, or preparation. The cost of ice blocks used in decorative carvings and not charged to banquet customers is recorded as Decorations.

Kitchen Fuel. Includes the cost of fuels such as Sterno, propane, and charcoal used in the warming, or sometimes specialized cooking, of food.

Laundry and Dry Cleaning. Includes the cost of laundry and dry cleaning services applicable to the Food department, whether the services are performed by an in-house facility or are contracted to an outside company. If the services are performed by an in-house laundry, an allocation from House Laundry is charged to Laundry and Dry Cleaning. If the services are performed by an outside company, the amount charged to Laundry and Dry Cleaning should be based on invoices sent by the outside laundry. The cost of cleaning employee uniforms is charged to the Uniform Laundry account.

Licenses and Permits. Includes the cost of federal, state, and local licenses, including costs of inspections needed for licensing, for all activities of the Food department.

Linen. Includes the cost, whether purchased or rented, of table cloths, napkins, table runners, and skirting used by the Food department.

Management Fees. Includes any amounts paid to a third-party individual or company to operate or manage a food outlet within the property, whether the fees are computed as a fixed amount or a percentage of revenues or profit.

Menus and Beverage Lists. Includes all costs of designing and printing menus for the Food department. The costs of decorative and protective covers are also charged to this line item.

Miscellaneous. Includes any expenses of the Food department that do not apply to the other line items discussed in this section.

Music and Entertainment. Includes all costs of providing live or recorded entertainment within the Food department. Entertainment costs charged to banquet customers are recorded as Cost of Other Revenue.

Operating Supplies. Includes the cost of operating and general office supplies needed to operate the Food department that are not included in the descriptions of specific supply accounts such as Cleaning Supplies, Menus, Paper and Plastics, and Printing and Stationery.

Paper and Plastics. Includes the cost of all general supplies for the Food department made from paper, plastic, and Styrofoam that are not specifically assigned by definition to other line items. Items charged to this line include chef hats, paper bags, aluminum foil, can liners, disposable plastic utensils, and disposable paper plates.

Printing and Stationery. Includes the cost of printed forms used in the Food department, whether they are purchased from an outside source or produced internally. The cost of producing menus is charged to Menus and Beverage Lists.

Royalty Fees. Includes all costs associated with the right to use a brand name in connection with a Food department activity. For example, the fees paid for use of a brand name to identify a property food outlet, including franchise fees, are charged to this line item. If the food outlet serves both food and beverage, then the fees should be split between the departments on a reasonable basis.

Telecommunications. Includes any telecommunications expenditures that can be directly related to the Food department, including the costs of local, long distance, and Internet communications. Telecommunications includes not only traditional telephone systems, but also the cost of cellular phones, including the equipment and periodic service charges, used in the Food department. Telecommunications charged to banquet customers is recorded in the Telecommunications department.

Training. Includes the cost, other than time, that can be directly attributed to the training of employees in the Food department. Examples include the costs of training materials, supplies, and instructor fees. The cost of employee wages incurred during training is charged to Salaries and Wages.

Travel—Meals and Entertainment. Includes the reimbursable cost of food and beverage expenditures for travel and entertainment, by employees of the Food department traveling on property business.

Travel—Other. Includes the cost of travel and reimbursable expenditures, other than food, beverage, and entertainment by employees of the Food department traveling on property business.

Uniform Laundry. Includes the cost of cleaning uniforms for employees of the Food department whether performed by an in-hotel facility or contracted to an outside company.

Uniforms. Includes the cost of employee uniforms used in the Food department, whether purchased or rented. Repair costs are also included in this line item. The cost of cleaning uniforms is charged to the Uniform Laundry account.

Utensils. Includes the cost of kitchen utensils used in food preparation, whether purchased or rented.

Total Other Expenses

Total Other Expenses is calculated by adding all items listed under Other Expenses. The percentage for each line item expense as well as Total Other Expenses is calculated by dividing the line item amount by Total Revenue for the Food department.

Total Expenses

Total Expenses is calculated by adding Total Payroll and Related Expenses to Total Other Expenses. The percentage for Total Expenses is calculated by dividing Total Expenses by Total Revenue for the Food department.

The sum of Total Cost of Food Sales and Other Revenue and Total Expenses for the Food department and Total Cost of Beverage Sales and Other Revenue and Total Expenses for the Beverage department is the amount that appears on the Summary Operating Statement under Departmental Expenses—Food and Beverage.

Departmental Income (Loss)

Departmental Income (Loss) is calculated by subtracting Total Expenses from Gross Profit. The percentage for Departmental Income (Loss) is calculated by dividing Departmental Income (Loss) by Total Revenue for the Food department.

BEVERAGE—SUB-SCHEDULE 2-2

	CURRENT MONTH			YEAR-TO-DATE		
	ACTUAL	FORECAST	PRIOR YEAR	ACTUAL	FORECAST	PRIOR YEAR
	$ | %	$ | %	$ | %	$ | %	$ | %	$ | %
REVENUE						
Outlet Beverage Revenue						
In-Room Dining Beverage Revenue						
Banquet/Catering Beverage Revenue						
Mini Bar Beverage Revenue						
Other Beverage Revenue						
Less: Allowances						
Total Beverage Revenue						
OTHER REVENUE						
Audiovisual						
Public Room Rentals						
Cover Charges						
Service Charges						
Miscellaneous Other Revenue						
Less: Allowances						
Total Other Revenue						
TOTAL REVENUE						
COST OF BEVERAGE SALES						
COST OF OTHER REVENUE						
Audiovisual Cost						
Miscellaneous Cost						
Total Cost of Other Revenue						
TOTAL COST OF BEVERAGE SALES AND OTHER REVENUE						
GROSS PROFIT (LOSS)						
EXPENSES						
Payroll and Related Expenses						
Salaries, Wages, and Bonuses						
Salaries and Wages						
Bonuses and Incentives						
Total Salaries, Wages, and Bonuses						
Payroll-Related Expenses						
Payroll Taxes						
Supplemental Pay						
Employee Benefits						
Total Payroll-Related Expenses						
Total Payroll and Related Expenses						
Other Expenses						
Banquet Expense						
China						
Cleaning Supplies						
Complimentary Services and Gifts						
Contract Services						
Corporate Office Reimbursables						
Decorations						
Dishwashing Supplies						

(continued)

BEVERAGE—SUBSCHEDULE 2-2 *(continued)*

	CURRENT MONTH			YEAR-TO-DATE		
	ACTUAL	FORECAST	PRIOR YEAR	ACTUAL	FORECAST	PRIOR YEAR
	$ | %	$ | %	$ | %	$ | %	$ | %	$ | %
Dues and Subscriptions						
Equipment Rental						
Flatware						
Glassware						
Ice						
Kitchen Fuel						
Laundry and Dry Cleaning						
Licenses and Permits						
Linen						
Management Fees						
Menus and Beverage Lists						
Miscellaneous						
Music and Entertainment						
Operating Supplies						
Paper and Plastics						
Printing and Stationery						
Royalty Fees						
Telecommunications						
Training						
Travel—Meals and Entertainment						
Travel—Other						
Uniform Laundry						
Uniforms						
Utensils						
Total Other Expenses						
TOTAL EXPENSES						
DEPARTMENTAL INCOME (LOSS)						

Beverage—Sub-schedule 2-2 presents the proper format for a separate Beverage department. When separate schedules for food and beverage are prepared, it must be noted that whether a sale is classified as food or beverage revenue is decided by definition of those revenues and is not dependent on the type of outlet in which the sale occurs or the department whose staff is performing service. Moreover, proper recording of payroll costs, other expenses, and other income must occur when Food and Beverage departments are separate in order to match revenues and expenses on departmental schedules.

Revenue

Beverage Revenue includes all sales of alcoholic beverages for consumption by customers. Non-alcoholic beverages are recorded as food revenue in the Food department unless served in a normally pure beverage outlet (bar or lounge) and without food. Non-consumable items sold in the Beverage department are recorded as Other Revenue.

Outlet Beverage Revenue

Outlet Beverage Revenue includes beverage sales in specific dining areas in the property. Examples of outlets are restaurants, lounges, bars, and pool areas. Banquet rooms and guestrooms are not considered outlets.

In-Room Dining Beverage Revenue

In-Room Dining Beverage Revenue includes beverage sales that require delivery to customers in their guestroom. In-Room Dining Beverage Revenue can also include sales that require delivery to other areas inside the hotel or outside as in the example of condominiums that may be located near a property. Group beverage sales ordered from and serviced by the Banquet/Catering department and delivered to outside locations are recorded as Banquet/Catering Beverage Revenues.

Banquet/Catering Beverage Revenue

Banquet/Catering Beverage Revenue includes beverage sales in the property's banquet rooms and for group functions outside the hotel. The banquet designation is used for sales related to groups of customers occupying guestrooms, while catering sales are related to groups of customers who are not occupying guestrooms. Banquet/Catering Beverage Revenues also include sales from beverage service performed by the Banquet/ Catering department in a guestroom/suite.

Mini Bar Beverage Revenue

Mini Bar Beverage Revenue includes sales of packaged beverages (bottles and cans) placed in a guestroom.

Other Beverage Revenue

Other Beverage Revenue includes sales of consumable beverage items not designated as Outlet, In-Room Dining, Banquet/Catering, or Mini Bar revenues. An example of Other Beverage Revenue is beverages sold at the property's front desk or in a tennis shop.

Allowances

Allowances refers to a reduction in revenue due to a service problem, and not an error in posting. Errors in posting, such as charging an incorrect amount on a guest check, are treated as an adjustment to revenue, regardless of the accounting period in which the error occurred.

Total Beverage Revenue

Total Beverage Revenue is calculated by adding together Outlet Beverage Revenue, In-Room Dining Beverage Revenue, Banquet/Catering Beverage Revenue, Mini Bar Beverage Revenue, and Other Beverage Revenue and subtracting Allowances.

Other Revenue

Other Revenue includes sales of services and all products that are not consumable beverage items.

Audiovisual

Audiovisual includes revenues and commissions derived from supplying audiovisual equipment and services to customers, whether the equipment is owned by the property or rented from a third party. If the services and equipment are obtained from an outside company, then the costs incurred are charged to Audiovisual Cost.

Public Room Rentals

Public Room Rentals includes revenues derived from the rental of public meeting rooms to customers. If a guestroom/suite is used as a meeting room and Banquet/Catering Beverage Revenue occurs, the meeting room revenue is recorded as Public Room Rentals. If Banquet/Catering Beverage Revenue does not occur in the guestroom/suite, meeting room revenue is recorded as Other Rooms Revenue in the Rooms department.

Cover Charges

Cover Charges includes charges to customers for entrance to special events where beverage is sold.

Service Charges

Service Charges includes automatic charges added to any beverage sale to help cover the cost of staff service to the customer. Service Charges must be recorded as revenue and may not be credited to any expense account. Discretionary amounts added to a beverage sale as a gratuity to an employee by the customer are treated as tip income to the employee.

Miscellaneous Other Revenue

Miscellaneous Other Revenue includes all non-beverage items or services sold to customers in the Beverage department that are not included in Audiovisual, Public Room Rentals, Cover Charges, or Service Charges. Costs associated with providing these items and services is charged to Miscellaneous Cost. Temporary Internet connection service fees are included in the Telecommunications department.

Allowances

Allowances refers to a reduction in revenue due to a service problem, and not an error in posting. Errors in posting, such as charging an incorrect amount, are treated as an adjustment to revenue.

Total Other Revenue

Total Other Revenue is calculated by adding together Audiovisual, Public Room Rentals, Cover Charges, Service Charges, and Miscellaneous Other Revenue and subtracting Allowances.

Total Revenue

Total Revenue is the sum of Total Beverage Revenue and Total Other Revenue. The sum of Total Revenue from the Beverage department and Total Revenue from the Food department is amount that appears on the Summary Operating Statement under Revenue—Food and Beverage.

In completing the revenue section of Schedule 2 or Sub-schedule 2-2, the Total Revenue line is considered to be 100 percent, and the percentage for each source of revenue is determined by dividing the dollar amount for that revenue source by Total Revenue for the Food and Beverage department (on Schedule 2) or for the Beverage department (on Sub-schedule 2-2).

Cost of Beverage Sales

Cost of Beverage Sales includes the cost of alcoholic beverages served to guests in all segments of beverage revenues. Cost of Beverage Sales also includes the cost of food items transferred from the food department and used in alcoholic beverage preparation and service (this includes the cost of non-alcoholic beverages such as soft drinks whose sales are included in the definition of beverage revenue). Spoilage, waste, and spillage are included in Cost of Beverage Sales and are not charged to Other Expenses. Cost of Beverage Sales does not include costs of beverage items that have been transferred to other departments to be used in preparation or decoration in those departments. Such transfers are charged directly to the appropriate cost accounts in the departments receiving the items. If beverage items are sold at cost and revenue is not recorded (commissary or steward's sales), the sale is credited to the Cost of Beverage Sales. Cost of Beverage Sales does not include the cost associated with beverage inventory items being used for gratis presentation to customers, vendors, and employees of all departments in a hotel. The cost of this complimentary beverage is charged as an expense to Complimentary Services and Gifts in the department that makes the gratis presentation. Finally, if beverage vendor rebates are legal within a jurisdiction and a vendor provides a rebate on beverage purchased, it is subtracted from the Cost of Beverage Sales.

The percentage for Cost of Beverage Sales is calculated by dividing Cost of Beverage Sales by Total Beverage Revenue.

Cost of Other Revenue

Cost of Other Revenue includes the costs associated with the sales of services and all products that are not consumable beverage items. The percentage for each item under Cost of Other Revenue is calculated by dividing the dollar cost by its corresponding revenue amount.

Audiovisual Cost

Audiovisual Cost includes the cost associated with providing audiovisual services to customers in the Beverage department. The income received from charging customers for these services is recorded as Audiovisual revenue.

Miscellaneous Cost

Miscellaneous Cost includes the cost associated with providing non-beverage items and services other than audiovisual services to customers in the Beverage department. The income received from charging customers for these items and services is recorded as Miscellaneous Other Revenue. The cost of providing temporary Internet connections is reported in the Telecommunications department.

Total Cost of Other Revenue

Total Cost of Other Revenue is calculated by adding Audiovisual Cost and Miscellaneous Cost. The percentage for Total Cost of Other Revenue is calculated by dividing Total Cost of Other Revenue by Total Other Revenue.

Total Cost of Beverage Sales and Other Revenue

Total Cost of Beverage Sales and Other Revenue is the sum of Cost of Beverage Sales and Total Cost of Other Revenue. The percentage for Total Cost of Beverage Sales and Other Revenue is calculated by dividing Total Cost of Beverage Sales and Other Revenue by Total Revenue for the Beverage department.

Gross Profit (Loss)

Gross Profit (Loss) is calculated by subtracting Total Cost of Sales and Other Revenue from Total Revenue for the Beverage department. The percentage for Gross Profit (Loss) is calculated by dividing Gross Profit (Loss) by Total Revenue for the Beverage department.

Expenses

Beverage department expenses are separated into two major categories: Payroll and Related Expenses and Other Expenses.

Payroll and Related Expenses

Payroll and Related Expenses for the Beverage department comprises the expenses associated with Salaries, Wages, and Bonuses and Payroll-Related Expenses for employees of the Beverage department. A list of the positions typically included in the Beverage department is shown on page 175.

Salaries, Wages, and Bonuses. This grouping includes (1) Salaries and Wages and (2) Bonuses and Incentives. Salaries and Wages includes only earnings paid to an employee for duties that relate to the operation of the property, such as regular pay, overtime pay, and shift differential pay. If an employee works in a department other than his or her regular home department, his or her earnings must be charged as Salaries and Wages in that other department, regardless of the duties being performed. For example, if a Beverage department employee works as a server for an employee awards banquet, his or her earnings are charged to Salaries and Wages in Administrative and General, and not to this line item. Payroll-Related Expenses (described below) for the above example are treated similarly and charged as Payroll-Related Expenses in Administrative and General.

Salaries and Wages also includes contract or leased labor. Contract or leased labor refers to those situations in which a property enters into an agreement with an outside service to provide employees to fill positions that would normally be held by individuals paid on the regular payroll. In these situations, the property usually supervises the individuals and records or tracks their hours worked and pays them on an hourly basis. A typical example is the use of individuals brought into the property through an employment agency to fill in for a shortage of bartending staff. This situation differs from a contract service in which a property has an agreement with an outside company to provide some type of service. In this case, the contracted organization typically provides the supervision and ensures that the work is performed. The costs associated with this type of agreement are charged under Contract Services for the department receiving the service.

Bonuses and Incentives includes bonuses, incentive pay, and other types of performance pay designed to drive revenue through sales, profit, or guest satisfaction measures.

Total Salaries, Wages, and Bonuses. Calculated by adding together Salaries and Wages and Bonuses and Incentives.

Payroll-Related Expenses. Payroll-Related Expenses includes amounts paid for an employee for duties that relate to the operation of the property and amounts paid for an employee who works in a department other than his or her regular home department regardless of the duties being performed. Payroll-Related Expenses includes the following items:

- *Payroll Taxes.* Includes Federal Retirement and Medicare (FICA), Federal and State Unemployment Taxes (FUTA and SUTA), State Disability Insurance (SDI), and other mandated payroll-related taxes or social insurance items. (See *Payroll-Related Expenses—Schedule 13.*)

- *Supplemental Pay.* Includes personal days, vacation pay, sick pay, holiday pay, jury duty pay, relocation pay, paid time off, and severance pay. Supplemental Pay also includes bonuses and incentive payments that are discretionary and not determined by results from operations.

- *Employee Benefits.* Includes all other payroll-related expenses, such as employer-paid health insurance expenses, cost of meals furnished to employees, pension contributions, and union fees. (See *Payroll-Related Expenses—Schedule 13.*) The distribution of employee meal costs from *Employee Cafeteria—Schedule 12* is charged to this line.

Total Payroll-Related Expenses. Calculated by adding together Payroll Taxes, Supplemental Pay, and Employee Benefits.

Total Payroll and Related Expenses

Total Payroll and Related Expenses is calculated by adding together Total Salaries, Wages and Bonuses and Total Payroll-Related Expenses. The percentage for each payroll and related expense line item as well as Total Payroll and Related Expenses is calculated by dividing the line item amount by Total Revenue for the Beverage department.

Other Expenses

This expense grouping includes the significant Beverage department expenses approved as Other Expenses in the *Uniform System.* Individual properties may delete irrelevant line items, but the *Uniform System* does not provide for the addition or substitution of other expense line items. Rather, properties may choose to develop a sub-account/sub-schedule to provide more detail related to a particular expense item. This sub-account/sub-schedule is then to be rolled into the appropriate line item listed below.

Banquet Expense. Includes the cost of items used in providing banquet service for which matching Other Revenue and Cost of Other Revenue accounts cannot be identified. If expenses can be matched to specific other revenue accounts (audiovisual or miscellaneous), they are recorded as Cost of Other Revenue.

China. Includes the cost of purchased or rented plates, bowls, serving platters, etc., constructed from any material (ceramic, glass, metal, non-disposable plastic, etc.) and used in providing complimentary food service in the Beverage department.

Cleaning Supplies. Includes the cost of products used in cleansing, sweeping, polishing, waxing, and disinfecting areas associated with the Beverage department. The cost of cleaning supplies used in dishwashing is charged to Dishwashing Supplies.

Complimentary Services and Gifts. Includes the cost of providing gift items used in gratis presentations for promotional purposes to guests and vendors of the Beverage department, such as the cost of food provided to guests on a complimentary basis during "Happy Hour."

Contract Services. Includes expenses for activities performed for the Beverage department by outside companies rather than hotel employees. The cost of contracting an outside company to clean the carpet in a lounge area is an example. If supplies are purchased for contract companies to use, the supplies are charged to the appropriate supply account. The cost of contracts for Beverage department laundry and dry cleaning is charged to Laundry and Dry Cleaning.

Corporate Office Reimbursables. Includes the allocations of salaries and expenses of corporate or management company beverage personnel billed to the property by the regional or corporate office or by the management company. Travel expenses of corporate or management company beverage personnel that are incurred while visiting the property, including the costs of meals and other applicable services or amenities provided to corporate or management company staff while on business in the property for the benefit of the property, are also charged to this account.

Decorations. Includes the cost of decorative items used in Beverage department areas for holidays and special events that are not charged directly to banquet customers. (The cost of decorations charged to banquet customers is recorded as Cost of Other Revenue.) Decorations also includes the costs of ice blocks used in decorative carvings.

Dishwashing Supplies. Includes the cost of cleaning, rinsing, and soaking agents used specifically in washing china, glassware, silver, and utensils in the Beverage department.

Dues and Subscriptions. Includes the cost of representation of the Beverage department, or of members of the staff when authorized to represent the Beverage department, in business or professional organizations. Dues and Subscriptions is also charged with the cost of subscriptions to newspapers, magazines, and books for use by the staff of the Beverage department.

Equipment Rental. Includes the cost of renting any type of equipment that may be used either sporadically in the Beverage department or as a replacement for equipment out of service on a temporary basis. Equipment that is rented on a continuous basis and, if purchased, would qualify as a capital purchase is charged to Other Property and Equipment under the Rent section of *Rent, Property and Other Taxes, and Insurance—Schedule 10*. The costs of equipment rental charged to banquet customers is recorded as Cost of Other Revenue.

Flatware. Includes the cost of all flatware and serving pieces (serving spoons, cake knives, ladles, etc.), either purchased or rented, used in providing complimentary food service in the Beverage department.

Glassware. Includes the cost of purchased or rented containers constructed from any material (glass, ceramic, metal, non-disposable plastic, etc.) used in consumption of beverages as defined in the definition of beverage revenue.

Ice. Includes the cost of ice used in beverage service, storage, or preparation. The cost of ice blocks used in decorative carvings and not charged to banquet customers is recorded as Decorations.

Kitchen Fuel. Includes the cost of fuels such as Sterno used in the warming of complimentary food provided to guests during "Happy Hour."

Laundry and Dry Cleaning. Includes the cost of laundry and dry cleaning services applicable to the Beverage department, whether the services are performed by an in-house facility or are contracted to an outside company. If the services are performed by an in-house laundry, an allocation from House Laundry is charged to Laundry and Dry Cleaning. If the services are performed by an outside company, the amount charged to Laundry and Dry Cleaning should be based on invoices sent by the outside laundry. The cost of cleaning employee uniforms is charged to the Uniform Laundry account.

Licenses and Permits. Includes the cost of federal, state, and local licenses, including costs of inspections needed for licensing, for all activities of the Beverage department.

Linen. Includes the cost, whether purchased or rented, of tablecloths, napkins, table runners, and skirting used by the Beverage Department.

Management Fees. Includes any amounts paid to a third-party individual or company to operate or manage a beverage outlet within the property, whether the fees are computed as a fixed amount or a percentage of revenues or profit.

Menus and Beverage Lists. Includes all costs of designing and printing menus for the Beverage department. The costs of decorative and protective covers are also charged to this line item.

Miscellaneous. Includes any expenses of the Beverage department that do not apply to the other line items discussed in this section.

Music and Entertainment. Includes all costs of providing live or recorded entertainment within the Beverage department. Entertainment costs charged to banquet customers is recorded as Cost of Other Revenue.

Operating Supplies. Includes the cost of operating and general office supplies needed to operate the Beverage department that are not included in the descriptions of specific supply accounts such as Cleaning Supplies, Menus, Paper and Plastics, and Printing and Stationery. An example of an item included in this expense is bottle stoppers.

Paper and Plastics. Includes the cost of all general supplies for the Beverage department made from paper, plastic, and Styrofoam that are not specifically assigned by definition to other line items. Items charged to this line include stir sticks, cocktail picks, paper bags, aluminum foil, can liners, disposable plastic utensils, and disposable paper plates.

Printing and Stationery. Includes the cost of printed forms used in the Beverage department, whether they are purchased from an outside source or produced internally. The cost of producing beverage lists is charged to Menus and Beverage Lists.

Royalty Fees. Includes all costs associated with the right to use a brand name in connection with a Beverage department activity. For example, the fees paid for use of a brand name to identify a property beverage outlet, including franchisee fees, are charged to this line item. If the beverage outlet serves both food and beverage, then the fees should be split between the departments on a reasonable basis.

Telecommunications. Includes any telecommunications expenditures that can be directly related to the Beverage department, including the costs of local, long distance, and Internet communications. Telecommunications includes not only traditional telephone systems, but also the cost of cellular phones, including the equipment and periodic service charges, used in the Beverage department. Telecommunications charged to banquet customers is recorded in the Telecommunications department.

Training. Includes the cost, other than time, that can be directly attributed to the training of employees in the Beverage department. Examples include the costs of training materials, supplies, and instructor fees. The cost of employee wages incurred during training is charged to Salaries and Wages.

Travel—Meals and Entertainment. Includes the reimbursable cost of food and beverage expenditures for travel and entertainment by employees of the Beverage department traveling on property business.

Travel—Other. Includes the cost of travel and reimbursable expenditures, other than food, beverage, and entertainment, by employees of the Beverage department traveling on property business.

Uniform Laundry. Includes the cost of cleaning uniforms for employees of the Beverage department whether performed by an in-hotel facility or contracted to an outside company.

Uniforms. Includes the cost of employee uniforms used in the Beverage department, whether purchased or rented. Repair costs are also included in this line item. The cost of cleaning uniforms is charged to the Uniform Laundry account.

Utensils. Includes the cost of utensils (strainers, wine openers, cutting boards/knives) used in providing beverage service, whether purchased or rented.

Total Other Expenses

Total Other Expenses is calculated by adding all items listed under Other Expenses. The percentage for each line item expense as well as Total Other Expenses is calculated by dividing the line item amount by Total Revenue for the Beverage department.

Total Expenses

Total Expenses is calculated by adding Total Payroll and Related Expenses to Total Other Expenses. The percentage for Total Expenses is calculated by dividing Total Expenses by Total Revenue for the Beverage department.

The sum of Total Cost of Beverage Sales and Other Revenue and Total Expenses for the Beverage department and Total Cost of Food Sales and Other Revenue and Total Expenses for the Food department is the amount that appears on the Summary Operating Statement under Departmental Expenses—Food and Beverage.

Departmental Income (Loss)

Departmental Income (Loss) is calculated by subtracting Total Expenses from Gross Profit. The percentage for Departmental Income (Loss) is calculated by dividing Departmental Income (Loss) by Total Revenue for the Beverage department.

OTHER OPERATED DEPARTMENTS—SCHEDULE 3

	CURRENT MONTH			YEAR-TO-DATE		
	ACTUAL	FORECAST	PRIOR YEAR	ACTUAL	FORECAST	PRIOR YEAR
	$ | %	$ | %	$ | %	$ | %	$ | %	$ | %
DEPARTMENTAL REVENUE						
Other Operated Department 1						
Other Operated Department 2						
...						
Other Operated Department *x*						
Minor Operated Departments						
Total Departmental Revenue						
DEPARTMENTAL EXPENSES[1]						
Other Operated Department 1						
Other Operated Department 2						
...						
Other Operated Department *x*						
Minor Operated Departments						
Total Departmental Expenses						
DEPARTMENTAL INCOME (LOSS)						
Other Operated Department 1						
Other Operated Department 2						
...						
Other Operated Department *x*						
Minor Operated Departments						
TOTAL OTHER OPERATED DEPARTMENT INCOME (LOSS)						

1. Departmental Expenses is the sum of Cost of Sales (when applicable) and Total Expenses.

Other Operated Departments—Schedule 3 illustrates the proper format for reporting the summary of the Revenue and Expense amounts for the Other Operated and Minor Operated Departments. Only the revenues and expenses from the Other Operated and Minor Operated Departments that exist at an individual property are included on Schedule 3. To provide more detail, properties must prepare a sub-schedule for each major Other Operated Department as well as a summary sub-schedule for all Minor Operated Departments. The totals from these sub-schedules are then to be incorporated into the appropriate line items on Schedule 3. The names of the line items under Revenue and Departmental Expenses should be changed to the names of the actual Other Operated Department (e.g., Telecommunications). Properties may choose to delete some of the columns or to show them in a different order and remain "in conformity with the *Uniform System.*"

Total Departmental Revenue is the same amount that appears on the Summary Operating Statement under Revenue—Other Operated Departments. Total Departmental Expenses is the same amount that appears on the Summary Operating Statement under Departmental Expenses—Other Operated Departments. All operated departments, exclusive of the Rooms, Food, and Beverage, are classified on the Summary Operating Statement as Other Operated Departments. The following guidelines define an Other Operated Department:

- The department should generate revenue, have direct operating expenses, and be operated with a motivation to make a profit or limit the loss.

- Revenues are reported on a gross basis without the deduction of operating expenses, commissions, or fees. (See below for guidance regarding gross versus net revenue.)

- A department that has minor or no revenue and is operated primarily to provide a complimentary guest service is not classified as an Other Operated Department. The net expense of such a department is allocated to the department(s) that benefits most from the service. For example, if a property provides complimentary guest parking, all expenses for the complimentary parking operation would be charged to the Rooms and/or Food and Beverage departments.

- If the majority of income to the property is "net revenue" (percent of income, percent of profit, commission revenue, etc.), then the net revenues received by the property are classified under *Rentals and Other Income—Schedule 4.* (See below for guidance regarding gross versus net revenue.)

- All of the expenses cannot be paid by third-party operators. If all of the expenses result from a third party performing the services, the activity cannot be classified as an "operated department." (See below for guidance regarding gross versus net revenue.)

- If the vast majority of financial risk and liability for an operating department are assumed by a third-party management company (even though the department and equipment are owned by the hotel's owner), then the "net income" of that department is classified as *Rentals and Other Income—Schedule 4.* (See below for guidance regarding gross versus net revenue.)

Reporting Revenue on a Gross Versus Net Basis

The determination to report revenue on a gross or net basis influences the classification of a revenue source as an Other Operated Department or as Rentals and Other Income. In addition, reporting revenues on a gross or net basis can affect the amount of management, franchise, and other fees and costs that are a function of gross revenues.

The decision to recognize revenue based on the gross amount billed to a customer or the net amount retained (the amount billed to the customer less the amount paid to a supplier) is based on a comparison of the relevant facts and circumstances of the property's revenue source to a series of indicators provided by a variety of accounting authorities. The following paragraphs summarize the indicators that provide guidance for the determination of reporting hotel revenues on a gross or net basis.

Indicators of Gross Revenue Reporting

1. The property is responsible for fulfillment, including the acceptability of the product or service ordered or purchased by the customer.

2. The property takes title to a product before that product is ordered by a customer or will take title to the product if the customer returns it.

3. The property has latitude in establishing price.

4. The property modifies the product, other than packaging, or performs part of the service ordered by a customer.

5. The property has multiple suppliers for a product or service ordered by a customer and discretion to select the supplier.

6. The property determines the nature, type, characteristics, or specifications of the product(s) or service(s) ordered by the customer

7. Title to the product is transferred to the property at the shipping point and is transferred from the property to the customer upon delivery.

8. The property has credit risk. The property is responsible for collecting the sales price from a customer but must pay the amount owed to a supplier after the supplier performs, regardless of whether the sales price is fully collected. Credit risk is not present if:

    - a property returns or refunds only the net amount it earned in the transaction if the transaction is cancelled or reversed;

    - a property fully collects the sales price prior to the delivery of the product or service to the customer (in other words, before the property incurs an obligation to the supplier); and

    - a customer pays by credit card and a property obtains authorization for the charge in advance of product shipment or service performance.

Indicators of Net Revenue Reporting

1. The supplier (not the property) is the primary obligor in the arrangement.

    - The supplier (and not the property) is responsible for fulfillment, including the acceptability of the product(s) or service(s) ordered or purchased by a customer.

    - Representations (written or otherwise) made by a property during marketing and the terms of the sales contract generally will provide evidence as to a customer's understanding of whether the property or the supplier is responsible for fulfilling the ordered product or service.

2. The amount the property earns is fixed.

    - The property earns a fixed dollar amount per customer transaction regardless of the amount billed to a customer.

- The property earns a stated percentage of the amount billed to a customer.

3. The supplier (and not the property) has credit risk.

The determination to classify a property's revenue source as an Other Operated Department or as Rentals and Other Income is based on the balance of the preceding indicators that exist given the facts and circumstances for the production, execution, and delivery of each revenue source. If the predominance of indicators favors the reporting of revenue on a gross basis, then the revenue source is classified as an Other Operated Department. If the predominance of indicators favors the reporting of revenue on a net basis, then the net revenue is recorded as Rentals and Other Income.

Case Study Examples of Gross Versus Net Revenue Reporting

The following "case studies" are presented to provide examples of applications of the preceding indicators to common property revenue sources. Many more revenue instances will fall into these types of determinations. In each case, it is the reporting entity that determines if the revenues are reported as gross or net and each case will depend on the facts and circumstances of the arrangement, written or otherwise, between the property and the supplier.

Laundry and Dry Cleaning

Scenario One: In-House Operation

Structure. Property A operates a laundry facility that performs laundry and dry cleaning services for the guests of the hotel. All employees are employed by the property. In addition, the equipment and supplies are also owned (or leased) by the property.

Evaluation. Since Property A is responsible for providing the service to the guest, sets the prices charged, and assumes the risk of collection, the revenues and expenses under Scenario One are reported on a gross basis within a Guest Laundry Operated Department.

Scenario Two: Outside Contract

Structure. Property A issues an RFP to several local laundries that specifies quality standards, delivery and pickup times, and other elements of providing laundry and dry cleaning services to its guests. After evaluation of all proposals submitted, Property A contracts with XYZ Cleaners to launder and dry clean clothing of its guests. Property A collects the clothing from the guest, passes the clothing on to XYZ Cleaners for laundering or dry cleaning, and then returns the clothing to the guest's room. XYZ Cleaner charges Property A the contracted amount to clean each item of clothing. Property A then marks up the cost charged by XYZ (by a fixed dollar amount or percentage) and charges the guest the higher amount. Property A is the primary obligor in providing the service and takes all responsibility for resolving guest service issues. Property A also has discretion in selecting which outside laundry service to use.

Evaluation. Since Property A is the primary obligor, does provide a moderate degree of service to the guest (pick up and return of the clothing), sets the standards of service and prices charged to the guest, and assumes the risk of collection, the revenues and expenses under Scenario Two are reported on a gross basis as either an Other Operated Department or as a Minor Operated Department.

Scenario Three: Outside Concessionaire

Structure. XYZ Cleaners approaches Property A to provide laundry and dry cleaning services for the property's guests. Guests of Property A bring their clothing to the front desk. The property then passes the clothing on to XYZ Cleaners for laundering or dry cleaning. Upon return to the property, the clothing is stored at the front desk for guest pick-up. Property A passes on the cost of the charge received from XYZ Cleaners directly to the guest without a mark up. Property A then pays XYZ Cleaners the amount of laundry/dry cleaning revenue collected by property, minus a commission (percent of revenue or fixed dollar amount per item).

Evaluation. Since Property A provides only a limited degree of service to the guest, does not mark up the price from that charged by XYZ Cleaners, and receives a fixed commission, the revenue to the property under Scenario Three (the commission) is reported in Rental and Other Income on a net basis.

In-Room TV Entertainment

Scenario One: In-House Operation

Structure. Property A owns its own TVs and MATV system and provides free local and basic and some premium cable channels to guests. Each room has its own VCR/DVD player and the property maintains a library of tapes and DVDs for rent by guests. In-room promotions list the titles available and the charges to rent a tape or DVD.

Evaluation. Since Property A is responsible for providing the service to the guest, sets the prices charged, carries the inventory of tapes and DVDs, and assumes the risk of collection, the revenues and expenses under Scenario One are reported on a gross basis as either an Other Operated Department or as a Minor Operated Department.

Scenario Two: Outside TV Entertainment Service Agreement

Structure. Property B enters into a service agreement with XYZ Video Corporation (XYZ Video) to provide pay-per-view movies and other electronic guest services which may include on-demand music, video games, TV on demand, music on demand, and Internet access, all charged to the guest on a per-usage basis. The guest is made aware through in-room literature and/or video content that XYZ Video is providing these electronic video and guest services. XYZ Video sets the pricing of all services charged to the guest.

Property B owns or leases its TV and MATV system. XYZ Video owns and maintains its "system" of in-room electronic services.

Property B bills the guests the gross amount of the pay-per-view service as recorded by XYZ Video's monitoring system plus any applicable sales and use taxes. On a monthly basis, XYZ Video invoices Property B for the pay-per-view/usage fees recorded by its monitoring device. Property B is allowed to deduct a commission from its remittance to XYZ Video that is typically a percentage of the pay-per-view/usage fees.

XYZ Video provides training to Property B's personnel in the operation of the system, use of in-room electronic services, managing guest issues and complaints, and programming content, among other things. XYZ Video may permit a set number of monthly adjustments to guest pay-per-view charges, a flat percentage of total pay-per-view revenue to be adjusted off the monthly invoice, or it may allow Property B's management to determine all rebates to accommodate guest complaints depending on the contract.

Evaluation. Since Property B receives a percentage commission of the pay-per-view/usage fees charged to the guest, it would record the net commission in Rentals and Other Income. Although it does provide some level of service, Property B has no inventory risk, little collection risk, and also has the adjustments allowed by XYZ Video to mitigate guests' disputes. To the guest, XYZ Video is prominently featured in all in-room advertising and equipment as the provider (primary obligor) of the movies and other electronic guest services.

Garage/Parking

Scenario One: Property Operation

Structure. Property A operates the parking garage and performs all services for guests using the facility. Property A employs the garage employees and is responsible for the costs of operating the facility.

Evaluation. As Property A directly provides the services to the guest, controls the pricing, and has retained the risks and rewards of ownership, the revenue and expenses under this scenario are properly recorded on a gross basis and the Garage is considered an operating department.

Scenario Two: Outside Contractor

Structure. Property A contracts with Contractor Z to provide garage administration and valet parking services for Property A's guests. Property A owns the garage structure, employs the personnel, is responsible for costs of maintenance of the facility (including liability insurance), and has approval rights over the price to be charged to guests. Contractor Z charges the Property a contracted amount (percent of revenue or fixed amount) to provide the garage services. Property A is responsible for collecting the amounts charged to guests' folios.

Evaluation. As Property A provides the facility for the service, assumes the risk of collection, retains control over pricing, and bears the risk of departmental loss, the revenues and expenses are reported on a gross basis under this scenario and the Garage is considered an operating department.

Scenario Three: Outside Concessionaire

Structure. Property A contracts with Company Z to provide parking facilities in a preferred provider relationship with the property. Company Z owns and operates the garage. Property A passes the charge set by Company Z on to the guest without a mark-up and is responsible for the collection from the guest. The amounts collected on behalf of Company Z are remitted back to Garage Z on a periodic basis net of a contracted commission.

Evaluation. As Property A has not assumed the risk and rewards of operating the parking garage, the revenues are recorded on a net basis, with Property A only recording the amount of the commission in Rentals and Other Income.

Scenario Four: Lease to Outside Concessionaire

Structure. Property A leases a garage facility to a third party (Company Z) that operates the garage. Under the terms of the lease, the garage is to provide parking services for the property. Company Z establishes the price to be charged for the service. Guests are able to charge the parking fees to their folio, in which case Property A remits the amount of collections back to Company Z on a periodic basis.

Evaluation. Property A includes the rental income as part of its revenues in Rentals and Other Income.

Other Operated Department Schedule Formats

A property must include a sub-schedule for each of the Other Operated Departments that it runs or manages, and a consolidated schedule for all Minor Operated Departments. The total revenue and expenses for each Other Operated Department are added to the total revenues and expenses from all Minor Operated Departments on Schedule 3. The combined revenues and expenses for all Other Operated Departments as shown on Schedule 3 are then listed on the Summary Operating Statement.

The format for an Other Operated Department sub-schedule follows the same base outline as the departmental schedules for the Rooms and Food and Beverage departments. The following pages contain sample sub-schedules for Telecommunications, Golf Course and Pro Shop, Health Club/Spa, and Parking Garage. In addition, a generic sub-schedule is presented to provide guidance on the format of a sub-schedule for potential Other Operated Departments (e.g., Guest Laundry, Business Center, Retail Store). Finally, a schedule is provided that summarizes and aggregates all revenues and expenses for Minor Operated Departments.

TELECOMMUNICATIONS—SUB-SCHEDULE 3-1

	CURRENT MONTH			YEAR-TO-DATE		
	ACTUAL	FORECAST	PRIOR YEAR	ACTUAL	FORECAST	PRIOR YEAR
	$ | %	$ | %	$ | %	$ | %	$ | %	$ | %
REVENUE						
Local Call Revenue						
Long Distance Revenue						
Internet Revenue						
Other Revenue						
Less: Allowances						
Total Telecommunications Revenue						
COST OF CALLS						
Cost of Local Calls						
Cost of Long Distance Calls						
Cost of Internet Service						
Other Cost						
Total Cost of Calls						
GROSS PROFIT (LOSS)						
EXPENSES						
Payroll and Related Expenses						
Salaries, Wages, and Bonuses						
Salaries and Wages						
Bonuses and Incentives						
Total Salaries, Wages, and Bonuses						
Payroll-Related Expenses						
Payroll Taxes						
Supplemental Pay						
Employee Benefits						
Total Payroll-Related Expenses						
Total Payroll and Related Expenses						
Other Expenses						
Contract Services						
Corporate Office Reimbursables						
Decorations						
Dues and Subscriptions						
Equipment Rental						
Laundry and Dry Cleaning						
Miscellaneous						
Operating Supplies						
Printing and Stationery						
Professional Fees						
Telecommunications						
Training						
Travel—Meals and Entertainment						
Travel—Other						
Uniform Laundry						
Uniforms						
Total Other Expenses						
TOTAL EXPENSES						
DEPARTMENTAL INCOME (LOSS)						

Telecommunications—Sub-schedule 3-1 illustrates the proper format for reporting the Revenue, Cost of Calls, Payroll and Related Expenses, Other Expenses, and Income (Loss) amounts for a Telecommunications department. Individual properties may delete irrelevant line items, but the *Uniform System* does not provide for the addition or substitution of other revenue or expense line items. Rather, properties may choose to develop further sub-accounts/sub-schedules to provide more detail related to a particular revenue or expense item. These additional sub-accounts/sub-schedules are then to be rolled into the appropriate line item on Sub-schedule 3-1. Additionally, properties may choose to delete some of the columns or to show them in a different order and remain "in conformity with the *Uniform System.*"

The Total Telecommunications Revenue, Total Expenses (including Total Cost of Calls), and Departmental Income (Loss) shown on Sub-schedule 3-1 are then reported on Schedule 3.

Revenue

Telecommunications Revenue is categorized into Local Call Revenue, Long Distance Revenue, Internet Revenue, and Other Revenue.

Local Call Revenue

Local Call Revenue includes revenue from calls made by guests that are designated as non-toll calls by the service provider.

Long Distance Revenue

Long Distance Revenue includes revenue from calls made by guests that are designated as toll calls by the service provider.

Internet Revenue

Internet Revenue includes revenue generated from the guest use of Internet services when the cost of providing these services is incurred directly by the hotel. This includes the guest use of Internet services in both guestrooms and public rooms. The commission received from a third-party operator of Internet service is recorded in *Rentals and Other Income—Schedule 4.*

Other Revenue

Other Revenue includes revenue from service charges, owned pay stations, and from other telecommunications services not included in Local Call Revenue, Long Distance Revenue, or Internet Revenue. Revenue derived from guests using facsimile services is also credited to this line item, unless the property has a Business Center, in which case the revenue is recorded as Business Center Revenue. Commissions from non-owned pay stations are recorded in *Rentals and Other Income—Schedule 4.*

Allowances

Allowances refers to a reduction in revenue due to a service problem, and not an error in posting. Errors in posting, such as posting an incorrect charge, are treated as an adjustment to revenue, regardless of the accounting period in which the error occurred.

Total Telecommunications Revenue

Total Telecommunications Revenue is calculated by adding together Local Call Revenue, Long Distance Revenue, Internet Revenue, and Other Revenue and subtracting Allowances. This amount is shown on Schedule 3 as Departmental Revenue—Telecommunications.

In completing the revenue section of Schedule 3-1, the Total Telecommunications Revenue line is considered to be 100 percent, and the percentage for each source of revenue is determined by dividing the dollar amount for that revenue source by Total Telecommunications Revenue.

Cost of Calls

Cost of Calls is divided into Cost of Local Calls, Cost of Long Distance Calls, Cost of Internet Service, and Other Cost. The Telecommunications department is not charged with any expenses for telecommunication, Internet, or facsimile services used by management or other departments of the property. The percentage for each item under Cost of Calls is calculated by dividing the cost by its corresponding revenue amount.

Cost of Local Calls

Cost of Local Calls includes the cost of calls designated as non-toll calls by the service provider, such as the associated costs for trunk lines, access charges, usage fees, and utility taxes. The cost of complimentary guest local phone calls is charged to this account, unless the complimentary offering is part of a Marketing department promotion.

Cost of Long Distance Calls

Cost of Long Distance Calls includes the cost of calls designated as toll calls by the service provider, such as the associated costs for trunk lines, access charges, usage fees, and utility taxes. The cost of complimentary guest long distance phone calls is charged to this account, unless the complimentary offering is part of a Marketing department promotion.

Cost of Internet Service

Cost of Internet Service includes the cost of providing Internet service, such as access charges, miscellaneous equipment not eligible for capitalization, and interchange fees.

Other Cost

Other Cost includes any cost incurred in generating Other Revenue.

Total Cost of Calls

Total Cost of Calls is calculated by adding together Cost of Local Calls, Cost of Long Distance Calls, Costs of Internet Service, and Other Cost. The percentage for

Total Cost of Calls is calculated by dividing Total Cost of Calls by Total Telecommunications Revenue.

Gross Profit (Loss)

The Gross Profit (Loss) is calculated by subtracting the Total Cost of Calls from Total Telecommunications Revenue. The percentage for Gross Profit (Loss) is calculated by dividing Gross Profit (Loss) by Total Telecommunications Revenue.

Expenses

Telecommunications department expenses are separated into two major categories: Payroll and Related Expenses and Other Expenses.

Payroll and Related Expenses

Payroll and Related Expenses for the Telecommunications department comprises the expenses associated with Salaries, Wages, and Bonuses and Payroll-Related Expenses for employees of the Telecommunications department. A list of the positions typically included in the Telecommunications department is shown on page 176.

Salaries, Wages, and Bonuses. This grouping includes (1) Salaries and Wages and (2) Bonuses and Incentives. Salaries and Wages includes only earnings paid to an employee for duties that relate to the operation of the property, such as regular pay, overtime pay, and shift differential pay. If an employee works in a department other than his or her regular home department, his or her earnings are charged as Salaries and Wages in that other department, regardless of the duties being performed. For example, if a Telecommunications department employee works as a server for an employee awards banquet, his or her earnings are charged to Salaries and Wages in Administrative and General, and not to this line item. Payroll-Related Expenses (described below) for the above example are treated similarly and charged as Payroll-Related Expenses in Administrative and General.

Salaries and Wages also includes contract or leased labor. Contract or leased labor refers to those situations in which a property enters into an agreement with an outside service to provide employees to fill positions that would normally be held by individuals paid on the regular payroll. In these situations, the property usually supervises the individuals and records or tracks their hours worked and pays them on an hourly basis. An example is the use of individuals brought into the property to fill in for a shortage of telephone operators. This situation differs from a contract service in which a property has an agreement with an outside company to provide some type of service, such as maintenance of the telephone equipment. In this case, the contracted organization typically provides the supervision and ensures that the work is performed. The costs associated with this type of agreement are charged under Contract Services for the department receiving the service.

Bonuses and Incentives includes bonuses, incentive pay, and other types of performance pay designed to drive revenue through sales, profit, or guest satisfaction measures.

Total Salaries, Wages, and Bonuses. Calculated by adding together Salaries and Wages and Bonuses and Incentives.

Payroll-Related Expenses. Payroll-Related Expenses includes amounts paid for an employee for duties that relate to the operation of the property and amounts paid for an employee who works in a department other than his or her regular home department regardless of the duties being performed. Payroll-Related Expenses includes the following items:

- *Payroll Taxes.* Includes Federal Retirement and Medicare (FICA), Federal and State Unemployment Taxes (FUTA and SUTA), State Disability Insurance (SDI), and other mandated payroll-related taxes or social insurance items. (See *Payroll-Related Expenses—Schedule 13.*)

- *Supplemental Pay.* Includes personal days, vacation pay, sick pay, holiday pay, jury duty pay, relocation pay, paid time off, and severance pay. Supplemental Pay also includes bonuses and incentive payments that are discretionary and not determined by results from operations.

- *Employee Benefits.* Includes all other payroll-related expenses, such as employer-paid health insurance expenses, cost of meals furnished to employees, pension contributions, and union fees. (See *Payroll-Related Expenses—Schedule 13.*) The distribution of employee meal costs from *Employee Cafeteria—Schedule 12* is charged to this line.

Total Payroll-Related Expenses. Calculated by adding together Payroll Taxes, Supplemental Pay, and Employee Benefits.

Total Payroll and Related Expenses

Total Payroll and Related Expenses is calculated by adding together Total Salaries, Wages and Bonuses and Total Payroll-Related Expenses. The percentage for each payroll and related expense line item as well as Total Payroll and Related Expenses is calculated by dividing the line item amount by Total Telecommunications Revenue.

Other Expenses

This expense grouping includes the significant Telecommunications department expenses approved as Other Expenses in the *Uniform System*. Individual properties may delete irrelevant line items, but the *Uniform System* does not provide for the addition or substitution of other expense line items. Rather, properties may choose to develop a sub-account/sub-schedule to provide more detail related to a particular expense item. This sub-account/sub-schedule is then to be rolled into the appropriate line item listed below.

Contract Services. Includes expenses for activities performed for the Telecommunications department by outside companies rather than hotel employees. Exceptions include contracts for the maintenance of the telephone system. The costs associated with contracting telecommunications maintenance is charged to Information Systems within the Administrative and General Department.

Corporate Office Reimbursables. Includes the allocations of salaries and expenses of corporate or management company telecommunications personnel billed to the property by the regional or corporate office or by the management company. Travel expenses of such corporate or management company personnel that are incurred while visiting the property, including the costs of meals and other applicable services or amenities provided to corporate or management company staff while on business in the property for the benefit of the property, are also charged to this account.

Decorations. Includes the cost of decorative items used in Telecommunications department areas for holidays and special events.

Dues and Subscriptions. Includes the cost of representation of the Telecommunications department, or of members of the staff when authorized to represent the Telecommunications department, in business or professional organizations. Dues and Subscriptions is also charged with the cost of subscriptions to newspapers, magazines, and books for use by the staff of the Telecommunications department.

Equipment Rental. Includes the costs of renting any type of equipment that may be used either sporadically in the Telecommunications department or as a replacement for equipment out of service on a temporary basis. Equipment that is rented on a continuous basis and, if purchased, would qualify as a capital purchase is charged to Other Property and Equipment under the Rent section of *Rent, Property and Other Taxes, and Insurance—Schedule 10*. The costs of equipment rental charged to banquet customers is recorded as Cost of Other Revenue in Food and Beverage.

Laundry and Dry Cleaning. Includes the cost of laundry and dry cleaning services applicable to the Telecommunications department, whether the services are performed by an in-house facility or are contracted to an outside company. If the services are performed by an in-house laundry, an allocation from House Laundry is charged to Laundry and Dry Cleaning. If the services are performed by an outside company, the amount charged to Laundry and Dry Cleaning should be based on invoices sent by the outside laundry. The cost of cleaning employee uniforms is charged to the Uniform Laundry account.

Miscellaneous. Includes any expenses of the Telecommunications department that do not apply to the other line items discussed in this section.

Operating Supplies. Includes the cost of operating and general office supplies needed to operate the Telecommunications department other than those assigned to Printing and Stationery. An example of an item included in Operating Supplies is a telephone headset.

Printing and Stationery. Includes the cost of printed forms used in the Telecommunications department, whether they are purchased from an outside source or produced internally.

Professional Fees. Includes the cost of specialists, whether certified or not, engaged to assist management in Telecommunications operations.

Telecommunications. Includes any telecommunications expenditures that can be directly related to the Telecommunications department, including the costs of local, long distance, and Internet communications. Telecommunications includes not only traditional telephone systems, but also the cost of cellular phones, including the equipment and periodic service charges, used in the Tele-communications department. The costs directly associated with guest use of tele-phones, Internet service, fax machines, and other electronic communication devices are charged to Cost of Calls in the Telecommunications department.

Training. Includes the costs, other than time, that can be directly attributed to the training of employees in the Telecommunications department. Examples include the costs of training materials, supplies, and instructor fees. The cost of employee wages incurred during training is charged to Salaries and Wages.

Travel—Meals and Entertainment. Includes the reimbursable cost of food and beverage expenses for travel and entertainment by employees of the Telecom-munications department traveling on property business.

Travel—Other. Includes the cost of travel and reimbursable expenses, other than food, beverage, and entertainment, by employees of the Telecommunications department traveling on property business.

Uniform Laundry. Includes the cost of cleaning uniforms for employees of the Telecommunications department whether performed by an in-hotel facility or contracted to an outside company.

Uniforms. Includes the cost of employee uniforms used in the Telecommu-nications department, whether purchased or rented. Repair costs are also included in this line item. The cost of cleaning uniforms is charged to the Uniform Laundry account.

Total Other Expenses

Total Other Expenses is calculated by adding all items listed under Other Expenses. The percentage for each line item expense as well as Total Other Expenses is calculated by dividing the line item amount by Total Telecommunica-tions Revenue.

Total Expenses

Total Expenses is calculated by adding Total Payroll and Related Expenses to Total Other Expenses. The percentage for Total Expenses is calculated by dividing Total Expenses by Total Telecommunications Revenue.

The sum of Total Cost of Calls and Total Expenses is shown on Schedule 3 as Departmental Expenses—Telecommunications.

Departmental Income (Loss)

Departmental Income (Loss) is calculated by subtracting Total Expenses from Gross Profit. The percentage for Departmental Income (Loss) is calculated by dividing Departmental Income (Loss) by Total Telecommunications Revenue. Departmental Income (Loss) is shown on Schedule 3 as Departmental Income (Loss)—Telecommunications.

GOLF COURSE AND PRO SHOP—SUB-SCHEDULE 3-2

	CURRENT MONTH			YEAR-TO-DATE		
	ACTUAL	FORECAST	PRIOR YEAR	ACTUAL	FORECAST	PRIOR YEAR
	$ %	$ %	$ %	$ %	$ %	$ %
REVENUE						
Greens Fee Revenue						
Tournament Fee Revenue						
Golf Cart Rental Revenue						
Golf Equipment Rental Revenue						
Practice Range Fee Revenue						
Lesson Fee Revenue						
Golf Club Maintenance Revenue						
Storage Fee Revenue						
Membership Fee Revenue						
Merchandise Revenue						
Clothing Revenue						
Other Revenue						
Less: Allowances						
Total Golf Course and Pro Shop Revenue						
COST OF SALES						
Cost of Merchandise Sales						
Cost of Clothing Sales						
Total Cost of Sales						
GROSS PROFIT (LOSS)						
EXPENSES						
Payroll and Related Expenses						
Salaries, Wages, and Bonuses						
Salaries and Wages						
Bonuses and Incentives						
Total Salaries, Wages, and Bonuses						
Payroll-Related Expenses						
Payroll Taxes						
Supplemental Pay						
Employee Benefits						
Total Payroll-Related Expenses						
Total Payroll and Related Expenses						
Other Expenses						
Cleaning Supplies						
Complimentary Services and Gifts						
Contract Services						
Corporate Office Reimbursables						
Decorations						
Dues and Subscriptions						
Equipment Rental						
Gasoline and Lubricants						
Golf Cart Batteries/Electricity						
Golf Cart Repairs and Maintenance						
Grounds Maintenance and Landscaping						
Irrigation						
Laundry and Dry Cleaning						
Licenses and Permits						

(continued)

GOLF COURSE AND PRO SHOP—SUB-SCHEDULE 3-2 *(continued)*

	CURRENT MONTH			YEAR-TO-DATE		
	ACTUAL	FORECAST	PRIOR YEAR	ACTUAL	FORECAST	PRIOR YEAR
	$ %	$ %	$ %	$ %	$ %	$ %
Linen						
Management Fees						
Miscellaneous						
Operating Supplies						
Printing and Stationery						
Professional Fees						
Royalty Fees						
Telecommunications						
Tournament Expenses						
Training						
Transportation						
Travel—Meals and Entertainment						
Travel—Other						
Uniform Laundry						
Uniforms						
Water						
Total Other Expenses						
TOTAL EXPENSES						
DEPARTMENTAL INCOME (LOSS)						

Golf Course and Pro Shop—Sub-schedule 3-2 illustrates the proper format for reporting the Revenue, Cost of Sales, Payroll and Related Expenses, Other Expenses, and Income (Loss) amounts for a separate Golf Course and Pro Shop. Individual properties may delete irrelevant line items, but the *Uniform System* does not provide for the addition or substitution of other revenue or expense line items. Rather, properties may choose to develop further sub-accounts/sub-schedules to provide more detail related to a particular revenue or expense item. These additional sub-accounts/sub-schedules are then to be rolled into the appropriate line item on Sub-schedule 3-2. Additionally, properties may choose to delete some of the columns or to show them in a different order and remain "in conformity with the *Uniform System.*"

The Total Golf Course and Pro Shop Revenue, Total Expenses (including Total Cost of Sales), and Departmental Income (Loss) shown on Sub-schedule 3-2 are then reported on Schedule 3.

Revenue

Revenue from the Golf Course and Pro Shop is classified into the following categories.

Greens Fee Revenue

Greens Fee Revenue includes revenue derived from charges to customers for playing golf on the golf course. Examples of Greens Fees charged to this account are those for hotel guests, club members, and general public. Revenues collected for tournament play are recorded as Tournament Fee Revenue. Revenues derived from rental of golf carts are recorded as Golf Cart Rental Revenue.

Tournament Fee Revenue

Tournament Fee Revenue includes revenue derived from charges to customers for the playing of golf in organized tournaments.

Golf Cart Rental Revenue

Golf Cart Rental Revenue includes revenue derived from the rental of electric or gasoline-powered golf carts to customers of the Golf department. Pull cart rental revenue is recorded as Golf Equipment Rental Revenue.

Golf Equipment Rental Revenue

Golf Equipment Rental Revenue includes revenue derived from rental of all items used to play golf, such as clubs and pull carts. Power cart rental revenues are recorded as Golf Cart Rental Revenue.

Practice Range Fee Revenue

Practice Range Fee Revenue includes revenue derived from the use of golf practice facilities of any kind (driving, putting, etc.) whether the facilities are located indoors or outdoors.

Lesson Fee Revenue

Lesson Fee Revenue includes revenue derived from all golf lessons given to customers whether on the golf course or practice range.

Golf Club Maintenance Revenue

Golf Club Maintenance Revenue includes revenue derived from the cleaning and repair of golf clubs for customers.

Storage Fee Revenue

Storage Fee Revenue includes revenue derived from renting personal lockers or golf cart space to customers.

Membership Fee Revenue

Membership Fee Revenue includes revenue derived from charging customers for a "membership" at the golf course, which normally allows the customer "member" to exercise privileges not given to the general public. Examples of privileges might be preferred tee times or discounts for golf or merchandise.

Merchandise Revenue

Merchandise Revenue includes revenue derived from all sales of non-clothing items in the golf shop or anywhere on the golf course. Examples of merchandise would be clubs, bags, and balls.

Clothing Revenue

Clothing Revenue includes revenues derived from all sales of clothing items in the golf shop or anywhere on the golf course.

Other Revenue

Other Revenue includes revenue from providing any other services not previously specified. Revenue from food and beverage sales sold on the golf course is reported in Food and Beverage.

Allowances

Allowances refers to a reduction in revenue due to a service problem, and not an error in posting. Errors in posting, such as charging an incorrect amount, are treated as an adjustment to revenue, regardless of the accounting period in which the error occurred.

Total Golf Course and Pro Shop Revenue

Total Golf Course and Pro Shop Revenue is calculated by adding together each of the revenue items listed above and subtracting Allowances. This amount is shown on Schedule 3 as Departmental Revenue—Golf Course and Pro Shop.

In completing the revenue section of Schedule 3-2, the Total Golf Course and Pro Shop Revenue line is considered to be 100 percent, and the percentage for each source of revenue is determined by dividing the dollar amount for that revenue source by Total Golf Course and Pro Shop Revenue.

Cost of Sales

Cost of Sales is divided into two categories: Cost of Merchandise Sales and Cost of Clothing Sales. The percentage for each of the Costs of Sales is calculated by dividing the dollar cost by its corresponding revenue amount.

Cost of Merchandise Sales

Cost of Merchandise Sales includes the cost of non-clothing items sold to customers of the Golf Course and Pro Shop. Inventory losses due to damaged or missing items are also charged to the Cost of Merchandise Sales and are not charged to Other Expenses. Cost of Merchandise Sales does not include the cost associated with non-clothing items used for gratis presentation to customers, vendors, and employees of any department in the property. The cost of any complimentary items is charged as an expense to Complimentary Services and Gifts expense for the department that makes the gratis presentation.

Cost of Clothing Sales

Cost of Clothing Sales includes the cost of clothing items sold to customers of the Golf Course and Pro Shop. Inventory losses due to damaged or missing items are also charged to the Cost of Clothing Sales and are not charged to Other Expenses. Cost of Clothing Sales does not include the cost associated with clothing items used for gratis presentation to customers, vendors, and employees of any department in the property. The cost of any complimentary clothing items is charged as an expense to Complimentary Services and Gifts expense for the department that makes the gratis presentation.

Total Cost of Sales

Total Cost of Sales is the sum of Cost of Merchandise Sales and Cost of Clothing Sales. The percentage for Total Cost of Sales is calculated by dividing Total Cost of Sales by the sum of Merchandise Revenue and Clothing Revenue.

Gross Profit (Loss)

Gross Profit (Loss) is calculated by subtracting Total Cost of Sales from Total Golf Course and Pro Shop Revenue. The percentage for Gross Profit (Loss) is calculated by dividing Gross Profit (Loss) by Total Golf Course and Pro Shop Revenue.

Expenses

Golf Course and Pro Shop expenses are separated into two major categories: Payroll and Related Expenses and Other Expenses.

Payroll and Related Expenses

Payroll and Related Expenses for the Golf Course and Pro Shop comprises the expenses associated with Salaries, Wages, and Bonuses and Payroll-Related Expenses for employees of the Golf Course and Pro Shop. A list of the positions typically included in the Golf Course and Pro Shop is shown on page 176.

Salaries, Wages, and Bonuses. This grouping includes (1) Salaries and Wages and (2) Bonuses and Incentives. Salaries and Wages includes only earnings paid to an employee for duties that relate to the operation of the property, such as regular pay, overtime pay, and shift differential pay. If an employee works in a department other than his or her regular home department, his or her earnings are charged as Salaries and Wages in that other department, regardless of the duties being performed. For example, if a Pro Shop employee works as a server for an employee awards banquet, his or her earnings are charged to Salaries and Wages in Administrative and General, and not to this line item. Payroll-Related Expenses (described below) for the above example are treated similarly and charged as Payroll-Related Expenses in Administrative and General.

Salaries and Wages also includes contract or leased labor. Contract or leased labor refers to those situations in which a property enters into an agreement with an outside service to provide employees to fill positions that would normally be held by individuals paid on the regular payroll. In these situations, the property usually supervises the individuals and records or tracks their hours worked and pays them on an hourly basis. A typical example is the use of individuals brought into the property to fill in for a shortage of caddies or bag attendants. This situation differs from a contract service in which a property has an agreement with an outside company to provide some type of service, such as landscaping. In this case, the contracted organization typically provides the supervision and ensures that the work is performed. The costs associated with this type of agreement are charged under Contract Services for the department receiving the service.

Bonuses and Incentives includes bonuses, incentive pay, and other types of performance pay designed to drive revenue through sales, profit, or guest satisfaction measures.

Total Salaries, Wages, and Bonuses. Calculated by adding together Salaries and Wages and Bonuses and Incentives.

Payroll-Related Expenses. Payroll-Related Expenses includes amounts paid for an employee for duties that relate to the operation of the property and amounts paid for an employee who works in a department other than his or her regular home department regardless of the duties being performed. Payroll-Related Expenses includes the following items:

- *Payroll Taxes.* Includes Federal Retirement and Medicare (FICA), Federal and State Unemployment Taxes (FUTA and SUTA), State Disability Insurance (SDI), and other mandated payroll-related taxes or social insurance items. (See *Payroll-Related Expenses—Schedule 13.*)

- *Supplemental Pay.* Includes personal days, vacation pay, sick pay, holiday pay, jury duty pay, relocation pay, paid time off, and severance pay. Supplemental Pay also includes bonuses and incentive payments that are discretionary and not determined by results from operations.

- *Employee Benefits.* Includes all other payroll-related expenses, such as employer-paid health insurance expenses, cost of meals furnished to employees, pension contributions, and union fees. (See *Payroll-Related Expenses—Schedule 13.*) The distribution of employee meal costs from *Employee Cafeteria—Schedule 12* is charged to this line.

Total Payroll-Related Expenses. Calculated by adding together Payroll Taxes, Supplemental Pay, and Employee Benefits.

Total Payroll and Related Expenses

Total Payroll and Related Expenses is calculated by adding together Total Salaries, Wages, and Bonuses and Total Payroll-Related Expenses. The percentage for each payroll and related expense line item as well as Total Payroll and Related Expenses is calculated by dividing the line item amount by Total Golf Course and Pro Shop Revenue.

Other Expenses

This expense grouping includes the significant Golf Course and Pro Shop expenses approved as Other Expenses in the *Uniform System*. Individual properties may delete irrelevant line items, but the *Uniform System* does not provide for the addition or substitution of other expense line items. Rather, properties may choose to develop a sub-account/sub-schedule to provide more detail related to a particular expense item. This sub-account/sub-schedule is then to be rolled into the appropriate line item listed below.

Cleaning Supplies. Includes the cost of products used in cleansing, sweeping, polishing, waxing, and disinfecting areas associated with the Golf Course and Pro Shop.

Complimentary Services and Gifts. Includes the cost of providing gift items used in gratis presentations for promotional purposes to guests and vendors of the Golf Course and Pro Shop, such as golf balls and sun visors.

Contract Services. Includes expenses for activities performed for the Golf Course and Pro Shop by outside companies rather than hotel employees. The cost of contracting an outside company to maintain the golf carts is an example. If supplies are purchased for contract companies to use, the supplies are charged to the appropriate supply account. The cost of contracts for Golf Course and Pro Shop laundry and dry cleaning is charged to Laundry and Dry Cleaning.

Corporate Office Reimbursables. Includes the allocations of salaries and expenses of corporate or management company golf and pro shop personnel billed to the property by the regional or corporate office or by the management company. Travel expenses of such corporate or management company personnel that are incurred while visiting the property, including the costs of meals and other applicable services or amenities provided to corporate or management company staff while on business in the property for the benefit of the property, are also charged to this account.

Decorations. Includes the cost of decorative items used in Golf Course and Pro Shop areas for holidays and special events.

Dues and Subscriptions. Includes the cost of representation of the golf club, or of members of the staff when authorized to represent the golf club, in business or professional organizations. Dues and Subscriptions is also charged with the cost of subscriptions to newspapers, magazines, and books for use by the staff of the Golf Course and Pro Shop.

Equipment Rental. Includes the cost of renting any type of equipment that may be used either sporadically in the Golf Course and Pro Shop or as a replacement for equipment out of service on a temporary basis. Equipment that is rented on a continuous basis and, if purchased, would qualify as a capital purchase is charged to Other Property and Equipment under the Rent section of *Rent, Property and Other Taxes, and Insurance—Schedule 10.*

Gasoline and Lubricants. Includes the cost of gasoline and lubricants for gasoline-powered golf carts, mowers, tractors, and trucks used in operating the golf course.

Golf Cart Batteries/Electricity. Includes the cost of batteries for golf carts along with the costs associated with charging the batteries.

Golf Cart Repairs and Maintenance. Includes the cost of repairing and maintaining golf carts, mowers, tractors, and trucks used in operating the golf course.

Grounds Maintenance and Landscaping. Includes the cost of maintaining the golf course and related roads and paths. Examples include fertilizers, insecticides, other chemicals, sand, topsoil, seeds, flowers, and shrubs.

Irrigation. Includes the cost of repairing golf course water and drainage systems, sprinklers, water controllers, and computerized water systems. The cost of the water used for irrigation is charged to the Water line item below.

Laundry and Dry Cleaning. Includes the cost of laundry and dry cleaning services applicable to the Golf Course and Pro Shop, whether the services are performed by an in-house facility or are contracted to an outside company. If the services are performed by an in-house laundry, an allocation from House Laundry is charged to Laundry and Dry Cleaning. If the services are performed by an outside company, the amount charged to Laundry and Dry Cleaning is based on invoices sent by the outside laundry. The cost of cleaning employee uniforms is charged to the Uniform Laundry account.

Licenses and Permits. Includes the cost of federal, state, and local licenses, including costs of inspections needed for licensing, for all activities of the Golf Course and Pro Shop.

Linen. Includes the cost, whether purchased or rented, of towels, face cloths, bath mats, and table cloths used by the Golf Course and Pro Shop.

Management Fees. Includes the fees charged by an organization (other than the hotel's management company) to manage the Golf Course and Pro Shop operations.

Miscellaneous. Includes any expenses of the Golf Course and Pro Shop that do not apply to the other line items discussed in this section.

Operating Supplies. Includes the cost of operating and general office supplies needed to operate the Golf Course and Pro Shop that are not included in the descriptions of specific supply accounts such as Cleaning Supplies, Grounds Maintenance and Landscaping, Golf Cart Repairs and Maintenance, or Printing and Stationery. Examples of items included in Operating Supplies are practice range balls and containers, golf flag pins, ice chests and paper cups for use on golf carts, and course signage.

Printing and Stationery. Includes the cost of printed forms used in the Golf Course and Pro Shop, whether they are purchased from an outside source or produced internally. Examples of Printing and Stationary include scoring cards and pencils.

Professional Fees. Includes the cost of specialists, whether certified or not, engaged to assist management in Golf Course and Pro Shop operations, tournaments, and promotions.

Royalty Fees. Includes all costs associated with the right to use a brand name in connection with a Golf Course and Pro Shop activity. For example, the fees paid for use of a brand name to identify a golf course, including franchise fees, are charged to this line item.

Telecommunications. Includes any telecommunications expenditures that can be directly related to the Golf Course and Pro Shop, including the costs of local, long distance, and Internet communications. Telecommunications includes not only traditional telephone systems, but also the cost of cellular phones, including the equipment and periodic service charges, used in the Golf Course and Pro Shop.

Tournament Expenses. Includes all costs associated with administering a golf tournament.

Training. Includes the costs, other than time, that can be directly attributed to the training of employees in the Golf Course and Pro Shop. Examples include the costs of training materials, supplies, and instructor fees. The cost of employee wages incurred during training is charged to Salaries and Wages.

Transportation. Includes all costs associated with transporting guests to and from a remote golf course, such as fuel costs, costs of washing and cleaning vehicles, or the occasional rental of vehicles for transporting large groups, or the costs of contracting guest transportation services. The cost of mechanical maintenance of vehicles used to transport guests is charged to *Property Operation and Maintenance—Schedule 7*. If a vehicle used to transport guests is leased, the cost of the lease is charged to Rent under *Rent, Property and Other Taxes, and Insurance—Schedule 10.*

Not included in this account are the costs associated with the maintenance of golf carts owned by the hotel. These costs are charges to Golf Cart Repairs and Maintenance.

Travel—Meals and Entertainment. Includes the reimbursable cost of food and beverage expenditures for travel and entertainment by employees of the Golf Course and Pro Shop traveling on property business.

Travel—Other. Includes the cost of travel and reimbursable expenditures, other than food, beverage, and entertainment, by employees of the Golf Course and Pro Shop traveling on property business.

Uniform Laundry. Includes the cost of cleaning uniforms for employees of the Golf Course and Pro Shop whether performed by an in-hotel facility or contracted to an outside company.

Uniforms. Includes the cost of employee uniforms used in the Golf Course and Pro Shop, whether purchased or rented. Repair costs are also included in this line item. The cost of cleaning uniforms is charged to the Uniform Laundry account.

Water. Includes the cost of water used for irrigation and water features/hazards on the golf course.

Total Other Expenses

Total Other Expenses is calculated by adding all items listed under Other Expenses. The percentage for each line item expense as well as Total Other

Expenses is calculated by dividing the line item amount by Total Golf Course and Pro Shop Revenue.

Total Expenses

Total Expenses is calculated by adding Total Payroll and Related Expenses to Total Other Expenses. The percentage for Total Expenses is calculated by dividing Total Expenses by Total Golf Course and Pro Shop Revenue.

   The sum of Total Cost of Sales and Total Expenses is shown on Schedule 3 as Departmental Expenses—Golf Course and Pro Shop.

Departmental Income (Loss)

Departmental Income (Loss) is calculated by subtracting Total Expenses from Gross Profit (Loss). The percentage for Departmental Income (Loss) is calculated by dividing Departmental Income (Loss) by Total Golf Course and Pro Shop Revenue. Departmental Income (Loss) is then shown on Schedule 3 as Departmental Income (Loss)—Golf Course and Pro Shop.

HEALTH CLUB/SPA—SUB-SCHEDULE 3-3

	CURRENT MONTH			YEAR-TO-DATE		
	ACTUAL	FORECAST	PRIOR YEAR	ACTUAL	FORECAST	PRIOR YEAR
	$ %	$ %	$ %	$ %	$ %	$ %
REVENUE						
Club Use Revenue						
Fitness Lessons Revenue						
Health/Wellness Services Revenue						
Massage Revenue						
Membership Fee Revenue						
Personal Training Revenue						
Spa Treatment Revenue						
Salon Treatment Revenue						
Merchandise Revenue						
Clothing Revenue						
Other Revenue						
Less: Allowances						
Total Health Club/Spa Revenue						
COST OF SALES						
Cost of Merchandise Sales						
Cost of Clothing Sales						
Total Cost of Sales						
GROSS PROFIT (LOSS)						
EXPENSES						
Payroll and Related Expenses						
Salaries, Wages, and Bonuses						
Salaries and Wages						
Bonuses and Incentives						
Total Salaries, Wages, and Bonuses						
Payroll-Related Expenses						
Payroll Taxes						
Supplemental Pay						
Employee Benefits						
Total Payroll-Related Expenses						
Total Payroll and Related Expenses						
Other Expenses						
Ambience						
Athletic Supplies						
Cleaning Supplies						
Complimentary Services and Gifts						
Contract Services						
Corporate Office Reimbursables						
Decorations						
Dues and Subscriptions						
Equipment Rental						
Health and Beauty Products						
Laundry and Dry Cleaning						
Licenses and Permits						
Linen						
Management Fees						
Miscellaneous						

(continued)

HEALTH CLUB/SPA—SUB-SCHEDULE 3-3 *(continued)*

	CURRENT MONTH			YEAR-TO-DATE		
	ACTUAL	FORECAST	PRIOR YEAR	ACTUAL	FORECAST	PRIOR YEAR
	$ %	$ %	$ %	$ %	$ %	$ %
Operating Supplies						
Printing and Stationery						
Professional Fees						
Royalty Fees						
Telecommunications						
Training						
Travel—Meals and Entertainment						
Travel—Other						
Uniform Laundry						
Uniforms						
Total Other Expenses						
TOTAL EXPENSES						
DEPARTMENTAL INCOME (LOSS)						

Health Club/Spa—Sub-schedule 3-3 illustrates the proper format for reporting the Revenue, Cost of Sales, Payroll and Related Expenses, Other Expenses, and Income (Loss) amounts for a separate Health Club/Spa. Individual properties may delete irrelevant line items, but the *Uniform System* does not provide for the addition or substitution of other revenue or expense line items. Rather, properties may choose to develop further sub-accounts/sub-schedules to provide more detail related to a particular revenue or expense item. These additional sub-accounts/sub-schedules are then to be rolled into the appropriate line item on Sub-schedule 3-3. Additionally, properties may choose to delete some of the columns or to show them in a different order and remain "in conformity with the *Uniform System.*"

The Total Health Club/Spa Revenue, Total Expenses (including Total Cost of Sales), and Departmental Income (Loss) shown on Sub-schedule 3-3 are then reported on Schedule 3.

Revenue

Revenue from the Health Club/Spa is classified into the following categories.

Club Use Revenue

Club Use Revenue includes revenue derived from fees charged to customers for daily use of the health club facility.

Fitness Lessons Revenue

Fitness Lessons Revenue includes revenue derived from group exercise programs such as aerobic dance or martial arts.

Health/Wellness Services Revenue

Health/Wellness Services Revenue includes revenue derived from programs such as nutritional cooking classes, spiritual guidance, and personal life counseling.

Massage Revenue

Massage Revenue includes revenue derived from fees charged to customers for massage services.

Membership Fee Revenue

Membership Fee Revenue includes revenue derived from charging customers for a "membership" at the health club which normally allows the customer "member" unlimited daily use of the club facility without further payment.

Personal Training Revenue

Personal Training Revenue includes the revenue derived from fitness lessons given to an individual rather than for a group.

Spa Treatment Revenue

Spa Treatment Revenue includes revenue derived from health treatments such as facials, body wraps, and mud packs. Revenue derived from massages is recorded as Massage Revenue.

Salon Treatment Revenue

Salon Treatment Revenue includes revenue derived from hair and nail treatments such as cuts and coloring.

Merchandise Revenue

Merchandise Revenue includes revenue derived from all sales of non-clothing items in the health club/spa. Examples of merchandise would be skin care products, exercise mats, and herbal supplements.

Clothing Revenue

Clothing Revenue includes revenue derived from all sales of clothing items in the health club/spa.

Other Revenue

Other Revenue includes revenue from providing any other services not previously specified. Revenue from food and beverage sales sold in the health club/spa is reported in Food and Beverage.

Allowances

Allowances refers to a reduction in revenue due to a service problem, and not an error in posting. Errors in posting, such as charging an incorrect amount, are treated as an adjustment to revenue, regardless of the accounting period in which the error occurred.

Total Health Club/Spa Revenue

Total Health Club/Spa Revenue is calculated by adding together each of the revenue items listed above and subtracting Allowances. This amount is shown on Schedule 3 as Departmental Revenue—Health Club/Spa.

In completing the revenue section of Sub-schedule 3-3, the Total Health Club/Spa Revenue line is considered to be 100 percent, and the percentage for each source of revenue is determined by dividing the dollar amount for that revenue source by Total Health Club/Spa Revenue.

Cost of Sales

Cost of Sales is divided into two categories: Cost of Merchandise Sales and Cost of Clothing Sales. The percentage for each of the items under Costs of Sales is calculated by dividing the dollar cost by its corresponding revenue amount.

Cost of Merchandise Sales

Cost of Merchandise Sales includes the cost of non-clothing items sold to customers of the Health Club/Spa. Inventory losses due to damaged or missing items are also charged to the Cost of Merchandise Sales and are not charged to Other Expenses. Cost of Merchandise Sales does not include the cost associated with non-clothing items used for gratis presentation to customers, vendors, and employees of any department in the property. The cost of any complimentary items is charged as an expense to Complimentary Services and Gifts expense for the department that makes the gratis presentation.

Cost of Clothing Sales

Cost of Clothing Sales includes the cost of clothing items sold to customers of the Health Club/Spa. Inventory losses due to damaged or missing items are also charged to the Cost of Clothing Sales and are not charged to Other Expenses. Cost of Clothing Sales does not include the cost associated with clothing items used for gratis presentation to customers, vendors, and employees of any department in the property. The cost of any complimentary clothing items is charged as an expense to Complimentary Services and Gifts expense for the department that makes the gratis presentation.

Total Cost of Sales

Total Cost of Sales is the sum of Cost of Merchandise Sales and Cost of Clothing Sales. The percentage for Total Cost of Sales is calculated by dividing Total Cost of Sales by the sum of Merchandise Revenue and Clothing Revenue.

Gross Profit (Loss)

Gross Profit (Loss) is calculated by subtracting Total Cost of Sales from Total Health Club/Spa Revenue. The percentage for Gross Profit (Loss) is calculated by dividing Gross Profit (Loss) by Total Health Club/Spa Revenue.

Expenses

Health Club/Spa expenses are separated into two major categories: Payroll and Related Expenses and Other Expenses.

Payroll and Related Expenses

Payroll and Related Expenses for the Health Club/Spa comprises the expenses associated with Salaries, Wages, and Bonuses and Payroll-Related Expenses for employees of the Health Club/Spa. A list of the positions typically included in the Health Club/Spa is shown on page 176.

Salaries, Wages, and Bonuses. This grouping includes (1) Salaries and Wages and (2) Bonuses and Incentives. Salaries and Wages includes only earnings paid to an employee for duties that relate to the operation of the property, such as regular pay, overtime pay, and shift differential pay. If an employee works in a department other than his or her regular home department, his or her earnings are charged as Salaries and Wages in that other department, regardless of the duties being performed. For example, if a Health Club employee works as a server for an employee awards banquet, his or her earnings are charged to Salaries and Wages in Administrative and General, and not to this line item. Payroll-Related Expenses (described below) for the above example are treated similarly and charged as Payroll-Related Expenses in Administrative and General.

Salaries and Wages also includes contract or leased labor. Contract or leased labor refers to those situations in which a property enters into an agreement with an outside service to provide employees to fill positions that would normally be held by individuals paid on the regular payroll. In these situations, the property usually supervises the individuals and records or tracks their hours worked and pays them on an hourly basis. A typical example is the use of individuals brought into the property to fill in for a shortage of massage therapists or spa service technicians. This situation differs from a contract service in which a property has an agreement with an outside company to provide some type of service, such as cleaning the whirlpool. In this case, the contracted organization typically provides the supervision and ensures that the work is performed. The costs associated with this type of agreement are charged under Contract Services for the department receiving the service.

Bonuses and Incentives includes bonuses, incentive pay, and other types of performance pay designed to drive revenue through sales, profit, or guest satisfaction measures.

Total Salaries, Wages, and Bonuses. Calculated by adding together Salaries and Wages and Bonuses and Incentives.

Payroll-Related Expenses. Payroll-Related Expenses includes amounts paid for an employee for duties that relate to the operation of the property and amounts paid for an employee who works in a department other than his or her regular home department regardless of the duties being performed. Payroll-Related Expenses includes the following items:

- *Payroll Taxes.* Includes Federal Retirement and Medicare (FICA), Federal and State Unemployment Taxes (FUTA and SUTA), State Disability Insurance (SDI), and other mandated payroll-related taxes or social insurance items. (See *Payroll-Related Expenses—Schedule 13.*)

- *Supplemental Pay.* Includes personal days, vacation pay, sick pay, holiday pay, jury duty pay, relocation pay, paid time off, and severance pay. Supplemental Pay also includes bonuses and incentive payments that are discretionary and not determined by results from operations.

- *Employee Benefits.* Includes all other payroll-related expenses, such as employer-paid health insurance expenses, cost of meals furnished to employees, pension contributions, and union fees. (See *Payroll-Related Expenses—Schedule 13.*) The distribution of employee meal costs from *Employee Cafeteria—Schedule 12* is charged to this line.

Total Payroll-Related Expenses. Calculated by adding together Payroll Taxes, Supplemental Pay, and Employee Benefits.

Total Payroll and Related Expenses

Total Payroll and Related Expenses is calculated by adding together Total Salaries, Wages, and Bonuses and Total Payroll-Related Expenses. The percentage for each payroll and related expense line item as well as Total Payroll and Related Expenses is calculated by dividing the line item amount by Total Health Club/Spa Revenue.

Other Expenses

This expense grouping includes the significant Health Club/Spa expenses approved as Other Expenses in the *Uniform System.* Individual properties may delete irrelevant line items, but the *Uniform System* does not provide for the addition or substitution of other expense line items. Rather, properties may choose to develop a sub-account/sub-schedule to provide more detail related to a particular expense item. This sub-account/sub-schedule is then to be rolled into the appropriate line item listed below.

Ambience. Includes the cost to provide the sensory environment within the spa, including background music, candles, aromatherapy oils, and diffusers.

Athletic Supplies. Includes the cost of non-capitalized gym equipment, as well as supplies used during fitness classes.

Cleaning Supplies. Includes the cost of products used in cleansing, sweeping, polishing, waxing, and disinfecting areas associated with the Health Club/Spa.

Complimentary Services and Gifts. Includes the cost of providing gift items used in gratis presentations for promotional purposes to guests and vendors of the Health Club/Spa, such as razors and shaving cream, shampoo, q-tips and cotton balls, fruit juices, and herbal teas.

Contract Services. Includes expenses for activities performed for the Health Club/Spa by outside companies rather than hotel employees. The cost of contracting an outside company to clean the swimming pool, whirlpool, and spa is an example. If supplies are purchased for contract companies to use, the supplies are charged to the appropriate supply account. The cost of contracts for Health Club/Spa laundry and dry cleaning is charged to Laundry and Dry Cleaning.

Corporate Office Reimbursables. Includes the allocations of salaries and expenses of corporate or management company health club/spa personnel billed to the property by the regional or corporate office or by the management company. Travel expenses of such corporate or management company personnel that are incurred while visiting the property, including the costs of meals and other applicable services or amenities provided to corporate or management company staff while on business in the property for the benefit of the property, are also charged to this account.

Decorations. Includes the cost of decorative items used in Health Club/Spa areas for holidays and special events.

Dues and Subscriptions. Includes the cost of representation of the Health Club/Spa, or of members of the staff when authorized to represent the Health Club/Spa, in business or professional organizations. Dues and Subscriptions is also charged with the cost of subscriptions to newspapers, magazines, and books for use by the staff of the Health Club/Spa.

Equipment Rental. Includes the cost of renting any type of equipment that may be used either sporadically in the Health Club/Spa or as a replacement for equipment out of service on a temporary basis. Equipment that is rented on a continuous basis and, if purchased, would qualify as a capital purchase is charged to Other Property and Equipment under the Rent section of *Rent, Property and Other Taxes, and Insurance—Schedule 10*.

Health and Beauty Products. Includes the cost of items used in producing Massage, Spa Treatment, and Salon Treatment Revenues. Items charged to this line include nail polish, face cream, shampoo, and massage oils.

Laundry and Dry Cleaning. Includes the cost of laundry and dry cleaning services applicable to the Health Club/Spa, whether the services are performed by an in-house facility or are contracted to an outside company. If the services are performed by an in-house laundry, an allocation from House Laundry is charged to Laundry and Dry Cleaning. If the services are performed by an outside company, the amount charged to Laundry and Dry Cleaning should be based on invoices sent by the outside laundry. The cost of cleaning employee uniforms is charged to the Uniform Laundry account.

Licenses and Permits. Includes the cost of federal, state, and local licenses, including costs of inspections needed for licensing, for all activities of the Health Club/Spa.

Linen. Includes the cost, whether purchased or rented, of towels, face cloths, bath mats, and bathrobes used by the Health Club/Spa.

Management Fees. Includes the fees charged by an organization (other than the hotel's management company) to manage the Health Club/Spa operations.

Miscellaneous. Includes any expenses of the Health Club/Spa that do not apply to the other line items discussed in this section.

Operating Supplies. Includes the cost of operating and general office supplies needed to operate the Health Club/Spa that are not included in the descriptions of specific supply accounts such as Athletic Supplies or Health and Beauty Products. Examples of items included in Operating Supplies are chemicals used to treat a whirlpool, toilet paper, clothing hangers for merchandise, and a weight scale.

Printing and Stationery. Includes the cost of printed forms used in the Health Club/Spa, whether they are purchased from an outside source or produced internally. Examples of Printing and Stationary include forms to track exercise routines, file folders, and pencils.

Professional Fees. Includes the cost of specialists, whether certified or not, engaged to assist management in Health Club/Spa operations.

Royalty Fees. Includes all costs associated with the right to use a brand name in connection with a Health Club/Spa activity. For example, the fees paid for use of a brand name to identify the health club/spa, including franchise fees, are charged to this line item.

Telecommunications. Includes any telecommunications expenditures that can be directly related to the Health Club/Spa, including the costs of local, long distance, and Internet communications. Telecommunications includes not only traditional telephone systems, but also the cost of cellular phones, including the equipment and periodic service charges, used in the Health Club/Spa.

Training. Includes the cost, other than time, that can be directly attributed to the training of employees in the Health Club/Spa. Examples include the costs of training materials, supplies, and instructor fees. The cost of employee wages incurred during training is charged to Salaries and Wages.

Travel—Meals and Entertainment. Includes the reimbursable cost of food and beverage expenditures for travel and entertainment by employees of the Health Club/Spa traveling on property business.

Travel—Other. Includes the cost of travel and reimbursable expenditures, other than food, beverage, and entertainment, by employees of the Health Club/Spa traveling on property business.

Uniform Laundry. Includes the cost of cleaning uniforms for employees of the Health Club/Spa whether performed by an in-hotel facility or contracted to an outside company.

Uniforms. Includes the cost of employee uniforms used in the Health Club/Spa, whether purchased or rented. Repair costs are also included in this line item. The cost of cleaning uniforms is charged to the Uniform Laundry account.

Total Other Expenses

Total Other Expenses is calculated by adding all items listed under Other Expenses. The percentage for each line item expense as well as Total Other

Expenses is calculated by dividing the line item amount by Total Health Club/Spa Revenue.

Total Expenses

Total Expenses is calculated by adding Total Payroll and Related Expenses to Total Other Expenses. The percentage for Total Expenses is calculated by dividing Total Expenses by Total Health Club/Spa Revenue.

The sum of Total Cost of Sales and Total Expenses is shown on Schedule 3 as Departmental Expenses—Health Club/Spa.

Departmental Income (Loss)

Departmental Income (Loss) is calculated by subtracting Total Expenses from Gross Profit (Loss). The percentage for Departmental Income (Loss) is calculated by dividing Departmental Income (Loss) by Total Health Club/Spa Revenue. Departmental Income (Loss) is then shown on Schedule 3 as Departmental Income (Loss)—Health Club/Spa.

PARKING GARAGE—SUB-SCHEDULE 3-4

	CURRENT MONTH			YEAR-TO-DATE		
	ACTUAL	FORECAST	PRIOR YEAR	ACTUAL	FORECAST	PRIOR YEAR
	$　%	$　%	$　%	$　%	$　%	$　%
REVENUE						
Self-Parking Revenue						
Valet Parking Revenue						
Other Revenue						
Less: Allowances						
Total Parking Garage Revenue						
COST OF SALES						
GROSS PROFIT (LOSS)						
EXPENSES						
Payroll and Related Expenses						
Salaries, Wages, and Bonuses						
Salaries and Wages						
Bonuses and Incentives						
Total Salaries, Wages, and Bonuses						
Payroll-Related Expenses						
Payroll Taxes						
Supplemental Pay						
Employee Benefits						
Total Payroll-Related Expenses						
Total Payroll and Related Expenses						
Other Expenses						
Cleaning Supplies						
Complimentary Services and Gifts						
Contract Services						
Corporate Office Reimbursables						
Decorations						
Dues and Subscriptions						
Equipment Rental						
Laundry and Dry Cleaning						
Licenses and Permits						
Management Fees						
Miscellaneous						
Operating Supplies						
Printing and Stationery						
Professional Fees						
Rent						
Royalty Fees						
Telecommunications						
Training						
Travel—Meals and Entertainment						
Travel—Other						
Uniform Laundry						
Uniforms						
Total Other Expenses						
TOTAL EXPENSES						
DEPARTMENTAL INCOME (LOSS)						

Parking Garage—Sub-schedule 3-4 illustrates the proper format for reporting the Revenue, Cost of Sales, Payroll and Related Expenses, Other Expenses, and Income (Loss) amounts for a separate Parking Garage. Individual properties may delete irrelevant line items, but the *Uniform System* does not provide for the addition or substitution of other revenue or expense line items. Rather, properties may choose to develop further sub-accounts/sub-schedules to provide more detail related to a particular revenue or expense item. These sub-accounts/sub-schedules are then to be rolled into the appropriate line item on Sub-schedule 3-4. Additionally, properties may choose to delete some of the columns or to show them in a different order and remain "in conformity with the *Uniform System.*"

The Total Parking Garage Revenue, Total Expenses (including Cost of Sales), and Departmental Income (Loss) shown on Sub-schedule 3-4 are then reported on Schedule 3.

Revenue

Parking garage revenue is classified into Self-Parking Revenue, Valet Parking Revenue, and Other Revenue.

Self-Parking Revenue

Self-Parking Revenue includes revenue derived from use of the parking facilities by customers without valet service.

Valet Parking Revenue

Valet Parking Revenue includes revenue derived from use of the parking facility by customers with valet service.

Other Revenue

Other Revenue includes revenue from providing any other services not previously specified. Examples would include automobile repair, car washes, or gasoline sales.

Allowances

Allowances refers to a reduction in revenue due to a service problem, and not an error in posting. Errors in posting, such as charging an incorrect amount, are treated as an adjustment to revenue, regardless of the accounting period in which the error occurred.

Total Parking Garage Revenue

Total Parking Garage Revenue is calculated by adding together each of the revenue items listed above and subtracting Allowances. This amount is shown on Schedule 3 as Departmental Revenue—Parking Garage.

In completing the revenue section of Schedule 3-4, the Total Parking Garage Revenue line is considered to be 100 percent, and the percentage for each source of revenue is determined by dividing the dollar amount for that revenue source by Total Parking Garage Revenue.

Cost of Sales

Cost of Sales includes the cost for any items sold when the revenue is included in Other Revenue. The cost of gasoline sold would be an example of a Cost of Sales. The percentage for Cost of Sales is calculated by dividing Cost of Sales by Other Revenue.

Gross Profit (Loss)

Gross Profit (Loss) is calculated by subtracting Cost of Sales from Total Parking Garage Revenue. The percentage for Gross Profit (Loss) is calculated by dividing Gross Profit (Loss) by Total Parking Garage Revenue.

Expenses

Parking Garage expenses are separated into two categories: Payroll and Related Expenses and Other Expenses.

Payroll and Related Expenses

Payroll and Related Expense for the Parking Garage comprises the expenses associated with Salaries, Wages, and Bonuses and Payroll-Related Expenses for employees of the Parking Garage. A list of the positions typically included in the Parking Garage is shown on page 176.

Salaries, Wages, and Bonuses. This grouping includes (1) Salaries and Wages and (2) Bonuses and Incentives. Salaries and Wages includes only earnings paid to an employee for duties that relate to the operation of the property, such as regular pay, overtime pay, and shift differential pay. If an employee works in a department other than his or her regular home department, his or her earnings are charged as Salaries and Wages in that other department, regardless of the duties being performed. For example, if a Parking Garage employee works as a server for an employee awards banquet, his or her earnings are charged to Salaries and Wages in Administrative and General, and not to this line item. Payroll-Related Expenses (described below) for the above example are treated similarly and charged as Payroll-Related Expenses in Administrative and General.

Salaries and Wages also includes contract or leased labor. Contract or leased labor refers to those situations in which a property enters into an agreement with an outside service to provide employees to fill positions that would normally be held by individuals paid on the regular payroll. In these situations, the property usually supervises the individuals and records or tracks their hours worked and pays them on an hourly basis. A typical example is the use of individuals brought into the property to fill in for a shortage of valet parkers. This situation differs from a contract service in which a property has an agreement with an outside company to paint the lines on the parking surface. In this case, the contracted organization typically provides the supervision and ensures that the work is performed. The costs associated with this type of agreement are charged under Contract Services for the department receiving the service.

Bonuses and Incentives includes bonuses, incentive pay, and other types of performance pay designed to drive revenue through sales, profit, or guest satisfaction measures.

Total Salaries, Wages, and Bonuses. Calculated by adding together Salaries and Wages and Bonuses and Incentives.

Payroll-Related Expenses. Payroll-Related Expenses includes amounts paid for an employee for duties that relate to the operation of the property and amounts paid for an employee who works in a department other than his or her regular home department regardless of the duties being performed. Payroll-Related Expenses includes the following items:

- *Payroll Taxes.* Includes Federal Retirement and Medicare (FICA), Federal and State Unemployment Taxes (FUTA and SUTA), State Disability Insurance (SDI), and other mandated payroll-related taxes or social insurance items. (See *Payroll-Related Expenses—Schedule 13.*)

- *Supplemental Pay.* Includes personal days, vacation pay, sick pay, holiday pay, jury duty pay, relocation pay, paid time off, and severance pay. Supplemental Pay also includes bonuses and incentive payments that are discretionary and not determined by results from operations.

- *Employee Benefits.* Includes all other payroll-related expenses, such as employer-paid health insurance expenses, cost of meals furnished to employees, pension contributions, and union fees. (See *Payroll-Related Expenses—Schedule 13.*) The distribution of employee meal costs from *Employee Cafeteria—Schedule 12* is charged to this line.

Total Payroll-Related Expenses. Calculated by adding together Payroll Taxes, Supplemental Pay, and Employee Benefits.

Total Payroll and Related Expenses

Total Payroll and Related Expenses is calculated by adding together Total Salaries, Wages, and Bonuses and Total Payroll-Related Expenses. The percentage for each payroll and related expense line item as well as Total Payroll and Related Expenses is calculated by dividing the line item amount by Total Parking Garage Revenue.

Other Expenses

This expense grouping includes the significant Parking Garage expenses approved as Other Expenses in the *Uniform System*. Individual properties may delete irrelevant line items, but the *Uniform System* does not provide for the addition or substitution of other expense line items. Rather, properties may choose to develop a sub-account/sub-schedule to provide more detail related to a particular expense item. This sub-account/sub-schedule is then to be rolled into the appropriate line item listed below.

Cleaning Supplies. Includes the cost of products used in cleansing, polishing, and sweeping areas associated with the Parking Garage.

Complimentary Services and Gifts. Includes the cost of providing gift items used in gratis presentations for promotional purposes to guests and vendors of the Parking Garage.

Contract Services. Includes expenses for activities performed for the Parking Garage by outside companies rather than hotel employees. The cost of contracting an outside company to paint the lines on the parking surface is an example. If supplies are purchased for contract companies to use, the supplies are charged to the appropriate supply account. The cost of contracts for Parking Garage laundry and dry cleaning is charged to Laundry and Dry Cleaning.

Corporate Office Reimbursables. Includes the allocations of salaries and expenses of corporate or management company parking garage personnel billed to the property by the regional or corporate office or by the management company. Travel expenses of such corporate or management company personnel that are incurred while visiting the property, including the costs of meals and other applicable services or amenities provided to corporate or management company staff while on business in the property for the benefit of the property, are also charged to this account.

Decorations. Includes the cost of decorative items used in Parking Garage areas for holidays and special events.

Dues and Subscriptions. Includes the cost of representation of the Parking Garage, or of members of the staff when authorized to represent the Parking Garage, in business or professional organizations. Dues and Subscriptions is also charged with the cost of subscriptions to newspapers, magazines, and books for use by the staff of the Parking Garage.

Equipment Rental. Includes the costs of renting any type of equipment that may be used either sporadically in the Parking Garage or as a replacement for equipment out of service on a temporary basis. Equipment that is rented on a continuous basis and, if purchased would qualify as a capital purchase is charged to Other Property and Equipment under the Rent section of *Rent, Property and Other Taxes, and Insurance—Schedule 10.*

Laundry and Dry Cleaning. Includes the cost of laundry and dry cleaning services applicable to the Parking Garage, whether the services are performed by an in-house facility or are contracted to an outside company. If the services are performed by an in-house laundry, an allocation from House Laundry is charged to Laundry and Dry Cleaning. If the services are performed by an outside company, the amount charged to Laundry and Dry Cleaning should be based on invoices sent by the outside laundry. The cost of cleaning employee uniforms is charged to the Uniform Laundry account.

Licenses and Permits. Includes the cost of federal, state, and local licenses, including costs of inspections needed for licensing, for all activities of the Parking Garage.

Management Fees. Includes the fees charged by an organization (other than the hotel's management company) to manage Parking Garage operations.

Miscellaneous. Includes any expenses of the Parking Garage that do not apply to the other line items discussed in this section.

Operating Supplies. Includes the cost of operating and general office supplies needed to operate the Parking Garage that are not included in the descriptions of specific supply accounts such as Cleaning Supplies and Printing and Stationery. Examples include cleaning supplies for a car wash or auto parts for a repair operation.

Printing and Stationery. Includes the cost of printed forms used in the Parking Garage, whether they are purchased from an outside source or produced internally. Examples of Printing and Stationary include gate tickets and other department forms.

Professional Fees. Includes the cost of specialists, whether certified or not, engaged to assist management in Parking Garage operations.

Rent. Includes the costs associated with the temporary rental of additional parking spaces or a parking lot, usually to accommodate extra guests during special events or busy periods. Not included are the rental payments made for a long-term lease of parking spaces in a lot or garage that would be recorded in *Rent, Property and Other Taxes, and Insurance—Schedule 10*.

Royalty Fees. Includes all costs associated with the right to use a brand name in connection with the Parking Garage. For example, the fees paid for use of a brand name to identify a Parking Garage, including franchise fees, are charged to this line item.

Telecommunications. Includes any telecommunications expenditures that can be directly related to the Parking Garage, including the costs of local, long distance, and Internet communications. Telecommunications includes not only traditional telephone systems, but also the cost of cellular phones, including the equipment and periodic service charges, used in the Parking Garage.

Training. Includes the cost, other than time, that can be directly attributed to the training of employees in the Parking Garage. Examples include the costs of training materials, supplies, and instructor fees. The cost of employee wages incurred during training is charged to Salaries and Wages.

Travel—Meals and Entertainment. Includes the reimbursable cost of food and beverage expenditures for travel and entertainment by employees of the Parking Garage traveling on property business.

Travel—Other. Includes the cost of travel and reimbursable expenditures, other than food, beverage, and entertainment, by employees of the Parking Garage traveling on property business.

Uniform Laundry. Includes the cost of cleaning uniforms for employees of the Parking Garage whether performed by an in-hotel facility or contracted to an outside company.

Uniforms. Includes the cost of employee uniforms used in the Parking Garage, whether purchased or rented. Repair costs are also included in this line item. The cost of cleaning uniforms is charged to the Uniform Laundry account.

Total Other Expenses

Total Other Expenses is calculated by adding all items listed under Other Expenses. The percentage for each line item expense as well as Total Other Expenses is calculated by dividing the line item amount by Total Parking Garage Revenue.

Total Expenses

Total Expenses is calculated by adding Total Payroll and Related Expenses to Total Other Expenses. The percentage for Total Expenses is calculated by dividing Total Expenses by Total Parking Garage Revenue.

The sum of Cost of Sales and Total Expenses is shown on Schedule 3 as Departmental Expenses—Parking Garage.

Departmental Income (Loss)

Departmental Income (Loss) is calculated by subtracting Total Expenses from Gross Profit (Loss). The percentage for Departmental Income (Loss) is calculated by dividing Departmental Income (Loss) by Total Parking Garage Revenue. Departmental Income (Loss) is then shown on Schedule 3 as Departmental Income (Loss)—Parking Garage.

OTHER OPERATED DEPARTMENTS—SUB-SCHEDULE 3-X *(Generic)*

	CURRENT MONTH			YEAR-TO-DATE		
	ACTUAL	FORECAST	PRIOR YEAR	ACTUAL	FORECAST	PRIOR YEAR
	$ | %	$ | %	$ | %	$ | %	$ | %	$ | %
REVENUE						
Revenue						
Less: Allowances						
Total Revenue						
COST OF SALES						
GROSS PROFIT (LOSS)						
EXPENSES						
Payroll and Related Expenses						
Salaries, Wages, and Bonuses						
Salaries and Wages						
Bonuses and Incentives						
Total Salaries, Wages, and Bonuses						
Payroll-Related Expenses						
Payroll Taxes						
Supplemental Pay						
Employee Benefits						
Total Payroll-Related Expenses						
Total Payroll and Related Expenses						
Other Expenses						
Cleaning Supplies						
Complimentary Services and Gifts						
Contract Services						
Corporate Office Reimbursables						
Decorations						
Dues and Subscriptions						
Equipment Rental						
Laundry and Dry Cleaning						
Licenses and Permits						
Linen						
Management Fees						
Miscellaneous						
Operating Supplies						
[Other detailed expenses as warranted]						
Printing and Stationery						
Professional Fees						
Royalty Fees						
Telecommunications						
Training						
Travel—Meals and Entertainment						
Travel—Other						
Uniform Laundry						
Uniforms						
Total Other Expenses						
TOTAL EXPENSES						
DEPARTMENTAL INCOME (LOSS)						

The generic *Other Operated Departments—Sub-schedule 3-x* illustrates the proper format for reporting the Revenue, Cost of Sales, Payroll and Related Expenses, and Departmental Income (Loss) amounts for any Other Operated Departments that may be needed in addition to the four already detailed (Telecommunications, Golf Course and Pro Shop, Health Club/Spa, and Parking Garage)—for example, a Pool department, a Business Center, or a Tennis and Pro Shop. The hotel should define its additional departments.

When the need for an additional department exists, use the generic format set forth in Sub-schedule 3-x. Because each Other Operated Department may have significant costs that are unique to that department, hotels *are permitted* in this one area only to insert additional Other Expense line items in Sub-schedule 3-x. These unique expenses should be added under Other Expenses as appropriate. Examples of potential unique expenses are provided in the descriptive paragraph for the bracketed line item labeled [Other Detailed Expenses as warranted]. Properties may choose to develop further sub-accounts to provide even more detail related to a particular revenue or expense item. These additional sub-accounts/ sub-schedules are then to be rolled into the appropriate line item on Sub-schedule 3-x. Additionally, properties may choose to delete some of the columns or to show them in a different order and remain "in conformity with the *Uniform System*."

The Total Revenue, Total Expenses (including any applicable cost of sales), and Departmental Income (Loss) shown on Sub-schedule 3-x are then reported on Schedule 3.

The following presents a description of the base revenue and expense items that should be included in the sub-schedules for Other Operated Departments. In addition, examples of other revenue and expense items that are commonly found in Other Operated Departments are provided.

Special Notice for Condominium Hotels

The revenues and direct operating expenses associated with the management of condominium units is recorded as an Other Operated Department, unless the property has assumed an economic risk pursuant to a contractual relationship that extends beyond one year. If the property has assumed economic risk, then the revenues, expenses, and rooms statistics are recorded in their appropriate categories as prescribed by the *Uniform System.*

Special Notice for Casino Hotels

The *Uniform System of Accounts for the Lodging Industry* is not recommended for use by casino hotels with significant gaming operations. It is recommended that casino hotels use accounting classification systems specific to the gaming industry.

For hotels that receive minor revenue from gaming, revenues and direct operating expenses are recorded as an Other Operated Department. Examples include hotels with card rooms or gaming machines within the lounge.

Revenue

Revenue consists of the gross sales derived from the department. The following list describes the revenue typically found in select Other Operated Departments. The list is not intended to be all-inclusive. Additional significant revenues should be segregated in sub-schedules as warranted.

Operated Department	Revenue
Transportation:	Usage Revenue, Special Vehicle Rentals
Guest Laundry:	Guest Dry Cleaning/Laundry, Alterations and Repairs
Swimming Pool/Beach:	Usage Revenue, Membership Fees, Equipment Rental, Lessons
Tennis and Pro Shop:	Court Rental, Retail Revenue, Lessons, Merchandise, Equipment Rental
Business Center:	Typing Services, Document Printing
Marina:	Slip Rental, Gas, Groceries, Fishing Equipment Rental
Retail Store:	Clothing, Merchandise, Candy, Newspapers
Children's Camp:	Registration Fees, Day Care, Babysitting
Barber/Beauty Shop:	Hair Cuts/Styling, Merchandise
Condominium:	Room Rental, Condominium Sales
Gaming:	Card Games, Slot Machines

Allowances

Allowances refers to a reduction in revenue due to a service problem, and not an error in posting. Errors in posting, such as charging an incorrect amount, are treated as an adjustment to revenue, regardless of the accounting period in which the error occurred.

Total Revenue

Total Revenue is calculated by adding together each of the revenue items for a respective Other Operated Department and subtracting Allowances. This amount appears on Schedule 3 as Departmental Revenue—[Name of Department].

In completing the revenue section of Schedule 3-x, the Total Revenue line is considered to be 100 percent, and the percentage for each source of revenue is determined by dividing the dollar amount for that revenue source by Total Department x Revenue.

Cost of Sales

Cost of Sales includes the cost for any items sold. If individual merchandise items or categories of similar items are listed separately under Revenue, these same items or categories of items would also be listed separately under Cost of Sales. The percentage for Cost of Sales is calculated by dividing the dollar cost by its corresponding revenue amount.

Gross Profit (Loss)

Gross Profit (Loss) is calculated by subtracting Cost of Sales from Total Revenue. The percentage for Gross Profit (Loss) is calculated by dividing Gross Profit (Loss) by Total Revenue for Department x.

Expenses

Other Operated Department expenses are separated into two major categories: Payroll and Related Expenses and Other Expenses.

Payroll and Related Expenses

Payroll and Related Expenses for an Other Operated Department comprises the expenses associated with Salaries, Wages, and Bonuses and Payroll-Related Expenses for employees of the Other Operated Department.

Salaries, Wages, and Bonuses. This grouping includes (1) Salaries and Wages and (2) Bonuses and Incentives. Salaries and Wages includes only earnings paid to an employee for duties that relate to the operation of the property, such as regular pay, overtime pay, and shift differential pay. If an employee works in a department other than his or her regular home department, his or her earnings are charged as Salaries and Wages in that other department, regardless of the duties being performed. For example, if an Other Operated Department employee works as a server for an employee awards banquet, his or her earnings are charged to Salaries and Wages in Administrative and General, and not to this line item. Payroll-Related Expenses (described below) for the above example are treated similarly and charged as Payroll-Related Expenses in Administrative and General.

Salaries and Wages also includes contract or leased labor. Contract or leased labor refers to those situations in which a property enters into an agreement with an outside service to provide employees to fill positions that would normally be held by individuals paid on the regular payroll. In these situations, the property usually supervises the individuals and records or tracks their hours worked and pays them on an hourly basis. Examples include the use of individuals brought into the property to fill in for a shortage of bus drivers or lifeguards. This situation differs from a contract service in which a property has an agreement with an outside company to provide some type of service, such as cleaning the pool or fixing equipment in the Business Center. In this case, the contracted organization typically provides the supervision and ensures that the work is performed. The costs associated with this type of agreement are charged under Contract Services for the department receiving the service.

Bonuses and Incentives includes bonuses, incentive pay, and other types of performance pay designed to drive revenue through sales, profit, or guest satisfaction measures.

Total Salaries, Wages, and Bonuses. Calculated by adding together Salaries and Wages and Bonuses and Incentives.

Payroll-Related Expenses. Payroll-Related Expenses includes amounts paid for an employee for duties that relate to the operation of the property and amounts paid for an employee who works in a department other than his or her regular home department regardless of the duties being performed. Payroll-Related Expenses includes the following items:

- *Payroll Taxes.* Includes Federal Retirement and Medicare (FICA), Federal and State Unemployment Taxes (FUTA and SUTA), State Disability Insurance (SDI), and other mandated payroll-related taxes or social insurance items. (See *Payroll-Related Expenses—Schedule 13.*)

- *Supplemental Pay.* Includes personal days, vacation pay, sick pay, holiday pay, jury duty pay, relocation pay, paid time off, and severance pay. Supplemental Pay also includes bonuses and incentive payments that are discretionary and not determined by results from operations.

- *Employee Benefits.* Includes all other payroll-related expenses, such as employer-paid health insurance expenses, cost of meals furnished to employees, pension contributions, and union fees. (See *Payroll-Related Expenses—Schedule 13.*) The distribution of employee meal costs from *Employee Cafeteria—Schedule 12* is charged to this line.

Total Payroll-Related Expenses. Calculated by adding together Payroll Taxes, Supplemental Pay, and Employee Benefits.

Total Payroll and Related Expenses

Total Payroll and Related Expenses is calculated by adding together Total Salaries, Wages, and Bonuses and Total Payroll-Related Expenses. The percentage for each payroll and related expense line item as well as Total Payroll and Related Expenses is calculated by dividing the line item amount by Total Revenue for the Other Operated Department.

Other Expenses

This expense grouping includes the significant Other Operated Department expenses approved as Other Expenses in the *Uniform System.* As always, properties may delete irrelevant line items. For Sub-schedule 3-*x* only, properties *also may insert* additional Other Expenses that are substantial and unique to an Other Operated Department. Properties also may choose to develop a sub-account/sub-schedule to provide more detail related to a particular expense item. This sub-account/sub-schedule is then to be rolled into the appropriate line item listed below.

Cleaning Supplies. Includes the cost of products used in cleansing, sweeping, polishing, waxing, and disinfecting areas associated with the Other Operated Department.

Complimentary Services and Gifts. Includes the cost of providing gift items used in gratis presentations for promotional purposes to guests and vendors of the Other Operated Department.

Contract Services. Includes expenses for activities performed for the Other Operated Department by outside companies rather than hotel employees. The costs of contracting outside companies to clean the pool or maintain equipment in the Business Center are examples. If supplies are purchased for contract companies to use, the supplies are charged to the appropriate supply account. The cost of contracts for Other Operated Department laundry and dry cleaning is charged to Laundry and Dry Cleaning.

Corporate Office Reimbursables. Includes the allocations of salaries and expenses of corporate or management company personnel associated with specific other operated departments billed to the property by the regional or corporate office or by the management company. Travel expenses of such corporate or management company personnel that are incurred while visiting the property, including the costs of meals and other applicable services or amenities provided to corporate or management company staff while on business in the property for the benefit of the property, are also charged to this account.

Decorations. Includes the cost of decorative items used in Other Operated Department areas for holidays and special events.

Dues and Subscriptions. Includes the cost of representation of the Other Operated Department, or of members of the staff when authorized to represent the Other Operaated Department, in business or professional organizations. Dues and Subscriptions is also charged with the cost of subscriptions to newspapers, magazines, and books for use by the staff of the Other Operated Department.

Equipment Rental. Includes the costs of renting any type of equipment that may be used either sporadically in the Other Operated Department or as a replacement for equipment out of service on a temporary basis. Equipment that is rented on a continuous basis and, if purchased, would qualify as a capital purchase is charged to Other Property and Equipment under the Rent section of *Rent, Property and Other Taxes, and Insurance—Schedule 10.*

Laundry and Dry Cleaning. Includes the cost of laundry and dry cleaning services applicable to the Other Operated Department, whether the services are performed by an in-house facility or are contracted to an outside company. If the services are performed by an in-house laundry, an allocation from House Laundry is charged to Laundry and Dry Cleaning. If the services are performed by an outside company, the amount charged to Laundry and Dry Cleaning should be based on invoices sent by the outside laundry. The cost of cleaning employee uniforms is charged to the Uniform Laundry account.

Licenses and Permits. Includes the cost of federal, state, and local licenses, including costs of inspections needed for licensing, for all activities of the Other Operated Department.

Linen. Includes the cost, whether purchased or rented, of towels, face cloths, bath mats, and bathrobes used by the Other Operated Department.

Management Fees. Includes the fees charged by an organization (other than the hotel's management company) to manage the operations of the Other Operated Department.

Miscellaneous. Includes any expenses of the Other Operated Department that do not apply to the other line items discussed in this section or added to the Other Operated Department's sub-schedule.

Operating Supplies. Includes the cost of operating and general office supplies needed to operate the Other Operated Department that are not included in the descriptions of specific supply accounts such as Cleaning Supplies and Printing and Stationery.

Other Detailed Expenses (as warranted). Includes significant expenses commonly found in specific Other Operated Departments. The following expenses, if they exist, are presented as examples of separate expense line items typically found in the associated Other Operated Department. The list is not exhaustive. Additional significant expenses should be segregated as warranted.

Operated Department	Expense
Transportation:	Gas, Parts
Guest Laundry:	Cleaning Supplies, Chemicals
Swimming Pool/Beach:	Chemicals
Tennis and Pro Shop:	Nets and Tapes, Maintenance
Business Center:	Copier/Printer/Computer Parts & Supplies
Marina:	Maintenance
Barber/Beauty Shop:	Beauty Products
Retail Store:	Display Equipment
Children's Camp:	Arts and Crafts Equipment, Kids' Meals
Condominium:	Owner's Reimbursement
Gaming:	Cards, Chips

Printing and Stationery. Includes the cost of printed forms used in the Other Operated Department, whether they are purchased from an outside source or produced internally.

Professional Fees. Includes the cost of specialists, whether certified or not, engaged to assist management in the Other Operated Department.

Royalty Fees. Includes all costs associated with the right to use a brand name in connection with an Other Operated Department. For example, the fees paid for use of a brand name to identify a retail store, including franchise fees, are charged to this line item

Telecommunications. Includes any telecommunications expenditures that can be directly related to the Other Operated Department, including the costs of local, long distance, and Internet communications. Telecommunications includes not only traditional telephone systems, but also the cost of cellular phones, including the equipment and periodic service charges, used in the Other Operated Department.

Training. Includes the cost, other than time, that can be directly attributed to the training of employees in the Other Operated Department. Examples include the costs of training materials, supplies, and instructor fees. The cost of employee wages incurred during training is charged to Salaries and Wages.

Travel—Meals and Entertainment. Includes the reimbursable cost of food and beverage expenditures for travel and entertainment by employees of the Other Operated Department traveling on property business.

Travel—Other. Includes the cost of travel and reimbursable expenditures, other than food, beverage, and entertainment, by employees of the Other Operated Department traveling on property business.

Uniform Laundry. Includes the cost of cleaning uniforms for employees of the Other Operated Department whether performed by an in-hotel facility or contracted to an outside company.

Uniforms. Includes the cost of employee uniforms used in the Other Operated Department, whether purchased or rented. Repair costs are also included in this line item. The cost of cleaning uniforms is charged to the Uniform Laundry account.

Total Other Expenses

Total Other Expenses is calculated by adding all items listed under Other Expenses. The percentage for each line item expense as well as Total Other Expenses is calculated by dividing the line item amount by Total Revenue for the Other Operated Department.

Total Expenses

Total Expenses is calculated by adding Total Payroll and Related Expenses to Total Other Expenses. The percentage for Total Expenses is calculated by dividing Total Expenses by Total Revenue for the Other Operated Department.

The sum of Total Cost of Sales and Total Expenses is shown on Schedule 3 as Departmental Expenses—[Name of Department].

Departmental Income (Loss)

Departmental Income (Loss) is calculated by subtracting Total Expenses from Gross Profit (Loss). The percentage for Departmental Income (Loss) is calculated by dividing Departmental Income (Loss) by Total Revenue for the Other Operated Department. Departmental Income (Loss) is then shown on Schedule 3 as Departmental Income (Loss)—[Name of Department].

MINOR OPERATED DEPARTMENTS—SUB-SCHEDULE 3-XX

	CURRENT MONTH			YEAR-TO-DATE		
	ACTUAL	FORECAST	PRIOR YEAR	ACTUAL	FORECAST	PRIOR YEAR
	$ | %	$ | %	$ | %	$ | %	$ | %	$ | %
REVENUE						
Minor Operated Department 1						
Minor Operated Department 2						
...						
Minor Operated Department x						
Less: Allowances						
Total Revenue						
DEPARTMENTAL EXPENSES[1]						
Minor Operated Department 1						
Minor Operated Department 2						
...						
Minor Operated Department x						
Total Minor Operated Departmental Expenses						
DEPARTMENTAL INCOME (LOSS)						
Minor Operated Department 1						
Minor Operated Department 2						
...						
Minor Operated Department x						
TOTAL MINOR OPERATED DEPARTMENTAL INCOME (LOSS)						

1. Departmental Expenses is the sum of Cost of Sales (when applicable) and Total Expenses.

Minor Operated Departments—Sub-schedule 3-xx illustrates the proper format to summarize the Revenue, Departmental Expenses, and Income (Loss) amounts for all Minor Operated Departments. The revenue and expense items shown in Sub-schedule 3-*xx* are totally at the discretion of an individual hotel. However, each revenue item must have a matching expense item and vice versa. Properties may choose to delete some of the columns or to show them in a different order and remain "in conformity with the *Uniform System.*"

The Total Minor Operated Departmental Revenue and Total Minor Operated Departmental Expenses from Sub-Schedule 3-*xx* are then shown on Schedule 3.

Minor Operated Departments are sources of income that meet the guidelines to present revenues and expenses on a gross basis, yet generate limited income and incur minor direct operating expenses. Typically, Minor Operated Departments do not have any Payroll and Related Expenses. Examples of income sources that are frequently (but not always) classified as Minor Operated Departments are:

- Vending
- Retail kiosks operated by front desk personnel
- Video Games

- In-Room Movie Rental
- Guest Dry Cleaning (outside vendor)

For more information, see the discussion on reporting revenue on a gross or net basis presented at the beginning of this section. Some of the income sources may meet the requirement to be reported on a net basis in *Rentals and Other Income— Schedule 4.*

RENTALS AND OTHER INCOME—SCHEDULE 4

	CURRENT MONTH			YEAR-TO-DATE		
	ACTUAL	FORECAST	PRIOR YEAR	ACTUAL	FORECAST	PRIOR YEAR
	$ | %	$ | %	$ | %	$ | %	$ | %	$ | %
Space Rental and Concessions						
Commissions						
Cash Discounts Earned						
Cancellation Penalties						
Attrition Penalties						
Foreign Currency Transaction Gains (Losses)						
Guest Laundry and Dry Cleaning						
Interest Income						
Proceeds from Business Interruption Insurance						
Other						
TOTAL RENTALS AND OTHER INCOME						

Rentals and Other Income—Schedule 4 illustrates a format and identifies income sources that commonly appear on a supplemental schedule supporting the Net Revenue amounts reported on the Summary Operating Statement as Rentals and Other Income. Individual properties may delete irrelevant line items, but the *Uniform System* does not provide for the addition or substitution of other revenue line items. Rather, properties may choose to develop a sub-account/sub-schedule to provide more detail related to a particular revenue item. This sub-account/sub-schedule is then to be rolled into the appropriate line item. Additionally, properties may choose to delete some of the columns or to show them in a different order and remain "in conformity with the *Uniform System*."

In general, revenue is classified as Rental and Other Income if the following guidelines apply:

- The revenue the hotel receives is a fixed payment, percent of revenue, or a percent of profit, and "net" of any expenses.

- The hotel incurs no direct operating expenses associated with the generation of the revenue.

- The operation of the department generating the revenue is the responsibility of a third party. The hotel owner and/or operator do not participate in the operation of the department, and do not incur any direct liability for the expenses of the department.

For additional information, see Reporting Revenue on a Gross Versus Net Basis under *Other Operated Departments—Schedule 3.*

Space Rentals and Concessions

Many properties wish to offer their guests services and/or merchandise that are not provided by the operated departments previously discussed. In these cases, properties contract the operations of such activities through rental or concession agreements. Space Rentals and Concessions includes the revenue generated from the rental of space within the property. Examples are gifts shops, coffee kiosks, and car rental agencies that lease space from the hotel. The amount paid by tenants entering into leases with the property is amortized over the term of the lease and reported in Rentals and Other Income.

Commissions to renting agents are amortized over the term of the lease and are charged against Administrative and General—Professional Fees.

Commissions

Commissions received from third parties for services, such as leased telephone stations, leased gaming and vending machines, taxicab stands, garages and parking lots, automobile rentals, non-owned or non-operated audiovisual services, outside laundry services, and photography are included in this line item. Separate subcategories could be used to identify significant revenue items.

Cash Discounts Earned

Discounts earned by the payment of creditors' accounts within the discount period are included in this line item. Cash Discounts Earned does not include trade discounts that are more properly a deduction from cost of merchandise sales or an individual expense item.

Cancellation Penalties

Penalty income received from groups that cancel their reservations for guest rooms, food and beverage, and other services after a contracted date is included in this line item. "No-show" revenue from individual guests who do not show for a guaranteed reservation and "early departure fees" from the guests who check out earlier than the scheduled departure date are included in Other Revenue in the Rooms department.

Attrition Penalties

Penalty income received from groups that do not fulfill their guaranteed number of reservations for guestrooms, food and beverage, and other services is included in this line item.

Foreign Currency Transaction Gains (Losses)

Any foreign currency gains or losses generated from exchanging foreign currency into the local currency of the country used by the property to report its results of operations are included in this line item.

Guest Laundry and Dry Cleaning

The net income earned for cleaning guest laundry from third-party operated concessions is included in this line item.

Interest Income

Interest earned on cash investments, bank deposits, notes receivable, accounts receivable, and from other sources is included in this line item.

Proceeds from Business Interruption Insurance

Amounts received from an insurance company for a business interruption claim are included in this line item.

Other

This line item includes any income not classified under another caption. Included under Other are fees earned from managing mixed-ownership projects.

Total Rentals and Other Income

Total Rentals and Other Income is calculated by adding all of the amounts listed above. This amount appears on the Summary Operating Statement under Revenue—Rentals and Other Income.

In completing Schedule 4, Total Rentals and Other Income is considered to be 100 percent, and the percentage for each source of income is determined by dividing the dollar amount of that source by Total Rentals and Other Income.

ADMINISTRATIVE AND GENERAL—SCHEDULE 5

	CURRENT MONTH			YEAR-TO-DATE		
	ACTUAL	FORECAST	PRIOR YEAR	ACTUAL	FORECAST	PRIOR YEAR
	$ | %	$ | %	$ | %	$ | %	$ | %	$ | %
EXPENSES						
Payroll and Related Expenses						
Salaries, Wages, and Bonuses						
Salaries and Wages						
Bonuses and Incentives						
Total Salaries, Wages, and Bonuses						
Payroll-Related Expenses						
Payroll Taxes						
Supplemental Pay						
Employee Benefits						
Total Payroll-Related Expenses						
Total Payroll and Related Expenses						
Other Expenses						
Audit Charges						
Bank Charges						
Cash Overages and Shortages						
Centralized Accounting Charges						
Complimentary Services and Gifts						
Contract Services						
Corporate Office Reimbursables						
Credit and Collection						
Credit Card Commissions						
Decorations						
Donations						
Dues and Subscriptions						
Equipment Rental						
Human Resources						
Information Systems						
Laundry and Dry Cleaning						
Legal Services						
Licenses and Permits						
Loss and Damage						
Miscellaneous						
Operating Supplies						
Payroll Processing						
Postage and Overnight Delivery Charges						
Printing and Stationery						
Professional Fees						
Provision for Doubtful Accounts						
Security						
Settlement Costs						
Telecommunications						
Training						
Transportation						
Travel—Meals and Entertainment						
Travel—Other						
Uniform Laundry						
Uniforms						
Total Other Expenses						
TOTAL EXPENSES						

Administrative and General—Schedule 5 illustrates the proper format for reporting the Payroll and Related Expenses and Other Expenses for Administrative and General. Individual properties may delete irrelevant line items, but the *Uniform System* does not provide for the addition or substitution of expense line items. Rather, properties may choose to develop a sub-account/sub-schedule to provide more detail related to a particular expense item. This sub-account/sub-schedule is then to be rolled into the appropriate line item. Additionally, properties may choose to delete some of the columns or to show them in a different order and remain "in conformity with the *Uniform System*."

Expenses

Administrative and General expenses are separated into two major categories: Payroll and Related Expenses and Other Expense.

Payroll and Related Expenses

Payroll and Related Expenses for Administrative and General comprises the expenses associated with Salaries, Wages, and Bonuses and Payroll-Related Expenses for employees classified as Administrative and General. A list of the positions typically included in Administrative and General is shown on pages 176–177.

Salaries, Wages, and Bonuses. This grouping includes (1) Salaries and Wages and (2) Bonuses and Incentives. Salaries and Wages includes only earnings paid to an employee for duties that relate to the operation of the property, such as regular pay, overtime pay, and shift differential pay. If an employee works in a department other than his or her regular home department, his or her earnings are charged as Salaries and Wages in that other department, regardless of the duties being performed. For example, if a Food and Beverage department employee works as a server for an employee awards banquet, his or her earnings are charged to Salaries and Wages in Administrative and General, and not to this line item in the Food and Beverage department. Payroll-Related Expenses (described below) for the above example are treated similarly and charged as Payroll-Related Expenses in Administrative and General.

Salaries and Wages also includes contract or leased labor. Contract or leased labor refers to those situations in which a property enters into an agreement with an outside service to provide employees to fill positions that would normally be held by individuals paid on the regular payroll. In these situations, the property usually supervises the individuals and records or tracks their hours worked and pays them on an hourly basis. A typical example is the use of individuals brought into the property to fill a clerical function such as filing. This situation differs from a contract service in which a property has an agreement with an outside company to provide some type of service, such scanning documents in connection with digitizing records. In this case, the contracted organization typically provides the supervision and ensures that the work is performed. The costs associated with this type of agreement are charged under Contract Services for the department receiving the service.

Bonuses and Incentives includes bonuses, incentive pay, and other types of performance pay designed to drive revenue through sales, profit, or guest satisfaction measures.

Total Salaries, Wages, and Bonuses. Calculated by adding together Salaries and Wages and Bonuses and Incentives.

Payroll-Related Expenses. Payroll-Related Expenses includes amounts paid for an employee for duties that relate to the operation of the property and amounts paid for an employee who works in a department other than his or her regular home department regardless of the duties being performed. Payroll-Related Expenses includes the following items:

- *Payroll Taxes.* Includes Federal Retirement and Medicare (FICA), Federal and State Unemployment Taxes (FUTA and SUTA), State Disability Insurance (SDI), and other mandated payroll-related taxes or social insurance items. (See *Payroll-Related Expenses—Schedule 13.*)

- *Supplemental Pay.* Includes personal days, vacation pay, sick pay, holiday pay, jury duty pay, relocation pay, paid time off, and severance pay. Supplemental Pay also includes bonuses and incentive payments that are discretionary and not determined by results from operations.

- *Employee Benefits.* Includes all other payroll-related expenses, such as employer-paid health insurance expenses, cost of meals furnished to employees, pension contributions, and union fees. (See *Payroll-Related Expenses—Schedule 13.*) The distribution of employee meal costs from *Employee Cafeteria—Schedule 12* is charged to this line.

Total Payroll-Related Expenses. Calculated by adding together Payroll Taxes, Supplemental Pay, and Employee Benefits.

Total Payroll and Related Expenses

Total Payroll and Related Expenses is calculated by adding together Total Salaries, Wages, and Bonuses and Total Payroll-Related Expenses. The percentage for each payroll and related expense line item as well as Total Payroll and Related Expenses is calculated by dividing the line item amount by Total Revenue for the entire property.

Other Expenses

This expense grouping includes the significant Administrative and General expenses approved as Other Expenses in the *Uniform System.* Individual properties may delete irrelevant line items, but the *Uniform System* does not provide for the addition or substitution of other expense line items. Rather, properties may choose to develop a sub-account/sub-schedule to provide more detail related to a particular expense item. This sub-account/sub-schedule is then to be rolled into the appropriate line item listed below.

Audit Charges. Includes the cost of any accounting audits, whether internal or external, performed for the property.

Bank Charges. Includes bank charges assessed for miscellaneous banking services and transactions such as overdrafts, stop payments, check charges, and other related items.

Cash Overages and Shortages. Includes cashiers' overages and shortages.

Centralized Accounting Charges. Includes the cost of centralized accounting charges assessed by the corporate office or management company.

Complimentary Services and Gifts. Includes the cost of providing gift items used in gratis presentations for promotional purposes to guests and vendors associated with Administrative and General.

Contract Services. Includes expenses for activities performed for Administrative and General by outside companies rather than hotel employees. The costs of contracting outside companies for document retention services is an example. If supplies are purchased for contract companies to use, the supplies are charged to the appropriate supply account.

Corporate Office Reimbursables. Includes the allocations of salaries and expenses billed to the property by the regional or corporate office or by the management company only when these salaries and expenses cannot be billed to this account in any other department in the property. Travel expenses of such corporate or management company personnel that are incurred while visiting the property, including the costs of meals and other applicable services or amenities provided to corporate or management company staff while on business in the property for the benefit of the property, are also charged to this account.

Credit and Collection. Includes the cost of collecting guest accounts, such as attorney's fees and credit and check verification services.

Credit Card Commissions. Includes the cost of commissions paid to credit card organizations. Volume rebate payments received from credit card organizations would be credited to this account.

Decorations. Includes the cost of decorative items used in the Administrative and General areas for holidays and special events.

Donations. Includes the cost of any charitable contributions made by the property.

Dues and Subscriptions. Includes the cost of representation of the property, or of members of the staff when authorized to represent the property, in business or professional organizations. Dues and Subscriptions is also charged with the cost of subscriptions to newspapers, magazines, and books for use by property-wide staff.

Equipment Rental. Includes the cost of renting any type of equipment that may be used either sporadically in Administrative and General or as a replacement for equipment out of service on a temporary basis. Equipment that is rented on a continuous basis and, if purchased, would qualify as a capital purchase is charged to Other Property and Equipment under the Rent section of *Rent, Property and Other Taxes, and Insurance—Schedule 10.*

Human Resources. Includes all costs directly related to the human resources function, such as recruitment, relocation, employee housing (whether temporary or permanent), physician fees and medical supplies, and all expenses associated with the cost of house media, social and sports activities, employee awards, and events and activities intended to improve employee relations and morale. If these expenses are significant, a property may develop a sub-schedule to provide more detail, but the sub-schedule total must roll up into this line item.

Information Systems. Includes the cost of management information system services, supplies, and equipment, excluding equipment rental and capital items. Information Systems includes minor equipment, software, supplies, and peripheral equipment. The expenses associated with maintaining PMS, POS, and telecommunications systems are also charged to this line item. If these expenses are significant, a property may develop a sub-schedule to provide more detail, but the sub-schedule total must roll up into this line item.

Laundry and Dry Cleaning. Includes the cost of laundry and dry cleaning services applicable to Administrative and General, whether the services are performed by an in-house facility or are contracted to an outside company. If the services are performed by an in-house laundry, an allocation from House Laundry is charged to Laundry and Dry Cleaning. If the services are performed by an outside company, the amount charged to Laundry and Dry Cleaning should be based on invoices sent by the outside laundry. The cost of cleaning employee uniforms is charged to the Uniform Laundry account.

Legal Services. Includes court costs and the cost of attorney fees, expert witnesses, related travel, and other reimbursable expenses other than those incurred in connection with an insurance claim. Legal fees incurred for insurance-related matters are charged to the appropriate Insurance category in *Rent, Property and Other Taxes, and Insurance—Schedule 10.*

Licenses and Permits. Includes the cost of federal, state, and local licenses, including costs of inspections needed for licensing, for all Administrative and General activities.

Loss and Damage. Includes the payments made for guest property lost or damaged in excess of the amounts recovered from insurance companies.

Miscellaneous. Includes any expenses of Administrative and General that do not apply to the other line items discussed in this section.

Operating Supplies. Includes the cost of items needed to operate Administrative and General that are not included in Postage and Overnight Delivery Charges or Printing and Stationery. Examples of items included in Operating Supplies are general office supplies, such as facsimile machines, calculators, and expendable office supplies, such as notepads, pens, pencils, and paper clips.

Payroll Processing. Includes the cost incurred when a third-party service is used to process payroll.

Postage and Overnight Delivery Charges. Includes the cost of stamps and express mail charges, except amounts attributable to Sales and Marketing.

Printing and Stationery. Includes the cost of printed forms used in Administrative and General, whether they are purchased from an outside source or produced internally.

Professional Fees. Includes the cost of public accountants other than audit fees, tax advisors, and other professional consultants, excluding attorneys. The amount recorded includes professional fees, travel, and other reimbursable expenses. For example, amortization of commissions paid to rental agents who have assisted in securing tenants for space rented in the property is charged to this account. Consulting fees incurred for insurance-related matters are charged to the appropriate Insurance category in *Rent, Property and Other Taxes, and Insurance— Schedule 10.*

Provision for Doubtful Accounts. Includes any charge made to provide for the probable loss on accounts and notes receivable.

Security. Includes the cost of contract security and other related expenses, such as armored car service and safety and lock boxes.

Settlement Costs. Includes the cost associated with settling uninsurable claims, including damage awards in connection with the settling of a lawsuit, and contractual disputes. For example, the costs associated with Equal Employment Opportunities Commission and other discrimination claim settlements would be charged to this line item.

Telecommunications. Includes any telecommunications expenditures that can be directly related to Administrative and General, including the costs of local, long distance, and Internet communications. Telecommunications includes not only traditional telephone systems, but also the cost of cellular phones, including the equipment and periodic service charges, used in Administrative and General.

Training. Includes the costs, other than time, that can be directly attributed to the training of employees in Administrative and General. Examples include the costs of training materials, supplies, and instructor fees. The cost of employee wages incurred during training is charged to Salaries and Wages.

Transportation. Includes the cost of transportation other than that directly related to guests, such as the costs associated with transporting employees to the property or the cost of providing an automobile for the general manager.

Travel—Meals and Entertainment. Includes the reimbursable cost of food and beverage expenses for travel and entertainment by employees of Administrative and General traveling on property business.

Travel—Other. Includes the cost of travel and reimbursable expenses, other than food, beverage, and entertainment, by employees of Administrative and General traveling on property business.

Uniform Laundry. Includes the cost of cleaning uniforms for employees of Administrative and General whether performed by an in-hotel facility or contracted to an outside company.

Uniforms. Includes the cost of employee uniforms used in Administrative and General, whether purchased or rented. Repair costs are also included in this line item. The cost of cleaning uniforms is charged to the Uniform Laundry account.

Total Other Expenses

Total Other Expenses is calculated by adding all items listed under Other Expenses. The percentage for each line item expense as well as Total Other Expenses is calculated by dividing the line item amount by Total Revenue for the entire property.

Total Expenses

Total Expenses is calculated by adding Total Payroll and Related Expenses to Total Other Expenses. The percentage for Total Expenses is calculated by dividing Total Expenses by Total Revenue for the entire property.

Total Expenses is the same amount that appears on the Summary Operating Statement under Undistributed Operating Expenses—Administrative and General.

SALES AND MARKETING—SCHEDULE 6

	CURRENT MONTH						YEAR-TO-DATE					
	ACTUAL		FORECAST		PRIOR YEAR		ACTUAL		FORECAST		PRIOR YEAR	
	$	%	$	%	$	%	$	%	$	%	$	%
EXPENSES												
Payroll and Related Expenses												
Salaries, Wages, and Bonuses												
Salaries and Wages												
Bonuses and Incentives												
Total Salaries, Wages, and Bonuses												
Payroll-Related Expenses												
Payroll Taxes												
Supplemental Pay												
Employee Benefits												
Total Payroll-Related Expenses												
Total Payroll and Related Expenses												
Other Expenses												
Sales Expenses												
Complimentary Services and Gifts												
Contract Services												
Corporate Office Reimbursables												
Decorations												
Dues and Subscriptions												
Equipment Rental												
Fam (Familiarization) Trips												
Laundry and Dry Cleaning												
Miscellaneous												
Operating Supplies												
Outside Sales Representation												
Postage and Overnight Delivery Charges												
Printing and Stationery												
Promotion												
Telecommunications												
Trade Shows												
Training												
Travel—Meals and Entertainment												
Travel—Other												
Total Sales Expenses												
Marketing Expenses												
Agency Fees												
Collateral Material												
Contract Services												
Direct Mail												
E-Commerce												
Franchise and Affiliation Advertising												
Franchise Fees												
In-House Graphics												
Loyalty Programs and Affiliation Fees												
Media												
Miscellaneous												
Outdoor												
Outside Services												
Photography												
Total Marketing Expenses												
Total Other Expenses												
TOTAL EXPENSES												

Sales and Marketing—Schedule 6 illustrates the proper format for reporting the Payroll and Related Expenses and Other Expenses for Sales and Marketing. Individual properties may delete irrelevant line items, but the *Uniform System* does not provide for the addition or substitution of expense line items. Rather, properties may choose to develop a sub-account/sub-schedule to provide more detail related to a particular expense item. This sub-account/sub-schedule is then to be rolled into the appropriate line item. Additionally, properties may choose to delete some of the columns or to show them in a different order and remain "in conformity with the *Uniform System*."

Expenses

Sales and Marketing expenses are separated into two major categories: Payroll and Related Expenses and Other Expenses.

Payroll and Related Expenses

Payroll and Related Expenses for Sales and Marketing comprises the expenses associated with Salaries, Wages, and Bonuses and Payroll-Related Expenses for employees classified as Sales and Marketing. A list of the positions typically included in Sales and Marketing is shown on page 177.

Salaries, Wages, and Bonuses. This grouping includes (1) Salaries and Wages and (2) Bonuses and Incentives. Salaries and Wages includes only earnings paid to an employee for duties that relate to the operation of the property, such as regular pay, overtime pay, and shift differential pay. If an employee works in a department other than his or her regular home department, his or her earnings are charged as Salaries and Wages in that other department, regardless of the duties being performed. For example, if a Sales department employee works as a server for an employee awards banquet, his or her earnings are charged to Salaries and Wages in Administrative and General, and not to this line item. Payroll-Related Expenses (described below) for the above example are treated similarly and charged as Payroll-Related Expenses in Administrative and General.

Salaries and Wages also includes contract or leased labor. Contract or leased labor refers to those situations in which a property enters into an agreement with an outside service to provide employees to fill positions that would normally be held by individuals paid on the regular payroll. In these situations, the property usually supervises the individuals and records or tracks their hours worked and pays them on an hourly basis. A typical example is the use of individuals brought into the property to fill a clerical function such as filing. This situation differs from a contract service in which a property has an agreement with an outside company to provide some type of service, such as such scanning documents in connection with digitizing records. In this case, the contracted organization typically provides the supervision and ensures that the work is performed. The costs associated with this type of agreement are charged under Contract Services for the department receiving the service.

Bonuses and Incentives includes bonuses, incentive pay, and other types of performance pay designed to drive revenue through sales, profit, or guest satisfaction measures.

Total Salaries, Wages, and Bonuses. Calculated by adding together Salaries and Wages and Bonuses and Incentives.

Payroll-Related Expenses. Payroll-Related Expenses includes amounts paid for an employee for duties that relate to the operation of the property and amounts paid for an employee who works in a department other than his or her regular home department regardless of the duties being performed. Payroll-Related Expenses includes the following items:

- *Payroll Taxes.* Includes Federal Retirement and Medicare (FICA), Federal and State Unemployment Taxes (FUTA and SUTA), State Disability Insurance (SDI), and other mandated payroll-related taxes or social insurance items. (See *Payroll-Related Expenses—Schedule 13.*)

- *Supplemental Pay.* Includes personal days, vacation pay, sick pay, holiday pay, jury duty pay, relocation pay, paid time off, and severance pay. Supplemental Pay also includes bonuses and incentive payments that are discretionary and not determined by results from operations.

- *Employee Benefits.* Includes all other payroll-related expenses, such as employer-paid health insurance expenses, cost of meals furnished to employees, pension contributions, and union fees. (See *Payroll-Related Expenses—Schedule 13.*) The distribution of employee meal costs from *Employee Cafeteria—Schedule 12* is charged to this line.

Total Payroll-Related Expenses. Calculated by adding together Payroll Taxes, Supplemental Pay, and Employee Benefits.

Total Payroll and Related Expenses

Total Payroll and Related Expenses is calculated by adding together Total Salaries, Wages, and Bonuses and Total Payroll-Related Expenses. The percentage for each payroll and related expense line item as well as Total Payroll and Related Expenses is calculated by dividing the line item amount by Total Revenue for the entire property.

Other Expenses

This expense grouping includes the significant Sales and Marketing expenses approved as Other Expenses in the *Uniform System.* Other Expenses for Sales and Marketing are divided into two groups: Sales Expenses and Marketing Expenses. Individual properties may delete irrelevant line items, but the *Uniform System* does not provide for the addition or substitution of other expense line items. Rather, properties may choose to develop a sub-account/sub-schedule to provide more detail related to a particular expense item. This sub-account/sub-schedule is then to be rolled into the appropriate line item listed below.

Sales Expenses

Complimentary Services and Gifts. Includes the cost of providing gift items used in gratis presentations for promotional purposes to guests and vendors associated with Sales and Marketing, such as pens, golf balls, shirts, and key chains.

Contract Services. Includes expenses for activities performed for Sales and Marketing by outside companies rather than hotel employees. The costs of contracting outside companies to clean carpets and rugs or to disinfect areas associated with Sales and Marketing are typical examples. If supplies are purchased for contract companies to use, the supplies are charged to the appropriate supply account. The cost of contracts for Sales and Marketing laundry and dry cleaning is charged to Laundry and Dry Cleaning.

Corporate Office Reimbursables. Includes the allocations of salaries and expenses of corporate or management company sales and marketing personnel billed to the property by the regional or corporate office or by the management company. Travel expenses of such corporate or management company personnel that are incurred while visiting the property, including the costs of meals and other applicable services or amenities provided to corporate or management company staff while on business in the property for the benefit of the property, are also charged to this account.

Decorations. Includes the cost of decorative items used in the Sales and Marketing areas for holidays and special events.

Dues and Subscriptions. Includes the cost of membership of the Sales and Marketing staff, when authorized to represent the property, in business or professional organizations. Dues and Subscriptions is also charged with the cost of subscriptions to newspapers, magazines, and books for use by the Sales and Marketing staff.

Equipment Rental. Includes the cost of renting any type of equipment that may be used either sporadically in Sales and Marketing or as a replacement for equipment out of service on a temporary basis. Equipment that is rented on a continuous basis and, if purchased, would qualify as a capital purchase is charged to Other Property and Equipment under the Rent section of *Rent, Property and Other Taxes, and Insurance—Schedule 10.*

Fam (Familiarization) Trips. Includes all costs associated with travel agents or meeting planners coming to a property for the purpose of familiarizing them with the property and gaining additional sales business from them. Rooms are recorded as complimentary and food and beverage consumed at the property is recorded at cost for fam trips.

Laundry and Dry Cleaning. Includes the cost of laundry and dry cleaning services applicable to Sales and Marketing, whether the services are performed by an in-house facility or are contracted to an outside company. If the services are performed by an in-house laundry, an allocation from House Laundry is charged to Laundry and Dry Cleaning. If the services are performed by an outside company, the amount charged to Laundry and Dry Cleaning should be based on invoices sent by the outside laundry. The cost of cleaning employee uniforms is charged to the Uniform Laundry account.

Miscellaneous. Includes any expenses related to Sales that do not apply to the other line items discussed in this section. Items given as inducements to book rooms (e.g., a bottle of wine, dinner for two, etc.) are charged to Complimentary Services and Gifts in the Rooms department.

Operating Supplies. Includes the cost of items needed to operate Sales and Marketing that are not included in Postage and Overnight Delivery Charges or Printing and Stationery. Examples of items included in Operating Supplies are general office supplies, such as facsimile machines, calculators, and expendable office supplies, such as notepads, pens, pencils, and paper clips.

Outside Sales Representation. Includes the fees, commissions, and expenses paid to third parties, other than travel agents and meeting planners, whose services are retained for the purpose of selling and generating revenue for the property.

Postage and Overnight Delivery Charges. Includes the cost of stamps and express mail charges attributable to Sales and Marketing except those costs associated with direct mail campaigns.

Printing and Stationery. Includes the cost of printed forms used in Sales and Marketing, whether they are purchased from an outside source or produced internally.

Promotion. Includes the cost of goods and services provided to any individual or organization to promote the property in the community and the industry other than media advertising. Examples include entry fees to events held by civic groups to create a presence and awareness of the property, sponsoring gift certificates for non-profit and other organizations, participation in charity golf tournaments, and client appreciation parties. If food and beverage is involved, it is recorded at the cost of the food and beverage items provided.

Telecommunications. Includes any telecommunications expenditures that can be directly related to Sales and Marketing, including the costs of local, long distance, and Internet communications. Telecommunications includes not only traditional telephone systems, but also the cost of cellular phones, including the equipment and periodic service charges, used in Sales and Marketing.

Trade Shows. Includes the cost of promoting the property at various trade shows, excluding travel expenses of attending representatives, but including the cost of the booth, registration fees, promotional logo items, and rental of exhibition space.

Training. Includes the costs, other than time, that can be directly attributed to the training of employees in Sales and Marketing. Examples include the costs of training materials, supplies, and instructor fees. The cost of employee wages incurred during training is charged to Salaries and Wages.

Travel—Meals and Entertainment. Includes the reimbursable cost of food and beverage expenses for travel and entertainment by employees of Sales and Marketing traveling on property business.

Travel—Other. Includes the cost of travel and reimbursable expenses, other than food, beverage, and entertainment, by employees of Sales and Marketing traveling on property business.

Total Sales Expenses. Calculated by adding together all items listed under Sales Expenses.

Marketing Expenses

Agency Fees. Includes fees paid to advertising and/or public relations agencies.

Collateral Material. Includes the cost of brochures, salespersons' kits, maps, floor plans, and similar materials used to describe the property's services.

Contract Services. Includes expenses for activities related to Advertising that are performed by outside companies rather than hotel employees. The costs of equipment maintenance contracts and other service contracts related to Advertising are typical examples. If supplies are purchased for contract companies to use, the supplies are charged to the appropriate supply account.

Direct Mail. Includes the cost of mailing lists, letter writing, postage, addressing envelopes or cards, and other work of this nature.

E-Commerce. Includes the cost of Web site development and maintenance, including Web site registration fees, link costs, and the cost of producing a virtual tour.

Franchise and Affiliation Advertising. Includes any costs paid to a franchise or affiliation entity for the purpose of advertising on a national or regional basis.

Franchise Fees. Includes all fees except those related to national advertising, loyalty programs, and reservations charged by a franchisor or affiliation entity, including royalties for the licensing/branding/naming of the property itself. Fees paid for national advertising are charged to Franchise and Affiliation Advertising. Room reservation fees paid to the franchise company are charged to the Rooms department.

In-House Graphics. Includes the cost of directories, signs, brochures, and other costs associated with merchandising the services of the property. Computer software programs and applications purchased to produce these items in-house are also charged to this account.

Loyalty Programs and Affiliation Fees. Includes any costs associated with programs designed to build guest loyalty to the property or brand. Costs associated with cooperative frequent traveler programs, such as frequent flyer programs, are also charged to this account. Additionally, this account is charged with any fees associated with the administration of the property's frequent guest stay or similar programs. The actual cost of executing the frequent guest stay or similar programs, such as the charge based on revenue or sold room nights, is charged to this account.

Media. Includes the cost of advertising on radio and television, including production costs, as well as advertising in newspapers, magazines, directories, and third-party Web sites. When such costs are significant, a property may break out the items in a series of sub-accounts, such as consumer media, newspapers, prep and production, radio, trade media, brochures, and telephone directories, but the total of each of these items must be rolled into this line item.

Miscellaneous. Includes any expenses of Marketing that do not apply to the other line items discussed in this section.

Outdoor. Includes the cost of posters, painted billboards, reader boards, and other signs, including rental costs and service charges.

Outside Services. Includes the cost of any analysis prepared by independent research or consulting firms for the purpose of reviewing demographic characteristics or analyzing guest history.

Photography. Includes the cost of photographs used in various types of promotional and publicity programs, including the cost of using professional models.

Total Marketing Expenses. Calculated by adding all items listed under Marketing Expenses.

Total Other Expenses

Total Other Expenses is calculated by adding all items listed under Other Expenses. The percentage for each line item expense as well as Total Other Expenses is calculated by dividing the line item amount by Total Revenue for the entire property.

Total Expenses

Total Expenses is calculated by adding Total Payroll and Related Expenses to Total Other Expenses. The percentage for Total Expenses is calculated by dividing Total Expenses by Total Revenue for the entire property.

Total Expenses is the same amount that appears on the Summary Operating Statement under Undistributed Operating Expenses—Sales and Marketing.

PROPERTY OPERATION AND MAINTENANCE—SCHEDULE 7

	CURRENT MONTH			YEAR-TO-DATE		
	ACTUAL	FORECAST	PRIOR YEAR	ACTUAL	FORECAST	PRIOR YEAR
	$ | %	$ | %	$ | %	$ | %	$ | %	$ | %
EXPENSES						
Payroll and Related Expenses						
Salaries, Wages, and Bonuses						
Salaries and Wages						
Bonuses and Incentives						
Total Salaries, Wages, and Bonuses						
Payroll-Related Expenses						
Payroll Taxes						
Supplemental Pay						
Employee Benefits						
Total Payroll-Related Expenses						
Total Payroll and Related Expenses						
Other Expenses						
Building						
Complimentary Services and Gifts						
Contract Services						
Corporate Office Reimbursables						
Decorations						
Dues and Subscriptions						
Electrical and Mechanical Equipment						
Elevators and Escalators						
Engineering Supplies						
Equipment Rental						
Floor Covering						
Furniture and Equipment						
Grounds Maintenance and Landscaping						
Heating, Ventilation, and Air Conditioning Equipment						
Kitchen Equipment						
Laundry and Dry Cleaning						
Laundry Equipment						
Licenses and Permits						
Life/Safety						
Light Bulbs						
Miscellaneous						
Operating Supplies						
Painting and Decorating						
Plumbing						
Printing and Stationery						
Swimming Pool						
Telecommunications						
Training						
Travel—Meals and Entertainment						
Travel—Other						
Uniform Laundry						
Uniforms						
Waste Removal						
Total Other Expenses						
TOTAL EXPENSES						

Property Operation and Maintenance—Schedule 7 illustrates the proper format for reporting the Payroll and Related Expenses and Other Expenses for Property Operation and Maintenance. Individual properties may delete irrelevant line items, but the *Uniform System* does not provide for the addition or substitution of expense line items. Rather, properties may choose to develop a sub-account/sub-schedule to provide more detail related to a particular expense item. This sub-account/sub-schedule is then to be rolled into the appropriate line item. Additionally, properties may choose to delete some of the columns or to show them in a different order and remain "in conformity with the *Uniform System*."

Expenses

Property Operation and Maintenance expenses are separated into two major categories: Payroll and Related Expenses and Other Expenses.

Payroll and Related Expenses

Payroll and Related Expenses for Property Operation and Maintenance comprises the expenses associated with Salaries, Wages, and Bonuses and Payroll-Related Expenses for employees classified as Property Operation and Maintenance. A list of the positions typically included in Property Operation and Maintenance is shown on page 177.

Salaries, Wages, and Bonuses. This grouping includes (1) Salaries and Wages and (2) Bonuses and Incentives. Salaries and Wages includes only earnings paid to an employee for duties that relate to the operation of the property, such as regular pay, overtime pay, and shift differential pay. If an employee works in a department other than his or her regular home department, his or her earnings are charged as Salaries and Wages in that other department, regardless of the duties being performed. For example, if a maintenance department employee works as a server for an employee awards banquet, his or her earnings are charged to Salaries and Wages in Administrative and General, and not to this line item. Payroll-Related Expenses (described below) for the above example are treated similarly and charged as Payroll-Related Expenses in Administrative and General.

Salaries and Wages also includes contract or leased labor. Contract or leased labor refers to those situations in which a property enters into an agreement with an outside service to provide employees to fill positions that would normally be held by individuals paid on the regular payroll. In these situations, the property usually supervises the individuals and records or tracks their hours worked and pays them on an hourly basis. A typical example is the use of individuals brought into the property to fill a clerical function such as filing. This situation differs from a contract service in which a property has an agreement with an outside company to provide some type of service, such scanning documents in connection with digitizing records. In this case, the contracted organization typically provides the supervision and ensures that the work is performed. The costs associated with this type of agreement are charged under Contract Services for the department receiving the service.

Bonuses and Incentives includes bonuses, incentive pay, and other types of performance pay designed to drive revenue through sales, profit, or guest satisfaction measures.

Total Salaries, Wages, and Bonuses. Calculated by adding together Salaries and Wages and Bonuses and Incentives.

Payroll-Related Expenses. Payroll-Related Expenses includes amounts paid for an employee for duties that relate to the operation of the property and amounts paid for an employee who works in a department other than his or her regular home department regardless of the duties being performed. Payroll-Related Expenses includes the following items:

- *Payroll Taxes.* Includes Federal Retirement and Medicare (FICA), Federal and State Unemployment Taxes (FUTA and SUTA), State Disability Insurance (SDI), and other mandated payroll-related taxes or social insurance items. (See *Payroll-Related Expenses—Schedule 13.*)

- *Supplemental Pay.* Includes personal days, vacation pay, sick pay, holiday pay, jury duty pay, relocation pay, paid time off, and severance pay. Supplemental Pay also includes bonuses and incentive payments that are discretionary and not determined by results from operations.

- *Employee Benefits.* Includes all other payroll-related expenses, such as employer-paid health insurance expenses, cost of meals furnished to employees, pension contributions, and union fees. (See *Payroll-Related Expenses—Schedule 13.*) The distribution of employee meal costs from *Employee Cafeteria—Schedule 12* is charged to this line.

Total Payroll-Related Expenses. Calculated by adding together Payroll Taxes, Supplemental Pay, and Employee Benefits.

Total Payroll and Related Expenses

Total Payroll and Related Expenses is calculated by adding together Total Salaries, Wages, and Bonuses and Total Payroll-Related Expenses. The percentage for each line item as well as Total Payroll and Related Expenses is calculated by dividing the line item amount by Total Revenue for the entire property.

Other Expenses

This expense grouping includes the significant Property Operation and Maintenance expenses approved as Other Expenses in the *Uniform System.* Individual properties may delete irrelevant line items, but the *Uniform System* does not provide for the addition or substitution of other expense line items. Rather, properties may choose to develop a sub-account/sub-schedule to provide more detail related to a particular expense item. This sub-account/sub-schedule is then to be rolled into the appropriate line item listed below.

Building. Includes any cost of material and contracts related to repairing and maintaining the building, both interior and exterior. The cost of locksets, as well as the cost associated with sign maintenance, is charged to this account.

Complimentary Services and Gifts. Includes the cost of providing gift items used in gratis presentations for promotional purposes to guests and vendors associated with Property Operation and Maintenance.

Contract Services. Includes expenses for activities not otherwise identified in this department that are performed for Property Operations and Maintenance by outside companies. The cost of contracting outside companies for pest control is a typical example. If supplies are purchased for contract companies to use, the supplies are charged to the appropriate supply account.

Corporate Office Reimbursables. Includes the allocations of salaries and expenses of corporate or management company property operation and maintenance personnel billed to the property by the regional or corporate office or by the management company. Travel expenses of such corporate or management company personnel that are incurred while visiting the property, including the costs of meals and other applicable services or amenities provided to corporate or management company staff while on business in the property for the benefit of the property, are also charged to this account.

Decorations. Includes the cost of decorative items used in Property Operations and Maintenance areas for holidays and special events. The cost of exterior holiday decorations is also charged to this account.

Dues and Subscriptions. Includes the cost of membership of Property Operation and Maintenance staff, when authorized to represent the property, in business or professional organizations. Dues and Subscriptions is also charged with the cost of subscriptions to newspapers, magazines, and books for use by the Property Operation and Maintenance staff.

Electrical and Mechanical Equipment. Includes the cost of materials and contracts related to repairing and maintaining general equipment not specifically identified elsewhere. Maintenance contracts for telecommunications and information systems are charged to Administrative and General.

Elevators and Escalators. Includes the cost of materials and contracts related to repairing and maintaining elevators and escalators.

Engineering Supplies. Includes the cost related to any maintenance and chemical supplies and small tools used in Property Operation and Maintenance.

Equipment Rental. Includes the cost of renting any type of equipment that may be used either sporadically in Property Operation and Maintenance or as a replacement for equipment out of service on a temporary basis. Equipment that is rented on a continuous basis and, if purchased, would qualify as a capital purchase is charged to Other Property and Equipment under the Rent section of *Rent, Property and Other Taxes, and Insurance—Schedule 10.*

Floor Covering. Includes the cost of materials and contracts related to repairing floor covering for guestrooms, corridors, dining rooms, and public rooms.

Furniture and Equipment. Includes the cost of repairing and replacing furniture and equipment not specifically addressed elsewhere. For example, the cost of contracts, materials and supplies such as textiles, fibers, lumber, metal parts, and glass related to the repair of furniture, including beds, tables, dressers, chairs, curtains and draperies, and other articles of similar nature is charged to this account, as is the cost of repairing guestroom televisions.

Grounds Maintenance and Landscaping. Includes the cost of supplies and contracts related to the maintenance of grounds, such as parking lot resealing and stripping and snow removal. For properties located in an area where snow removal tends to be a significant operating expense, a sub-account may be established for snow removal, with the total cost of that account rolled into Grounds Maintenance and Landscaping.

Heating, Ventilation, and Air Conditioning Equipment. Includes the cost of materials and contracts related to repairing and maintaining all heating, ventilation, and air conditioning equipment.

Kitchen Equipment. Includes the cost of materials and contracts related to repairing and maintaining kitchen equipment.

Laundry and Dry Cleaning. Includes the cost of laundry and dry cleaning services applicable to Property Operation and Maintenance, whether the services are performed by an in-house facility or are contracted to an outside company. If the services are performed by an in-house laundry, an allocation from House Laundry is charged to Laundry and Dry Cleaning. If the services are performed by an outside company, the amount charged to Laundry and Dry Cleaning should be based on invoices sent by the outside laundry. The cost of cleaning employee uniforms is charged to the Uniform Laundry account.

Laundry Equipment. Includes the cost of materials and contracts related to repairing and maintaining laundry equipment.

Licenses and Permits. Includes the cost of federal, state, and local licenses, including costs of inspections needed for licensing, for activities associated with Property Operation and Maintenance.

Life/Safety. Includes the cost of regulatory inspection fees, certification tests, and materials and contracts to maintain fire control panels, tamper and flow switches, smoke detectors, and pull stations. The cost of inspections, repair, and maintenance of equipment and facilities required under the Americans with Disabilities Act is also charged to this account.

Light Bulbs. Includes the cost of replacement light bulbs.

Miscellaneous. Includes any expenses of Property Operation and Maintenance that do not apply to the other line items discussed in this section.

Operating Supplies. Includes the cost of operating and general office supplies needed to operate Property Operations and Maintenance that are not included in the descriptions of specific accounts.

Painting and Decorating. Includes the cost of materials, supplies, and contracts related to painting and wallpapering throughout the property.

Plumbing. Includes the cost of repairing and maintaining plumbing equipment and facilities throughout the property, including kitchen and bathroom fixtures, supply lines, and drains.

Printing and Stationery. Includes the cost of printed forms used in the Property Operation and Maintenance department, whether they are purchased from an outside source or produced internally.

Swimming Pool. Includes the cost of materials, supplies, and contracts relating to the maintenance and repair of swimming pools when a separate Other Operated Department does not exist.

Telecommunications. Includes any telecommunications expenditures that can be directly related to Property Operations and Maintenance, including the costs of local, long distance, and Internet communications. Telecommunications includes not only traditional telephone systems, but also the cost of cellular phones, including the equipment and periodic service charges, used in the Property Operations and Maintenance Department.

Training. Includes the cost, other than time, that can be directly attributed to the training of employees in Property Operation and Maintenance. Examples include the costs of training materials, supplies, and instructor fees. The cost of employee wages incurred during training is charged to Salaries and Wages.

Travel—Meals and Entertainment. Includes the reimbursable cost of food and beverage expenses for travel and entertainment by employees of Property Operation and Maintenance traveling on property business.

Travel—Other. Includes the cost of travel and reimbursable expenses, other than food, beverage, and entertainment, by employees of Property Operation and Maintenance traveling on property business.

Uniform Laundry. Includes the cost of cleaning uniforms for employees of the Property Operation and Maintenance whether performed by an in-hotel facility or contracted to an outside company.

Uniforms. Includes the cost of employee uniforms used in Property Operations and Maintenance, whether purchased or rented. Repair costs are also included in this line item. The cost of cleaning uniforms is charged to the Uniform Laundry account.

Waste Removal. Includes the costs of removing trash, rubbish, and any other types of garbage. Any costs associated with recycling of glass or other items as well as the rental charges for a trash container or compactor are also included in this line item.

Total Other Expenses

Total Other Expenses is calculated by adding all items listed under Other Expenses. The percentage for each line item expense as well as Total Other Expenses is calculated by dividing the line item amount by Total Revenue for the entire property.

Total Expenses

Total Expenses is calculated by adding Total Payroll and Related Expenses to Total Other Expenses. The percentage for Total Expenses is calculated by dividing Total Expenses by Total Revenue for the entire property.

Total Expenses is the same amount that appears on the Summary Operating Statement under Undistributed Operating Expenses—Property Operation and Maintenance.

UTILITIES—SCHEDULE 8

	CURRENT MONTH			YEAR-TO-DATE		
	ACTUAL	FORECAST	PRIOR YEAR	ACTUAL	FORECAST	PRIOR YEAR
	$ | %	$ | %	$ | %	$ | %	$ | %	$ | %
UTILITIES						
Electricity						
Gas						
Oil						
Steam						
Water						
Sewer						
Other Fuels						
Utility Taxes						
TOTAL UTILITIES						

Utilities—Schedule 8 illustrates the proper format for reporting Utilities. Individual properties may delete irrelevant line items, but the *Uniform System* does not provide for the addition or substitution of expense line items. Rather, properties may choose to develop a sub-account/sub-schedule to provide more detail related to a particular expense item. This sub-account/sub-schedule is then to be rolled into the appropriate line item. Additionally, properties may choose to delete some of the columns or to show them in a different order and remain "in conformity with the *Uniform System."*

Expenses

Electricity

The cost of electricity purchased from outside producers is charged to this account. If reimbursements for the cost of electricity are received from separate entities, such as managed condominiums, time-share units, or tenants of the property, they are credited to this account.

Gas

The cost of gas purchased from outside producers is charged to this account. If reimbursements for the cost of gas are received from separate entities, such as managed condominiums, time-share units, or tenants of the property, they are credited to this account.

Oil

The cost of oil purchased from outside producers is charged to this account. If reimbursements for the cost of oil are received from separate entities, such as managed condominiums, time-share units, or tenants of the property, they are credited to this account.

Steam

The cost of steam purchased from outside producers is charged to this account. If reimbursements for the cost of steam are received from separate entities, such as managed condominiums, time-share units, or tenants of the property, they are credited to this account.

Water

The cost of water, including the water specially treated for a circulating ice water system, is charged to this account. If reimbursements for the cost of water are received from separate entities, such as managed condominiums, time-share units, or tenants of the property, they are credited to this account.

If a property has a cogeneration or desalinization plant, a sub-schedule may be developed to provide more detail, but the sub-schedule total must roll up into this line item.

Sewer

The cost of sewer is charged to this account. If reimbursements for the cost of sewer are received from separate entities, such as managed condominiums, time-share units, or tenants of the property, they are credited to this account.

Other Fuels

The cost of other fuels (for example, propane, diesel, geothermal) purchased from outside producers, including the cost of breakdown service, is charged to this line item.

Utility Taxes

Taxes assessed by utilities, such as sewer taxes, are charged to this line item. If reimbursements for taxes assessed by utilities are received from separate entities, such as managed condominiums, time-share units, or tenants of the property, they are credited to this account.

Total Utilities

Total Utilities is calculated by adding all of the items listed under Utilities. The percentage for each line item expense as well as Total Utilities is calculated by dividing the line item amount by Total Revenue for the entire property.

Total Utilities is the same amount that appears on Summary Operating Statement under Undistributed Operating Expenses—Utilities.

MANAGEMENT FEES—SCHEDULE 9

	CURRENT MONTH			YEAR-TO-DATE		
	ACTUAL	FORECAST	PRIOR YEAR	ACTUAL	FORECAST	PRIOR YEAR
	$ | %	$ | %	$ | %	$ | %	$ | %	$ | %
MANAGEMENT FEES						
Base Fee						
Incentive Fees						
TOTAL MANAGEMENT FEES						

Management Fees—Schedule 9 illustrates the proper format for reporting Management Fees. Individual properties may delete irrelevant line items, but the *Uniform System* does not provide for the addition or substitution of expense line items. Rather, properties may choose to develop a sub-account/sub-schedule to provide more detail related to a particular expense item. This sub-account/sub-schedule is then to be rolled into the appropriate line item. Additionally, properties may choose to delete some of the columns or to show them in a different order and remain "in conformity with the *Uniform System.*"

Base Fees

Management fees computed as a fixed amount or a percentage of revenues or profit are charged to this item.

Incentive Fees

Management fees that are contingent upon achieving certain pre-defined levels of profitability are charged to this item.

Total Management Fees

Total Management Fees is the sum of Base Fees and Incentive Fees. The percentage for Total Management Fees is calculated by dividing Total Management Fees by Total Revenue for the entire property.

Total Management Fees is the same amount that appears on Summary Operating Statement under Management Fees.

RENT, PROPERTY AND OTHER TAXES, AND INSURANCE— SCHEDULE 10

	CURRENT MONTH			YEAR-TO-DATE		
	ACTUAL	FORECAST	PRIOR YEAR	ACTUAL	FORECAST	PRIOR YEAR
	$ | %	$ | %	$ | %	$ | %	$ | %	$ | %
RENT						
Land and Buildings						
Information Systems Equipment						
Telecommunications Equipment						
Other Property and Equipment						
Total Rent						
PROPERTY AND OTHER TAXES						
Real Estate Taxes						
Personal Property Taxes						
Business and Transient Occupation Taxes						
Other Taxes						
Total Property and Other Taxes						
INSURANCE						
Building and Contents						
Liability						
Total Insurance						
TOTAL RENT, PROPERTY AND OTHER TAXES, AND INSURANCE						

Rent, Property and Other Taxes, and Insurance—Schedule 10 illustrates the proper format for reporting Rent, Property and Other Taxes, and Insurance. Individual properties may delete irrelevant line items, but the *Uniform System* does not provide for the addition or substitution of other expense line items. Rather, properties may choose to develop a sub-account/sub-schedule to provide more detail related to a particular expense item. This sub-account/sub-schedule is then to be rolled into the appropriate line item. Additionally, properties may choose to delete some of the columns or to show them in a different order and remain "in conformity with the *Uniform System*."

Rent

The costs associated with the leasing and rental of property and equipment are charged to the Rent line item. Rent expense includes operating leases, ground lease rent, and rentals of property and equipment, other than those rented for a specific function or event, such as a specific banquet or New Year's Eve party. The rental of property or equipment for a specific event is generally short-term and the costs charged to the appropriate department. For example, tables and chairs rented for an outdoor wedding reception for a food and beverage client are charged to the appropriate line item/account in Food and Beverage. The costs associated with the following are examples of operating leases and rentals that are included in the Rent line item: land and building leases, information systems and telecommunications or audiovisual equipment, vehicle leases, copiers, and leased or rented items other than those related to a specific function.

Land and Buildings

If the property is leased under an operating lease, this line item is charged with the amount of the rental of the property. Rent is separated into base and participating rents.

Information Systems Equipment

Rental of information systems and related hardware is charged to this line item.

Telecommunications Equipment

This line item is charged with the rental of telecommunications equipment.

Other Property and Equipment

Other rentals include any other major items (for example, vehicles) which, had they not been rented, would be purchased and capitalized as property and equipment. Rental of miscellaneous equipment (copiers, projectors, and sound equipment) for a specific function, such as a banquet or similar function or merely to meet peak demand for a short-term period, is charged to the appropriate department and is not considered a rental expense chargeable to this line item.

Total Rent

Total Rent is calculated by adding all items listed under Rent. The percentage for each line item expense as well as Total Rent is calculated by dividing the dollar amount of that line item by Total Revenue for the entire property.

Total Rent is the same amount that appears on Summary Operating Statement under Fixed Charges—Rent.

Property and Other Taxes

Real Estate Taxes

This account is charged with all taxes assessed against the real property of the property by a state or political subdivision of the state, such as a county or city. Business Improvement District (BID) assessments are also included in this category. Assessments for public improvements are not to be included in this line item as they are generally capitalized as property and equipment. This account also includes any professional fees incurred by the property in appealing a tax assessment. Refunds received from an overpayment of taxes are recorded to this account as a contra item.

Personal Property Taxes

Taxes on furnishings, fixtures, and equipment are charged to this line item.

Business and Transient Occupation Taxes

Taxes such as gross receipts tax on sale of rooms, food, and beverage that cannot be passed along to customers are charged to this line item.

Other Taxes

Any taxes other than income and payroll taxes are charged to this line item and separately identified if material in a sub-schedule.

Total Property and Other Taxes

Total Property and Other Taxes is calculated by adding all items listed under Property and Other Taxes. The percentage for each line item expense as well as Total Property and Other Taxes is calculated by dividing the dollar amount of that line item by Total Revenue for the entire property.

Total Property and Other Taxes is the same amount that appears on Summary Operating Statement under Fixed Charges—Property and Other Taxes.

Insurance

Building and Contents

The cost of insuring the property's building and contents against damage or destruction by fire, weather, sprinkler leakage, boiler explosion, plate glass breakage, or any other cause is charged to this account. This account also includes amounts expended as a result of deductible provisions of insurance policies as well as costs incurred for underinsurance, such as costs incurred as a result of coinsurance and legal settlement costs.

Liability

General insurance costs, including premiums relating to liability, including Directors and Officers coverage and miscellaneous professional liability coverage, fidelity, and theft coverage, are charged to this account. Payroll-related insurance (workers' compensation) is included in Employee Benefits in the appropriate departmental schedule to which the associated payroll is charged. This account also includes amounts expended as a result of deductible provisions of insurance policies. Premium adjustments resulting from the audit of underwriting assumptions submitted to insurance carriers are reported here as are legal settlement costs.

Total Insurance

Total Insurance is calculated by adding all items listed under Insurance. The percentage for each line item expense as well as Total Insurance is calculated by dividing the dollar amount of that line item by Total Revenue for the entire property.

Total Insurance is the same amount that appears on Summary Operating Statement under Fixed Charges—Insurance.

Total Rent, Property and Other Taxes, and Insurance

Total Rent, Property and Other Taxes, and Insurance is calculated by adding Total Rent, Total Property and Other Taxes, and Total Insurance. The percentage for Total

Rent, Property and Other Taxes, and Insurance is calculated by dividing Total Rent, Property and Other Taxes, and Insurance by Total Revenue for the entire property.

Total Rent, Property and Other Taxes, and Insurance is the same amount that appears on Summary Operating Statement under Total Fixed Charges.

HOUSE LAUNDRY—SCHEDULE 11

	CURRENT MONTH			YEAR-TO-DATE		
	ACTUAL	FORECAST	PRIOR YEAR	ACTUAL	FORECAST	PRIOR YEAR
	$ %	$ %	$ %	$ %	$ %	$ %
EXPENSES						
Payroll and Related Expenses						
Salaries, Wages, and Bonuses						
Salaries and Wages						
Bonuses and Incentives						
Total Salaries, Wages, and Bonuses						
Payroll Related Expenses						
Payroll Taxes						
Supplemental Pay						
Employee Benefits						
Total Payroll Related Expenses						
Total Payroll and Related Expenses						
Other Expenses						
Cleaning Supplies						
Complimentary Services and Gifts						
Contract Services						
Corporate Office Reimbursables						
Decorations						
Dues and Subscriptions						
Equipment Rental						
Laundry and Dry Cleaning						
Laundry Supplies						
Licenses and Permits						
Miscellaneous						
Operating Supplies						
Printing and Stationery						
Telecommunications						
Training						
Travel—Meals and Entertainment						
Travel—Other						
Uniform Laundry						
Uniforms						
Total Other Expenses						
TOTAL EXPENSES						
CREDITS						
Cost of Guest and Outside Laundry						
Concessionaires' Laundry						
COST OF HOUSE LAUNDRY						

House Laundry—Schedule 11 illustrates the proper format for reporting the Payroll and Related Expenses and Other Expenses for the House Laundry. Individual properties may delete irrelevant line items, but the *Uniform System* does not provide for the addition or substitution of other expense line items. Rather, properties may choose to develop a sub-account/sub-schedule to provide more detail related to a particular revenue or expense item. This sub-account/sub-schedule is then to be rolled into the appropriate line item. Additionally, properties may choose to delete some of the columns or to show them in a different order and remain "in conformity with the *Uniform System.*"

This schedule is allocated to various departments on an equitable basis.

Expenses

House Laundry expenses are separated into two major categories: Payroll and Related Expenses and Other Expenses.

Payroll and Related Expenses

Payroll and Related Expenses for the House Laundry comprises the expenses associated with Salaries, Wages, and Bonuses and Payroll-Related Expenses for employees of the House Laundry. A list of the positions typically included in House Laundry is shown on pages 177–178.

Salaries, Wages, and Bonuses. This grouping includes (1) Salaries and Wages and (2) Bonuses and Incentives. Salaries and Wages includes only earnings paid to an employee for duties that relate to the operation of the property, such as regular pay, overtime pay, and shift differential pay. If an employee works in a department other than his or her regular home department, his or her earnings are charged as Salaries and Wages in that other department, regardless of the duties being performed. For example, if a House Laundry employee works as a server for an employee awards banquet, his or her earnings are charged to Salaries and Wages in Administrative and General, and not to this line item. Payroll-Related Expenses (described below) for the above example are treated similarly and charged as Payroll-Related Expenses in Administrative and General.

Salaries and Wages also includes contract or leased labor. Contract or leased labor refers to those situations in which a property enters into an agreement with an outside service to provide employees to fill positions that would normally be held by individuals paid on the regular payroll. In these situations, the property usually supervises the individuals and records or tracks their hours worked and pays them on an hourly basis. A typical example is the use of individuals brought into the property to fill in for a shortage of laundry staff. This situation differs from a contract service in which a property has an agreement with an outside company to provide some type of service, such as cleaning the laundry area during the early morning hours In this case, the contracted organization typically provides the supervision and ensures that the work is performed. The costs associated with this type of agreement are charged under Contract Services for the department receiving the service.

Bonuses and Incentives includes bonuses, incentive pay, and other types of performance pay designed to drive revenue through sales, profit, or guest satisfaction measures.

Total Salaries, Wages, and Bonuses. Calculated by adding together Salaries and Wages and Bonuses and Incentives.

Payroll-Related Expenses. Payroll-Related Expenses includes amounts paid for an employee for duties that relate to the operation of the property and amounts paid for an employee who works in a department other than his or her regular home department regardless of the duties being performed. Payroll-Related Expenses includes the following items:

- *Payroll Taxes.* Includes Federal Retirement and Medicare (FICA), Federal and State Unemployment Taxes (FUTA and SUTA), State Disability Insurance (SDI), and other mandated payroll-related taxes or social insurance items. (See *Payroll-Related Expenses—Schedule 13.*)

- *Supplemental Pay.* Includes personal days, vacation pay, sick pay, holiday pay, jury duty pay, relocation pay, paid time off, and severance pay. Supplemental Pay also includes bonuses and incentive payments that are discretionary and not determined by results from operations.

- *Employee Benefits.* Includes all other payroll-related expenses, such as employer-paid health insurance expenses, cost of meals furnished to employees, pension contributions, and union fees. (See *Payroll-Related Expenses—Schedule 13.*) The distribution of employee meal costs from *Employee Cafeteria—Schedule 12* is charged to this line.

Total Payroll-Related Expenses. Calculated by adding together Payroll Taxes, Supplemental Pay, and Employee Benefits.

Total Payroll and Related Expenses

Total Payroll and Related Expenses is calculated by adding together Total Salaries, Wages, and Bonuses and Total Payroll-Related Expenses. The percentage for each line item as well as Total Payroll and Related Expenses is calculated by dividing the line item amount by Total Revenue for the entire property.

Other Expenses

This expense grouping includes the significant House Laundry expenses approved as Other Expenses in the *Uniform System.* Individual properties may delete irrelevant line items, but the *Uniform System* does not provide for the addition or substitution of other expense line items. Rather, properties may choose to develop a sub-account/sub-schedule to provide more detail related to a particular expense item. This sub-account/sub-schedule is then to be rolled into the appropriate line item listed below.

Cleaning Supplies. Includes the cost of products used in cleansing, sweeping, polishing, waxing, and disinfecting areas associated with the House Laundry. The cost of materials or supplies used for laundering purposes is charged to Laundry Supplies.

Complimentary Services and Gifts. Includes the cost of providing gift items used in gratis presentations for promotional purposes to guests and vendors of the House Laundry.

Contract Services. Includes expenses for activities performed for the House Laundry by outside companies rather than hotel employees. The cost of contracting outside companies to clean areas associated with the House Laundry is an example. If supplies are purchased for contract companies to use, the supplies are charged to the appropriate supply account. The cost of contracts for the House Laundry laundry and dry cleaning is charged to Laundry and Dry Cleaning.

Corporate Office Reimbursables. Includes the allocations of salaries and expenses of corporate or management company house laundry personnel billed to the property by the regional or corporate office or by the management company. Travel expenses of such corporate or management company personnel that are incurred while visiting the property, including the costs of meals and other applicable services or amenities provided to corporate or management company staff while on business in the property for the benefit of the property, are also charged to this account.

Decorations. Includes the cost of decorative items used in House Laundry areas for holidays and special events.

Dues and Subscriptions. Includes the cost of membership of House Laundry staff, when authorized to represent the property, in business or professional organizations. Dues and Subscriptions is also charged with the cost of subscriptions to newspapers, magazines, and books for use by the House Laundry staff.

Equipment Rental. Includes the cost of renting any type of equipment that may be used either sporadically in the House Laundry or as a replacement for equipment out of service on a temporary basis. Equipment that is rented on a continuous basis and, if purchased, would qualify as a capital purchase is charged to Other Property and Equipment under the Rent section of *Rent, Property and Other Taxes, and Insurance—Schedule 10.*

Laundry and Dry Cleaning. Includes the cost of laundry and dry cleaning services applicable to the House Laundry that are contracted to an outside company. When services are performed by an outside company, the amount charged to Laundry and Dry Cleaning is based on invoices sent by the outside laundry. The cost of cleaning employee uniforms is charged to the Uniform Laundry account.

Laundry Supplies. Includes the cost of supplies used for laundering and dry cleaning purposes.

Licenses and Permits. Includes the cost of federal, state, and local licenses, including costs of inspections needed for licensing, for all activities of the House Laundry.

Miscellaneous. Includes any expenses of the House Laundry that do not apply to the other line items discussed in this section.

Operating Supplies. Includes the cost of operating and general office supplies needed to operate the House Laundry that are not included in the descriptions of specific supply accounts such as Cleaning Supplies, Laundry Supplies, or Printing and Stationery.

Printing and Stationery. Includes the cost of printed forms used in the House Laundry, whether they are purchased from an outside source or produced internally.

Telecommunications. Includes any telecommunications expenditures that can be directly related to the House Laundry, including the costs of local, long distance, and Internet communications. Telecommunications includes not only traditional telephone systems, but also the cost of cellular phones, including the equipment and periodic service charges, used in the House Laundry.

Training. Includes the cost, other than time, that can be directly attributed to the training of employees in the House Laundry. Examples include the costs of training materials, supplies, and instructor fees. The cost of employee wages incurred during training is charged to Salaries and Wages.

Travel—Meals and Entertainment. Includes the reimbursable cost of food and beverage expenses for travel and entertainment by employees of the House Laundry traveling on property business.

Travel—Other. Includes the cost of travel and reimbursable expenses, other than food, beverage, and entertainment, by employees of the House Laundry traveling on property business.

Uniform Laundry. Includes the cost of cleaning uniforms for employees of the House Laundry whether performed by an in-hotel facility or contracted to an outside company.

Uniforms. Includes the cost of employee uniforms used in the House Laundry, whether purchased or rented. Repair costs are also included in this line item. The cost of cleaning uniforms is charged to the Uniform Laundry account.

Total Other Expenses

Total Other Expenses is calculated by adding all items listed under Other Expenses. The percentage for each line item expense as well as Total Other Expenses is calculated by dividing the line item amount by Total Revenue for the entire property.

Total Expenses

Total Expenses is calculated by adding Total Payroll and Related Expenses to Total Other Expenses. The percentage for Total Expenses is calculated by dividing Total Expenses by Total Revenue for the entire property.

Credits

Cost of Guest and Outside Laundry

Where no separate guest laundry is maintained, this line item is credited on an equitable basis to reflect the cost of processing guest laundry.

Concessionaires' Laundry

Where laundering is done for concessionaires such as barber/beauty shops, the revenue received is usually deducted from the departmental expenses.

Cost of House Laundry

Cost of House Laundry is distributed to the departments using the House Laundry (Rooms, Food, Beverage, Health Club, etc.) on an equitable basis reflecting usage, such as cost-per-pound, number of pieces cleaned, etc.

EMPLOYEE CAFETERIA—SCHEDULE 12

	CURRENT MONTH			YEAR-TO-DATE		
	ACTUAL	FORECAST	PRIOR YEAR	ACTUAL	FORECAST	PRIOR YEAR
	$ | %	$ | %	$ | %	$ | %	$ | %	$ | %
NET REVENUE						
COST OF FOOD						
GROSS PROFIT (LOSS)						
EXPENSES						
Payroll and Related Expenses						
Salaries, Wages, and Bonuses						
Salaries and Wages						
Bonuses and Incentives						
Total Salaries, Wages, and Bonuses						
Payroll-Related Expenses						
Payroll Taxes						
Supplemental Pay						
Employee Benefits						
Total Payroll-Related Expenses						
Total Payroll and Related Expenses						
Other Expenses						
China						
Cleaning Supplies						
Contract Services						
Corporate Office Reimbursables						
Decorations						
Dishwashing Supplies						
Dues and Subscriptions						
Equipment Rental						
Flatware						
Glassware						
Ice						
Kitchen Fuel						
Laundry and Dry Cleaning						
Licenses and Permits						
Linen						
Miscellaneous						
Operating Supplies						
Paper and Plastics						
Printing and Stationery						
Telecommunications						
Training						
Travel—Meals and Entertainment						
Travel—Other						
Uniform Laundry						
Uniforms						
Utensils						
Total Other Expenses						
TOTAL EXPENSES						
DEPARTMENTAL INCOME (LOSS)						

Employee Cafeteria—Schedule 12 illustrates the proper format for reporting the Payroll and Related Expenses and Other Expenses for the Employee Cafeteria. Individual properties may delete irrelevant line items, but the *Uniform System* does not provide for the addition or substitution of other revenue or expense line items. Rather, properties may choose to develop a sub-account/sub-schedule to provide more detail related to a particular revenue or expense item. This sub-account/sub-schedule is then to be rolled into the appropriate line item. Additionally, properties may choose to delete some of the columns or to show them in a different order and remain "in conformity with the *Uniform System.*"

This schedule is allocated to various departments on an equitable basis.

Net Revenue

Net Revenue includes revenue derived from food sales, including sales of coffee, tea, milk, and soft drinks. In completing Schedule 12, the Net Revenue line is considered to be 100 percent.

Cost of Food

Cost of Food includes the cost of food items furnished for employee meals. Properties usually requisition the food items from either the storeroom or kitchen on a daily basis. Cost of Food is simply the cost of the products requisitioned each day, as evidenced on the respective vendor invoices. The percentage for Cost of Food is calculated by dividing Cost of Food by Net Revenue.

Gross Profit (Loss)

Gross Profit (Loss) is calculated by subtracting Cost of Food from Net Revenue. The percentage for Gross Profit (Loss) is calculated by dividing Gross Profit (Loss) by Net Revenue.

Expenses

Employee Cafeteria expenses are separated into two major categories: Payroll and Related Expenses and Other Expenses.

Payroll and Related Expenses

Payroll and Related Expenses for the Employee Cafeteria comprises the expenses associated with Salaries, Wages, and Bonuses and Payroll-Related Expenses for employees of the Employee Cafeteria. A list of the positions typically included in the Employee Cafeteria is shown on page 178.

Salaries, Wages, and Bonuses. This grouping includes (1) Salaries and Wages and (2) Bonuses and Incentives. Salaries and Wages includes only earnings paid to an employee for duties that relate to the operation of the property, such as regular pay, overtime pay, and shift differential pay. If an employee works in a department other than his or her regular home department, his or her earnings are charged as Salaries and Wages in that other department, regardless of the duties being performed. For example, if an Employee Cafeteria employee works as a server for an employee awards banquet, his or her earnings are charged to Salaries and Wages in Administrative and General, and not to this line item. Payroll-Related Expenses (described below) for the above example are treated similarly and charged as Payroll-Related Expenses in Administrative and General.

Salaries and Wages also includes contract or leased labor. Contract or leased labor refers to those situations in which a property enters into an agreement with an outside service to provide employees to fill positions that would normally be held by individuals paid on the regular payroll. In these situations, the property usually supervises the individuals and records or tracks their hours worked and pays them on an hourly basis. A typical example is the use of individuals brought into the property to fill in for a shortage of cafeteria staff. This situation differs from a contract service in which a property has an agreement with an outside company to provide some type of service, such as cleaning the cafeteria during the early morning hours. In this case, the contracted organization typically provides the supervision and ensures that the work is performed. The costs associated with this type of agreement are charged under Contract Services for the department receiving the service.

Bonuses and Incentives includes bonuses, incentive pay, and other types of performance pay designed to drive revenue through sales, profit, or guest satisfaction measures.

Total Salaries, Wages, and Bonuses. Calculated by adding together Salaries and Wages and Bonuses and Incentives.

Payroll-Related Expenses. Payroll-Related Expenses includes amounts paid for an employee for duties that relate to the operation of the property and amounts paid for an employee who works in a department other than his or her regular home department regardless of the duties being performed. Payroll-Related Expenses includes the following items:

- *Payroll Taxes.* Includes Federal Retirement and Medicare (FICA), Federal and State Unemployment Taxes (FUTA and SUTA), State Disability Insurance (SDI), and other mandated payroll-related taxes or social insurance items. (See *Payroll-Related Expenses—Schedule 13.*)

- *Supplemental Pay.* Includes personal days, vacation pay, sick pay, holiday pay, jury duty pay, relocation pay, paid time off, and severance pay. Supplemental Pay also includes bonuses and incentive payments that are discretionary and not determined by results from operations.

- *Employee Benefits.* Includes all other payroll-related expenses, such as employer-paid health insurance expenses, cost of meals furnished to employees, pension contributions, and union fees. (See *Payroll-Related Expenses—Schedule 13.*)

Total Payroll-Related Expenses. Calculated by adding together Payroll Taxes, Supplemental Pay, and Employee Benefits.

Total Payroll and Related Expenses

Total Payroll and Related Expenses is calculated by adding together Total Salaries, Wages, and Bonuses and Total Payroll-Related Expenses. The percentage for each line item as well as Total Payroll and Related Expenses is calculated by dividing the line item amount by Net Revenue.

Other Expenses

This expense grouping includes the significant Employee Cafeteria expenses approved as Other Expenses in the *Uniform System*. Individual properties may delete irrelevant line items, but the *Uniform System* does not provide for the addition or substitution of other expense line items. Rather, properties may choose to develop a sub-account/sub-schedule to provide more detail related to a particular expense item. This sub-account/sub-schedule is then to be rolled into the appropriate line item listed below.

China. Includes the cost of purchased or rented plates, bowls, serving platters, etc., constructed from any material (ceramic, glass, metal, non-disposable plastic, etc.) and used in providing food service to employees in the Employee Cafeteria, with the exception of non-alcoholic beverage items. The cost of containers for consumption of non-alcoholic beverages is charged to Glassware.

Cleaning Supplies. Includes the cost of products used in cleansing, sweeping, polishing, waxing, and disinfecting areas associated with the Employee Cafeteria.

Contract Services. Includes expenses for activities performed for the Employee Cafeteria by outside companies rather than hotel employees. The costs of contracting outside companies to clean carpets and rugs or to disinfect areas associated with the Employee Cafeteria are typical examples. Other examples include the cost of contracting outside companies to wash windows and degrease hoods. If supplies are purchased for contract companies to use, the supplies are charged to the appropriate supply account. The cost of contracts for the Employee Cafeteria laundry and dry cleaning is charged to Laundry and Dry Cleaning.

Corporate Office Reimbursables. Includes the allocations of salaries and expenses of corporate or management company employee food and beverage personnel billed to the property by the regional or corporate office or by the management company. Travel expenses of such corporate or management company personnel that are incurred while visiting the property, including the costs of meals and other applicable services or amenities provided to corporate or management company staff while on business in the property for the benefit of the property, are also charged to this account.

Decorations. Includes the cost of decorative items used in the Employee Cafeteria areas for holidays and special events.

Dishwashing Supplies. Includes the cost of cleaning, rinsing, and soaking agents used specifically in washing china, glassware, flatware, and utensils in the Employee Cafeteria.

Dues and Subscriptions. Includes the cost of representation of Employee Cafeteria staff when authorized to represent the property in business or professional organizations. Dues and Subscriptions is also charged with the cost of subscriptions to newspapers, magazines, and books for use by the staff of the Employee Cafeteria.

Equipment Rental. Includes the costs of renting any type of equipment that may be used either sporadically in the Employee Cafeteria or as a replacement for equipment out of service on a temporary basis. Equipment that is rented on a continuous basis and, if purchased, would qualify as a capital purchase, is charged to Other Property and Equipment under the Rent section of *Rent, Property and Other Taxes, and Insurance—Schedule 10.*

Flatware. Includes the cost of all flatware and serving pieces (serving spoons, cake knives, ladles, etc.), either purchased or rented, used in providing food service in the Employee Cafeteria.

Glassware. Includes the cost of purchased or rented containers constructed from any material (glass, ceramic, metal, non-disposable plastic) used in providing food service in the employee cafeteria.

Ice. Includes the cost of ice used in food service, storage, or preparation in the Employee Cafeteria.

Kitchen Fuel. Includes the cost of fuel used for cooking in the Employee Cafeteria.

Laundry and Dry Cleaning. Includes the cost of laundry and dry cleaning services applicable to the Employee Cafeteria, whether the services are performed by an in-house facility or are contracted to an outside company. If the services are performed by an in-house laundry, an allocation from House Laundry is charged to Laundry and Dry Cleaning. If the services are performed by an outside company, the amount charged to Laundry and Dry Cleaning should be based on invoices sent by the outside laundry. The cost of cleaning employee uniforms is charged to the Uniform Laundry account.

Licenses and Permits. Includes the cost of federal, state, and local licenses, including costs of inspections needed for licensing, for all activities of the Employee Cafeteria.

Linen. Includes the cost, whether purchased or rented, of table cloths, napkins, table runners, and skirting used by the Employee Cafeteria.

Miscellaneous. Includes any expenses of the Employee Cafeteria that do not apply to the other line items discussed in this section.

Operating Supplies. Includes the cost of operating and general office supplies needed to operate the Employee Cafeteria that are not included in the descriptions of specific supply accounts such as Cleaning Supplies and Printing and Stationery.

Paper and Plastics. Includes the cost of paper supplies used by the Employee Cafeteria.

Printing and Stationery. Includes the cost of printed forms used in the Employee Cafeteria, whether they are purchased from an outside source or produced internally. Examples of Printing and Stationary include placards identifying menu items.

Telecommunications. Includes any telecommunications expenditures that can be directly related to the Employee Cafeteria, including the costs of local, long distance, and Internet communications. Telecommunications includes not only traditional telephone systems, but also the cost of cellular phones, including the equipment and periodic service charges, used in the Employee Cafeteria.

Training. Includes the cost, other than time, that can be directly attributed to the training of employees in the Employee Cafeteria. Examples include the costs of training materials, supplies, and instructor fees. The cost of employee wages incurred during training is charged to Salaries and Wages.

Travel—Meals and Entertainment. Includes the reimbursable cost of food and beverage expenses for travel and entertainment by employees of the Employee Cafeteria traveling on property business.

Travel—Other. Includes the cost of travel and reimbursable expenses, other than food, beverage, and entertainment, by employees of the Employee Cafeteria traveling on property business.

Uniform Laundry. Includes the cost of cleaning uniforms for employees of the Employee Cafeteria whether performed by an in-hotel facility or contracted to an outside company.

Uniforms. Includes the cost of employee uniforms used in the Employee Cafeteria, whether purchased or rented. Repair costs are also included in this line item. The cost of cleaning uniforms is charged to the Uniform Laundry account.

Utensils. Includes the cost of all tools needed in the process of food preparation, such as butcher knives, spatulas, and whisks.

Total Other Expenses

Total Other Expenses is calculated by adding all items listed under Other Expenses. The percentage for each line item expense as well as Total Other Expenses is calculated by dividing the line item amount by Net Revenue.

Total Expenses

Total Expenses is calculated by adding Total Payroll and Related Expenses to Total Other Expenses. The percentage for Total Expenses is calculated by dividing Total Expenses by Net Revenue.

Departmental Income (Loss)

Departmental Income (Loss) is calculated by subtracting Total Expenses from Gross Profit (Loss). The percentage for Departmental Income (Loss) is calculated by dividing Departmental Income (Loss) by Net Revenue.

Department Income (Loss) is distributed to the various departments incurring a payroll expense (Rooms, Food, Beverage, Health Club, Administrative and General, etc.) on an equitable basis reflecting usage, such as number of employees fed, percentage of payroll, etc., and charged to Employee Benefits under Payroll-Related Expenses.

PAYROLL-RELATED EXPENSES—SCHEDULE 13

	CURRENT MONTH			YEAR-TO-DATE		
	ACTUAL	FORECAST	PRIOR YEAR	ACTUAL	FORECAST	PRIOR YEAR
	$ | %	$ | %	$ | %	$ | %	$ | %	$ | %
PAYROLL TAXES						
Federal Retirement (FICA)						
Federal Unemployment (FUTA)						
Medicare Tax (FICA)						
State Disability						
State Unemployment						
Total Payroll Taxes						
EMPLOYEE BENEFITS						
Automobile Allowance						
Child Care						
Contributory Savings Plan [401(k)]						
Dental Insurance						
Disability Pay						
Group Life Insurance						
Health Insurance						
Housing and Educational Allowances						
Meals						
Miscellaneous						
Nonunion Insurance						
Nonunion Pension						
Profit Sharing						
Stock Benefits						
Stock Options						
Union Insurance						
Union Pension						
Workers' Compensation Insurance						
Total Employee Benefits						
TOTAL PAYROLL TAXES AND EMPLOYEE BENEFITS						

Payroll systems in use today typically allow properties to charge payroll taxes and benefits directly to departments as salaries and wages are calculated, thus eliminating the need for allocation. *Payroll-Related Expenses—Schedule 13* illustrates a format for summarizing the total payroll taxes and employee benefits paid by a lodging property. Individual properties may delete irrelevant items, but the *Uniform System* does not permit combining or moving items between the two categories if the financial statements are to be "in conformity with the *Uniform System*."

Payroll Taxes

Federal Retirement (FICA). Includes taxes imposed on employers by Subchapter B, Chapter 21, of the Internal Revenue Code.

Federal Unemployment (FUTA). Includes taxes imposed by Chapter 23 of the Internal Revenue Code.

Medicare Tax (FICA). Includes taxes imposed on employers by Subchapter B, Chapter 2, of the Internal Revenue Code.

State Disability. Includes the contributions by employers to state agencies for disability purposes.

State Unemployment. Includes the contributions by employers to unemployment funds required by state unemployment compensation laws.

Employee Benefits

Automobile Allowance. Includes the cost of providing payment to employees for company-owned vehicles and flat allowances for the use of an auto.

Child Care. Includes the cost of providing discount in-house facilities for employees' children.

Contributory Savings Plan [401(k)]. Includes the cost of the employer's portion for any retirement matching programs offered by employees. This line item also includes any administrative costs associated with these programs.

Dental Insurance. Includes the cost of dental insurance coverage for employees less amounts reimbursed.

Disability Pay. Includes the cost of providing payment to employees for disability pay.

Group Life Insurance. Includes the employer's cost for any group life insurance programs.

Health Insurance. Includes the cost of health insurance coverage for employees less amounts reimbursed.

Housing and Educational Allowances. Includes the cost associated with covering some or all of the expenditures paid by employees for living off-property or sending family members, typically children, to school.

Meals. Includes the cost of providing meals to employees less amounts charged.

Miscellaneous. Includes the cost of providing employees with other benefits not included under other captions (e.g., daytimers or organizers, name tags, seminar, organization dues, etc.).

Nonunion Insurance. Includes the cost of life, health, accident, hospitalization and other insurance for employees not participating in a union fund.

Nonunion Pension. Includes the cost associated with nonunion pension plans.

Profit Sharing. Includes the cost of the employer's contribution to profit sharing plans.

Stock Benefits. Includes the cost (value) of company stock issued to employees as compensation.

Stock Options. Includes the cost related to the value of stock options issued to employees.

Union Insurance. Includes the cost associated with union employees' benefit funds for insurance on life, health, accident, hospitalization, and other purposes.

Union Pension. Includes the cost associated with union employees' pension benefit funds.

Workers' Compensation Insurance. Includes the cost for employee state compensation plans.

Departmental Payroll Titles

This section lists the typical job titles found in each of the departments of a lodging property. Individual properties may choose to use the same names or different names for the positions, but the *Uniform System* does not allow properties to combine departments other than what has been described earlier in this guide and remain "in conformity with the *Uniform System*."

"Manager" as used in any of these classifications is a proxy for manager, assistant manager, supervisor or other similar managerial/supervisory job classification. Management trainee and administrative assistant payroll is recorded in the department(s) where hours are worked.

Rooms

Management

Rooms director, director of revenue management, revenue manager, night manager

Front Office/Guest Service

Front desk: Front office manager, desk clerk

Bell service: Bell captain, bell/luggage attendant, door attendant, dispatcher

Guest services: Director of guest services, guest services manager, concierge, guest services representative, activities attendant, guest services coordinator

Housekeeping

Executive housekeeper, director of housekeeping, housekeeping manager, floor supervisor, room attendant, house attendant, public area attendant, turndown attendant, night attendant, housekeeping/linen runner, linen control supervisor, linen room attendant, sewing attendant, uniform room attendant

Reservations

Director of reservations, reservations manager, reservations agent

Transportation

Transportation manager, driver

Club Floor

Club floor manager, club floor attendant

Food

Management

Director of food and beverage, assistant food and beverage director/manager, food and beverage cost controller

F&B Purchasing/Storeroom

Food and beverage purchasing manager, food storeroom manager, food storeroom attendant

Food Preparation

Executive chef, executive sous chef, pastry chef, food production manager, chef de cuisine, chef garde manger, chef tournant, butcher, baker supervisor, baker, saucier, pantry supervisor, pantry attendant, cook

Stewarding

Stewarding manager, steward, potwasher, silver room supervisor, silver room attendant, kitchen cleaner

Restaurants

Director of outlets, director of restaurants, restaurant manager, restaurant server, sommelier, maître d', greeter, bus attendant, server, buffet attendant, food runner, restaurant cashier

Banquets/Catering

Banquet manager, banquet captain, banquet bus attendant, banquet server, banquet cashier, banquet houseperson, audiovisual manager

Director of catering, director of convention services, convention services manager, event manager

In-Room Dining

In-room dining manager, in-room dining captain, in-room dining server, in-room dining order taker, in-room dining cashier, bus attendant

Beverage

Management

Beverage manager

Beverage Service

Bartender, service bartender, banquet bartender, barback, beverage server, bar attendant

Beverage Storeroom

Beverage storeroom manager, beverage storeroom attendant

Telecommunications

Telecommunications manager, telecommunications attendant

Golf Course/Pro Shop

Maintenance

Director of golf course maintenance, golf course maintenance manager, greens supervisor, greens keeper, gardener, general maintenance, driver, mechanic

Operations

Director of golf, golf instructor, golf manager, golf marshal, golf course attendant, caddy, golf cashier, golf cart maintenance, golf ranger, golf pro, golf pro assistant, instructor, locker room attendant, club storage attendant, repair attendant, golf car storage attendant, ranger, starter

Golf Pro Shop

Golf pro shop manager, retail manager, golf pro, golf pro shop cashier, golf pro shop attendant, sales clerk

Health Club/Spa

Spa

Spa manager, spa director, spa sales manager, spa reception agent, fitness consultant, attendant, steam room/sauna attendant, hair stylist, manicurist, massage therapist, masseur/masseuse, salon supervisor, salon associate

Health Club

Health club sales manager, health club pool manager, health club director of retail, director of health club, health club manager, health club retail manager, health club attendant, health club cashier, health club pool attendant, health club pool supervisor, health club retail agent, health club technician, health club front desk agent, health club reservations agent

Swimming Pool

Pool manager, pool attendant, lifeguard

Garage and Parking

Garage manager, valet/parking attendant, garage cashier

Administrative and General

Manager's Office

Managing director, general manager, resident manager, hotel manager, quality assurance manager

Accounting

Controller, assistant controller, accounting manager, credit manager, chief accountant, accounts receivable manager, financial analyst, general cashier, paymaster, staff accountant, revenue audit manager, accounts payable manager, group billing clerk, accounting clerk

Cost Control

Cost controller, profit improvement manager

Storeroom and Receiving

General storeroom attendant, receiving clerk, package room manager, package room attendant

Purchasing

Director of purchasing, buyer, clerk, receiving agent, storekeeper, purchasing agent, purchasing coordinator

Information Systems

Director of information systems, MIS manager, systems manager, systems analyst, programmer, computer operator

Security

Director of security, security manager, security officer

Human Resources

Director of human resources, human resources manager, human resources coordinator, training director, benefits manager, benefits coordinator, employee relations manager, employment manager

Marketing and Sales

Director of marketing, sales manager, director of group sales, director of public relations, public relations manager, director of marketing communications, research analyst, pricing manager, catering sales manager

Property Operation and Maintenance

Director of engineering, chief engineer, engineering manager, groundskeeper, equipment operator, heavy machine operator, general maintenance engineer, general maintenance laborer, carpenter, electrician, painter, plumber, engineer, engineering coordinator, mechanic, environmental manager, energy manager

House Laundry

Management

Laundry/valet manager

Finishing

Folder, press machine operator, ironer, finisher

Washing

Washer, wringer, extractor, puller, tumbler

Other

Sorter, marker, checker, collection and delivery employee, linen attendant, chute attendant, sewing attendant

Employee Cafeteria

Employee cafeteria manager, employee cafeteria attendant, employee cafeteria cook

Part III
Ratios and Statistics

The use of ratios and statistics as a basis of comparison, measurement, and communication is prevalent within the lodging industry. The usefulness of these tools is predicated on a commonality of definition and understanding. The various ratios and statistics that can be developed and be useful are numerous. The intent of this section is to provide a consistent, uniform definition of basic lodging industry ratios and statistics. This section includes only those ratios and statistics that are in widespread general use within the industry. It is not intended to be a complete listing and definition of all possible relevant ratios and statistics.

Ratio Analysis

Financial statements issued by lodging properties contain a considerable amount of information. A thorough analysis of this information requires more than simply reading the reported figures and facts. Users of financial statements need to be able to interpret the figures and facts, and make them yield information that reveals aspects of the property's financial situation or operation that could otherwise go unnoticed. This is accomplished through ratio analysis, which compares related facts reported on financial statements. A ratio gives mathematical expression to a relationship between two figures, and is calculated by dividing one figure by the other.

Ratios are meaningful only when compared to useful criteria. Useful criteria with which to compare the results of ratio analysis include:

- Other properties and industry averages

- The corresponding ratio calculated for a prior period

- Planned ratio goals

Ratio analysis can be extremely useful. However, ratios are only indicators; they do not resolve problems or actually reveal what the problems may be. At best, when ratios vary significantly from past periods, budgeted standards, or industry averages, they indicate that problems may exist. When problems appear to exist, considerably more analysis and investigation is necessary to determine the appropriate corrective actions.

The following paragraphs are intended to provide the reader with guidance regarding the use of ratios to measure hotel financial performance.

Comparisons to Other Properties and Industry Averages

The comparison of financial performance measurements to other properties and industry averages can be valuable. However, care must be used when comparing the performance of one hotel's operation to the average performance of the industry at large, a competitive set of properties, or a comparable group or type of properties. Consider the following points:

- The data should be used as a benchmark to measure the performance of the subject hotel against properties of similar size, age, location, revenue mix, chain-segment, ownership structure, management, facilities and services offered, amenities offered, etc. Careful consideration should be given to the comparability of these criteria and the degree to which the criteria influence each revenue and expense item.

- Variances from the average should be used as an indication of the need for further investigation. There may be perfectly valid reasons why a particular hotel should be achieving a performance level above or below the industry-wide, competitive set, or comparable group average.

- The data presented are averages, not standards. You may wish to exceed the average income levels and achieve lower expense ratios.

Comparisons to Prior Periods or Budgets

While comparison to industry-wide, competitive set, or comparable property statistics has some use for general benchmarking of a property, an internal analysis of a hotel's operation from period to period or against planned goals (as expressed in the budget) is an invaluable practice. This discipline can provide insight to answer such questions as:

- How have revenues and expenses changed from period to period?

- What has been the correlation between movements in revenues, expenses, and rooms occupied?

- Which departments are ahead or behind budget?

- Which departments are operating efficiently or inefficiently?

- Was the budget realistic?

Methods of Analysis—Fixed vs. Variable

There are various ways to analyze ratios and compare statistics. The proper method used is often dictated by the fixed or variable nature of the revenue or expense item.

Fixed

In general, fixed revenues and expenses are those that are set by contractual agreement or established by third parties for periods of time, typically one year. The volume of business has little effect on the amount paid for these expense items or the revenues received. Examples of fixed expenses are property/liability insurance, property taxes, base annual salaries, and dues and subscriptions. Examples of fixed revenue could be rental payments from a restaurant or retail operation leasing space from the property.

Variable

Variable revenues and expenses are those that are driven by the volume of business at the hotel. In the lodging industry, volume of business is predominately measured by the number of rooms occupied, as well as number of food and beverage covers served. Variable expenses closely tied to the number of rooms occupied would include housekeeping costs, complimentary breakfast expense, laundry, and guest supplies. Rooms and telephone revenue are two examples of revenues that vary with the number of rooms occupied.

Some expenses vary directly with changes in revenue. Franchise fees, management fees, and credit card commissions are examples of expenses that frequently vary with changes in revenue.

Semi-Variable

There are some revenue and expense items that have both fixed and variable components to them. For instance, rooms departmental labor costs typically have a fixed component (management salaries), as well as a variable component (room attendant wages).

Methods of Calculation and Comparison

The most common calculations made to analyze lodging data are as follows:

- Per occupied room
- Per available room
- Percent of revenue
- Total dollars

Since the volume of rooms occupied most frequently drives *variable* revenues and expenses, these line items are most frequently analyzed on a per-occupied-room basis. On the other hand, *fixed* expenses are typically examined on a per-available-room or total dollar basis. Analysis of both fixed and variable expenses as a percent of revenue can be valuable. Each method will provide the analyst with a different perspective. Often, multiple methods are necessary to gain a comprehensive picture of a property's performance.

When making industry-wide, competitive property, or comparable property comparisons, total dollar comparisons should not be used. Instead, measurements need to be scaled to account for differences in room counts. Therefore, fixed revenue and expense comparisons among properties are frequently made on a dollar-per-available-room basis. Measurements calculated on a dollar-per-occupied-room or percent-of-revenue basis are already proportioned for comparable comparative analysis.

Liquidity Ratios

Liquidity ratios measure an operation's ability to meet its current, short-term obligations. Owners and stockholders often prefer relatively low current ratios because investments in many current assets may be less productive than investments in non-current assets. Creditors, on the other hand, normally prefer relatively high current ratios because this gives them assurance that the lodging property will be able to meet its short-term obligations. Management must try to satisfy both owners and creditors while maintaining adequate working capital and sufficient liquidity to ensure the smooth operation of the property.

Current Ratio

The most common liquidity ratio is the current ratio, which is the ratio of total current assets to total current liabilities:

$$\text{Current Ratio} = \frac{\text{Current Assets}}{\text{Current Liabilities}}$$

This ratio reveals the amount of current assets for every dollar of current liabilities.

Acid-Test Ratio

The acid-test ratio measures a property's liquidity by considering only "quick assets"—current assets minus inventories and prepaid expenses:

$$\text{Acid-Test Ratio} = \frac{\text{Quick Assets}}{\text{Current Liabilities}}$$

This ratio reveals the amount of quick assets for every dollar of current liabilities. This is often a more stringent measure of a property's liquidity because it may take several months for many properties to convert their inventories to cash.

Accounts Receivable Turnover

Accounts receivable can be the largest current asset of lodging properties because credit is often extended to guests. Therefore, any examination of a property's liquidity must consider how quickly accounts receivable are converted to cash. This is determined by the accounts receivable turnover ratio, which divides total revenue by the average accounts receivable. A refinement of this ratio uses only charge sales in the numerator; however, quite often charge sales figures are unavailable. Regardless of whether total revenue or charge sales are used as the numerator, the calculation should be consistent from period to period.

To calculate the accounts receivable turnover, it is first necessary to determine the average accounts receivable. This is accomplished by adding accounts receivable at the beginning and end of the period and then dividing that figure by two. The average accounts receivable figure is then divided into the total revenue for the period:

$$\text{Accounts Receivable Turnover} = \frac{\text{Total Revenue}}{\text{Average Accounts Receivable}}$$

Average Collection Period

This ratio reveals the number of days required to collect the average accounts receivable. The average collection period is calculated by dividing the number of days in the year by the accounts receivable turnover:

$$\text{Average Collection Period} = \frac{\text{Days in Year}}{\text{Accounts Receivable Turnover}}$$

Solvency Ratios

Solvency ratios measure the degree of debt financing used by the lodging property. These ratios reflect the ability of the property to meet its long-term obligations. Owners view solvency ratios as a measure of their leverage, and often prefer relatively low solvency ratios because their leverage increases as debt is used in place of equity dollars to increase the return on equity dollars already invested. Creditors, on the other hand, prefer relatively high solvency ratios because they reveal an equity cushion available to absorb any operating losses. Management is again caught in the middle, trying to satisfy owners by financing assets so as to maximize return on investments and trying to satisfy creditors by not unduly jeopardizing the property's ability to meet its long-term obligations.

Solvency Ratio

A lodging operation is solvent when its assets are greater than its liabilities. The solvency ratio compares total assets to total liabilities:

$$\text{Solvency Ratio} \ = \ \frac{\text{Total Assets}}{\text{Total Liabilities}}$$

This ratio reveals the amount of assets for every dollar of liabilities.

Debt-Equity Ratio

One of the most common solvency ratios is the debt-equity ratio, which compares the total debt of the operation to the total investment in the operation by the owners:

$$\text{Debt-Equity Ratio} = \frac{\text{Total Liabilities}}{\text{Total Owners' Equity}}$$

This ratio reveals the amount owed to creditors for every dollar of owners' equity.

Debt Service Coverage Ratio

This ratio measures the extent to which a hotel generates sufficient Adjusted Net Operating Income to cover its debt obligations (interest and/or principal payments):

$$\frac{\text{Debt Service}}{\text{Coverage Ratio}} = \frac{\text{Adjusted Net Operating Income}}{\text{Debt Service (i.e., Interest Expense + Principal Expense)}}$$

Activity Ratios

It is management's responsibility to generate earnings for owners while providing products and services to guests. Activity ratios measure the effectiveness with which management uses the resources of the property.

Inventory Turnover

This ratio measures the number of times inventory turns over during the period. Generally, the greater the number of times the better, because inventories can be expensive to maintain. Inventory turnovers are usually calculated separately for food items and beverage items. To calculate inventory turnover, it is first necessary to determine the average inventory. This is accomplished by adding inventory at the beginning and end of the period and then dividing that figure by two. An example of an inventory turnover ratio is the food inventory turnover ratio, calculated as follows:

$$\text{Food Inventory Turnover} = \frac{\text{Cost of Food Sales}}{\text{Average Food Inventory}}$$

Profitability Ratios

Profitability ratios allow management and owners to compare their profit performance to other competitive and/or comparable properties, to themselves over time, or to budget. Profitability ratios reflect the overall effectiveness of management in producing the bottom line figure expected by owners and creditors. Owners invest in lodging properties in order to increase their wealth through dividends and through increases in the value of the property. Dividends and values are highly dependent upon the present and future profits generated by the operation. Since future profits may be required to repay lenders, creditors normally perceive less risk to be involved in dealings with the more profitable businesses in their communities.

Caution should be used when using profitability ratios for comparison across competitive sets or comparable property groups. Several factors influence the relative profitability of one type of hotel (e.g., convention vs. limited service) or individual hotel compared to another or within its competitive set or comparable group.

Gross Operating Profit per Available Room (GOPAR)

GOPAR measures management's ability to produce profits by generating sales and controlling the operating expenses over which they have the most direct control. GOPAR is calculated by dividing gross operating profit by the rooms available in the hotel:

$$\text{GOPAR} = \frac{\text{Gross Operating Profit}}{\text{Rooms Available}}$$

GOPAR is somewhat useful in relating gross operating profits, on a proportional basis, across properties within a competitive set or comparable property groups. Because GOPAR is calculated before any deduction for management fees, this ratio can be used to compare comparable properties that are operated by a third-party management company with owner-operated properties.

Gross Operating Profit Margin Ratio

This ratio is another measure of management's overall ability to produce profits by generating sales and controlling the operating expenses over which they have the most direct control. It is calculated by dividing gross operating profit by total revenue:

$$\text{Gross Operating Profit Margin Ratio} = \frac{\text{Gross Operating Profit}}{\text{Total Revenue}}$$

Because gross operating profit is calculated before any deduction for management fees, this ratio can be used to compare comparable properties that are operated by a third-party management company with owner-operated properties. Care should be taken in comparing only gross operating profit margins among comparable properties as the revenue mix achieved can significantly influence these margins.

Income Before Fixed Charges per Available Room

This ratio measures management's ability to produce profits by generating sales and controlling all departmental costs, undistributed expenses, and management fees. It is calculated by dividing income before fixed charges by the rooms available in the hotel:

$$\frac{\text{Income Before Fixed Charges}}{\text{per Available Room}} = \frac{\text{Income Before Income Charges}}{\text{Rooms Available}}$$

Income Before Fixed Charges Margin Ratio

This ratio measures management's overall ability to produce profits by generating sales and controlling all departmental costs, undistributed expenses, and management fees. It is calculated by dividing income before fixed charges by total revenue:

$$\frac{\text{Income Before Fixed Charges}}{\text{Margin Ratio}} = \frac{\text{Income Before Fixed Charges}}{\text{Total Revenue}}$$

Net Operating Income per Available Room

This ratio measures management's ability to produce profits by generating sales and controlling all departmental costs, undistributed expenses, management fees, property taxes, insurance, and rent. Care should be taken in comparing only net operating income among comparable properties, since not all hotels have ground, building, or major equipment leases. This ratio is calculated by dividing net operating income (before capital reserves) by the rooms available in the hotel:

$$\text{Net Operating Income per Available Room} = \frac{\text{Net Operating Income}}{\text{Rooms Available}}$$

Net Operating Income Margin Ratio

This ratio measures management's overall ability to produce profits by generating sales and controlling all departmental costs, undistributed expenses, management fees, property taxes, insurance, and rent. Care should be taken in comparing only net operating income margins among comparable properties, since not all hotels have ground, building, or major equipment leases. This ratio is calculated by dividing net operating income (before capital reserves) by total revenue:

$$\text{Net Operating Income Margin Ratio} = \frac{\text{Net Operating Income}}{\text{Total Revenue}}$$

Cash on Cash Return

This calculation is one method of estimating return on investment. Cash on cash return is determined by dividing the adjusted net operating income, less debt-service, by the average owners' equity for a period of time. Average owners' equity is calculated by totaling owners' equity at the beginning and end of the period and then dividing that figure by two. Cash on cash return is calculated as follows:

$$\text{Cash on Cash Return} = \frac{\text{Adjusted Net Operating Income} - \text{Debt Service}}{\text{Average Owners' Equity}}$$

Note that owners, lenders, and analysts on specific investments frequently use other ratios and calculations, such as Internal Rate of Return (IRR).

Operating Ratios

Operating ratios assist owners and management in analyzing the operations of a lodging property. These ratios relate expenses to revenue and are useful for control purposes when the ratio results are compared to budgeted or planned ratio goals, as well as other properties and industry averages. Significant variations between actual ratio results and budgeted results, planned goals, or other properties and industry averages may indicate the need for further analysis and corrective action.

Caution should be used when using operating ratios for comparison across competitive sets or comparable property groups. Several factors influence the relative market position of one property compared to another.

Note for mixed-ownership hotels: For lodging properties that include units owned by third parties, it is appropriate to develop a supplemental schedule of ratios and statistics that includes the performance of these units. The performance measurements that would be affected are identified in the Definitions section of Part III by two asterisks (**).

Average Room Rate—Overall

Although room rates may vary seasonally, by market segment, or by room type within a property, most lodging properties calculate an overall average room rate, also called the average daily rate (ADR). The overall average room rate reveals the average rate charged per occupied room and is calculated by dividing total rooms revenue for a period by the number of rooms occupied during that period. Rooms occupied includes rooms occupied on a paid basis, as well as rooms occupied without charge in connection with a promotion or contract. Complimentary rooms are not included in the denominator of the ADR calculation. The overall average room rate is calculated as follows:

$$\text{Average Room Rate—Overall} = \frac{\text{Total Rooms Revenue}}{\text{Rooms Occupied}}$$

Average Room Rate—Revenue Segment

For analytical purposes, many lodging properties calculate an average room rate (ADR) for each revenue segment (transient, group, contract). The average room rate for a revenue segment reveals the average rate charged per occupied room and is calculated by dividing rooms revenue for a specific revenue segment for a period by the number of rooms occupied by guests in that revenue segment during that period. Rooms occupied by revenue segment includes rooms occupied on a paid basis, as well as rooms occupied without charge in connection with a promotion or contract. Complimentary rooms are not included in the denominator of the ADR per revenue segment calculation. The average room rate for a revenue segment is calculated as follows:

$$\text{Average Room Rate per Revenue Segment} = \frac{\text{Gross Rooms Revenue for Revenue Segment}}{\text{Rooms Occupied for that Revenue Segment}}$$

Rooms Revenue per Available Room (RevPAR)

Rooms revenue per available room (RevPAR) measures the rooms revenue yield a property achieves relative to the rooms available in the property for a period. RevPAR includes the influence of two factors—occupancy and overall average room rate. RevPAR can be used as a way to compare rooms revenue results with prior period results or to compare actual to budgeted results. In addition, since the rooms revenue is scaled by the number of rooms at the property, it can be used as one comparison of the rooms revenue yield of a property to its competitors or comparable properties. RevPAR is calculated as follows:

$$\text{RevPAR} = \frac{\text{Total Rooms Revenue}}{\text{Rooms Available}}$$

Total Revenue Per Available Room (Total RevPAR)

Total revenue per available room (Total RevPAR) measures the total revenue yield a property achieves relative to the rooms available in the property for a period. Total RevPAR can be used as one measure of total revenue change from prior period results or to compare actual to budgeted results. Since the total revenue is scaled by the number of rooms at the property, it can be used as one comparison of the revenue yield of a property to its competitors or comparable properties. For properties with significant revenue sources other than rooms revenue, this may be a better indicator of revenue yield or growth, as opposed to RevPAR. Total RevPAR is calculated as follows:

$$\text{Total RevPAR} = \frac{\text{Total Revenue}}{\text{Rooms Available}}$$

Average Food Check

This operating ratio reveals the amount of the average food check per cover and is calculated by dividing food revenue by the number of covers:

$$\text{Average Food Check} = \frac{\text{Total Food Revenue}}{\text{Number of Covers}}$$

Covers refers to the number of guests served in the food operation during the period. This analysis is typically carried out for each meal period and each outlet.

Food Cost Percentage

This operating ratio compares the cost of food sales to food revenue. It is frequently used in determining whether food costs are reasonable. Food cost percentage is calculated by dividing the cost of food sales by food revenue:

$$\text{Food Cost Percentage} = \frac{\text{Cost of Food Sales}}{\text{Food Revenue}}$$

Beverage Cost Percentage

This operating ratio compares the cost of beverage sales to beverage revenue. It is frequently used in determining whether beverage costs are reasonable. Beverage cost percentage is calculated by dividing the cost of beverage sales by beverage revenue:

$$\text{Beverage Cost Percentage} = \frac{\text{Cost of Beverage Sales}}{\text{Beverage Revenue}}$$

Labor Cost Percentage

Total labor expense includes the total payroll and related expenses for all departments and operational areas of the property. A total hotel labor cost percentage is calculated by dividing total labor expenses by total revenue. For control purposes, labor cost percentages also should be calculated and analyzed for each department and operational area of the property. The labor cost percentage is calculated as follows:

$$\text{Labor Cost Percentage} = \frac{\text{Total [or Department] Payroll and Related Expenses}}{\text{Total [or Department] Revenue}}$$

Labor Cost per Available or Occupied Room

An alternative method to measure labor costs is on a dollar per available room basis (PAR) or dollar per occupied room basis (POR). For those departments whose labor requirements are significantly influenced by the number of rooms occupied (e.g., rooms, telecommunications), labor cost per occupied room is one measure of labor efficiency. For departments whose labor requirements are not significantly influenced by the number of rooms occupied (e.g., undistributed), labor cost per available room is one measure of labor efficiency. The labor cost percentage is calculated as follows:

$$\frac{\text{Labor Cost per Available}}{\text{(or Occupied) Room}} = \frac{\text{Total [or Department] Payroll and Related Expenses}}{\text{Rooms Available (or Total Rooms Occupied)}}$$

Room Statistics and Occupancy Ratios

Lodging properties usually supplement the rooms operation information reported on the Statement of Income with occupancy ratio results. Occupancy ratios measure the success of the rooms operation in selling the primary product of the property. In order to calculate basic occupancy ratios, various rooms statistics must be kept during the period.

The following is a list with definitions of several common rooms statistics and occupancy ratios. Please note that the term "room nights" can be substituted for the word "rooms" in the following measurements and ratio definitions.

(1)   Total Room Inventory
        Rooms Not Available for Rent:
(2)   Seasonally Closed Rooms
(3)   Extended Closed Rooms
(4)   Rooms for Permanent House Use
(5)   Total Rooms Not Available for Rent
(6)   Rooms Available
        Number of Rooms Occupied:*
(7)   Transient
(8)   Group
(9)   Contract
(10)   Complimentary
(11)   Rooms Occupied
(12)   Total Rooms Occupied
(13)   Occupancy %
(14)   Vacant Rooms
        Percent of Occupancy:
(15)   Transient %
(16)   Group %
(17)   Contract %
(18)   Complimentary %
        Number of Guests:
(19)   Transient
(20)   Group
(21)   Contract
(22)   Complimentary
(23)   Total Guests
(24)   Number of Guests per Occupied Room
(25)   Number of Rooms with Multiple Guests
(26)   Multiple Occupancy %
(27)   Arrivals
(28)   Average Length of Stay

*See *Rooms—Schedule 1* for definitions of types of guests by revenue category.

DEFINITIONS:

(1)   **Total Room Inventory**
        Total number of guestrooms (keys) in a property whether available for sale or not. Included are (5) Rooms Not Available for Rent, (12) Total Rooms Occupied, and (14) Vacant Rooms.

(2)   **Seasonally Closed Rooms**
        When all operations of a hotel are closed for a minimum of 30 consecutive days due to seasonal demand patterns, then the rooms for this period should be removed from the annual salable inventory. The hotel must be consistently closed year-to-year.

(3) **Extended Closed Rooms**

Those rooms removed from salable inventory for a period of six consecutive months or more on a non-discretionary basis. Examples include rooms that are damaged due to a hurricane, earthquake, or fire, where there is intent to return the rooms to salable inventory.

(4) **Rooms for Permanent House Use**

Those rooms removed from salable inventory for a minimum of six consecutive months for use by a hotel employee (e.g., manager's apartment).

(5) **Total Rooms Not Available for Rent**

Total of rooms that are (2) Seasonally Closed, (3) Extended Closed, or used for (4) Permanent House Use.

(6) **Rooms Available****

Total Room Inventory (1) less (5) Total Rooms Not Available for Rent.

(7) **Transient Rooms Occupied**

Total rooms occupied by guests on an individual basis. Included are rooms occupied on a paid basis, as well as rooms occupied on a gratis basis in connection with a promotion or contract.

(8) **Group Rooms Occupied**

Total rooms occupied by guests as part of a group (10 rooms or more). Included are rooms occupied on a paid basis, as well as rooms occupied on a gratis basis in connection with a promotion or contract.

(9) **Contract Rooms Occupied**

Total rooms occupied by guests as part of a special contract, generally of a longer-term nature (i.e., multiple weeks or months). Included are rooms occupied on a paid basis, as well as rooms occupied on a gratis basis in connection with a promotion or contract.

(10) **Complimentary Rooms Occupied**

Free rooms provided to any guest, often for marketing purposes, but not related to an existing contractual relationship. Examples of complimentary rooms include rooms provided on a gratis basis to owners, employees, people on familiarization tours, friends, and family. Also included are rooms used by the hotel on a short-term basis (e.g., employee relocation, manager-on-duty, etc.).

Not classified as complimentary rooms are rooms provided due to a trade-out arrangement, rooms provided in connection with a promotion (e.g., stay two nights, get one free), or rooms provided as part of a group contract (e.g., book 50 rooms, get one free). These rooms should be classified as one of the revenue categories (transient, group, or contract).

(11) **Rooms Occupied****

Total rooms occupied by (7) Transient, (8) Group, and (9) Contract guests.

(12) **Total Rooms Occupied****

Total rooms occupied by (7) Transient, (8) Group, (9) Contract, and (10) Complimentary guests.

(14) **Vacant Rooms**

Total Rooms Available (6) less (12) Total Rooms Occupied. Vacant rooms can be classified into the following sub-categories:

Rooms Unoccupied: Those rooms available for sale, but not occupied by a paying or complimentary guest.

Rooms Out-of-Order: Those rooms removed from salable inventory for a period of less than six consecutive months due to renovation or a temporary fault or problem rendering them inadequate for occupancy.

Temporary Closed Rooms: Those rooms removed from salable inventory on a discretionary basis for a period of less than six consecutive months.

(19)   **Number of Guests—Transient**
Total guests traveling as individuals.

(20)   **Number of Guests—Group**
Total guests traveling as part of a group.

(21)   **Number of Guests—Contract**
Total guests who occupy their room through a special contract.

(22)   **Number of Guests—Complimentary**
Total persons staying on a complimentary basis as described in #10 above.

(23)   **Total Guests**
Total (19) Transient, (20) Group, (21) Contract, and (22) Complimentary guests.

(25)   **Number of Rooms with Multiple Guests**
Number of rooms occupied by more than one paying or gratis guest.

(27)   **Arrivals**
Number of room check-ins, both paying and complimentary.

FORMULAS

(13)   Occupancy Percentage $= \dfrac{(11) \quad \text{Rooms Occupied}}{(6) \quad \text{Rooms Available}} \times 100$

(15)   Percentage Occupancy Transient $= \dfrac{(7) \quad \text{Transient Rooms Occupied}}{(6) \quad \text{Rooms Available}} \times 100$

(16)   Percentage Occupancy Group $= \dfrac{(8) \quad \text{Group Rooms Occupied}}{(6) \quad \text{Rooms Available}} \times 100$

(17)   Percentage Occupancy Contract $= \dfrac{(9) \quad \text{Contract Rooms Occupied}}{(6) \quad \text{Rooms Available}} \times 100$

(18)   Percentage Occupancy Complimentary $= \dfrac{(10) \quad \text{Complimentary Rooms Occupied}}{(6) \quad \text{Rooms Available}} \times 100$

$$(24) \quad \begin{array}{l} \text{Number of Guests} \\ \text{per Occupied Room} \end{array} = \frac{(23)}{(12)} \quad \frac{\text{Total Guests}}{\text{Total Rooms Occupied}}$$

$$(26) \quad \text{Multiple Occupancy} = \frac{(25)}{(12)} \quad \frac{\text{Rooms with Multiple Guests}}{\text{Total Rooms Occupied}} \times 100$$

$$(28) \quad \text{Average Length of Stay} = \frac{(12)}{(27)} \quad \frac{\text{Total Rooms Occupied}}{\text{Arrivals}}$$

**Note for lodging properties with mixed-ownership units: When a lodging property includes rooms owned by parties other than the owner of the hotel, it is appropriate to develop a supplemental schedule of ratios and statistics that includes the performance of such elements. The ratios and statistics in this schedule can be used when providing data to independent industry reporting agencies in order to reflect the performance of the entire property.

The measurements that are affected include Rooms Available, Rooms Occupied, and Room Revenue. These measurements are used to calculate occupancy, average room rate, and RevPAR. When preparing the ratios and statistics in the supplemental schedule, please note the following guidance:

- *Rooms Available:* third-party-owned units under the control of hotel management for the purpose of renting to guests other than the unit owners should be added to the Rooms Available of the hotel.

- *Rooms Occupied*: third-party-owned units that are rented to guests other than the unit owners should be added to the Rooms Occupied of the hotel.

- *Room Revenue:* revenue earned for the rental of third-party-owned units to guests other than the unit owners should be added to Room Revenue as defined in the discussion of Schedule 1.

Food and Beverage Statistics

The following indicates the kind of food and beverage statistical information that the financial reports of hotels should contain:

Restaurant Facilities

Number of Seats
Meal Period Statistics

Meal Period	Covers	Average Check
Breakfast		
Lunch		
Dinner		
Total		

Beverage revenue % of food revenue
Combined food and beverage revenue per seat

Lounge Facilities

Number of Seats
Revenue per Seat

Room Service

Total Revenue per Occupied Room

Banquet

Total Square Feet
Banquet Revenue per Square Foot
Covers and Average Check Statistics

Inventory Turns and Number of Days of Inventory on Hand

These inventory statistics are calculated as follows for both food and beverage inventories:

Inventory Turns

Monthly Cost of Food and/or Beverage Sales divided by Average Inventory
Opening Inventory plus Closing Inventory divided by two.

Number of Days of Inventory on Hand

Number of days in the month divided by the inventory turns equals the average number of days it takes to turn the inventory over.

Part IV
Expense Dictionary

This dictionary is designed to help members of the lodging industry classify, in accordance with the *Uniform System of Accounts for the Lodging Industry*, the numerous expense items encountered in their daily work. It serves as a ready reference for accounting and non-accounting staff, indicating the proper department and line item/account for recording each expense item.

This Expense Dictionary is not intended to be a complete and comprehensive list of all items that can be expensed in a property. The intention is to present a representative list that is large enough to allow a user either to find the classification of an item or to find examples that will assist in classifying the item if it is not in the dictionary.

The Expense Dictionary does not deal with the question of when to capitalize versus when to expense. Generally Accepted Accounting Principles must be used to make this decision, as well as the "materiality" policies of the owner and/or management entity. One of the most common examples of how this decision affects the departmental statements deals with the recording of an expenditure made to repair property or equipment. Many properties make this decision based on the size of the expenditure when, in general, the expenditure should be capitalized only if it materially extends the life of the item being repaired or materially increases its value.

The Expense Dictionary is organized into two sections. Each section has three columns. In Section One, the Expense Dictionary presents the items to be expensed alphabetically in the first column. The second column designates the department or schedule, and the third column indicates the specific line item or account name to which the expense item is charged. In Section Two, the Expense Dictionary shows the department/schedule in the first column. The second column lists specific line items or account names for that department/schedule to which expense items are charged. Column three presents various expense items that apply to the second column's line item. Section Two begins with a listing of expense items that can apply to multiple departments/schedules, and then continues with an alphabetical listing of individual departments/schedules.

All department and account names used in the dictionary match those presented in the various sections of the *Uniform System of Accounts for the Lodging Industry*, with the following exceptions:

- Some items are shown to be charged to Food, Beverage, or Food or Beverage. This was done to make the classification easier for the user who wishes to maintain separate Food and Beverage Departments.

- Many items are shown to be charged to Multiple Departments. This was done to eliminate unnecessary repetition when a given item could apply to the same line item or account in several departments, depending on its actual use. When looking up an item by department or schedule in Section Two, remember to check under Multiple Departments when an expected item does not appear under a specific department.

Many items are listed in the dictionary under different names so that the user can more easily find an item based on what he/she may perceive as the correct item name. Finally, the user of the Expense Dictionary should refer to account definitions in the individual departments of the *Uniform System of Accounts for the Lodging Industry* in order to make expense classification decisions whenever an item being researched is not found in the dictionary.

Because of space considerations, the Expense Dictionary makes use of several abbreviations. The Guide to Abbreviations explains all but the most basic abbreviations used.

GUIDE TO ABBREVIATIONS

Abbreviation	Department/Function/Item
A&G	Administrative and General
B/TO Taxes	Business and Transient Occupant Taxes
Elec. & Mech.	Electrical and Mechanical Equipment
Empl. Caf.	Employee Cafeteria
Golf/Pro Shop	Golf Course and Pro Shop
Grounds M&L	Grounds Maintenance and Landscaping
IS Equip.	Information Systems Equipment
Mult. Depts.	Multiple Departments
P&ODC	Postage and Overnight Delivery Charges
POM	Property Operation and Maintenance
R/POT/I	Rent, Property and Other Taxes, and Insurance
Telecom.	Telecommunications

Expense Dictionary
Section One: Sorted by Item Name

Item Name	Department/ Schedule	Account Name
Accessibility Sign	POM	Life/Safety
Accountant's Fees (Consulting)	A&G	Professional Fees
Accountant's Fees (Replacing Hotel Employees)	A&G	Contract Services
Accounting Fees—Centralized (Management Company)	A&G	Cent. Acct. Charges
Accounting Fees—Centralized (Owner)	A&G	Cent. Acct. Charges
Acids	Mult. Depts.	Cleaning Supplies
ADA Compliance Items	POM	Life/Safety
Adapter Plug, Electrical	Mult. Depts.	Operating Supplies
Adding Machine Tape	Mult. Depts.	Operating Supplies
Adding Machines	Mult. Depts.	Operating Supplies
Address List Maintenance	Sales & Marketing	Direct Mail
Address List Purchase	Sales & Marketing	Direct Mail
Address List Rental	Sales & Marketing	Direct Mail
Adhesive Tape	Mult. Depts.	Operating Supplies
Adhesive, Stair Tread	POM	Floor Covering

Item Name	Department/ Schedule	Account Name
Advertising—Direct Mail	Sales & Marketing	Media
Advertising—Directories	Sales & Marketing	Media
Advertising—Internet	Sales & Marketing	Media
Advertising—Magazines	Sales & Marketing	Media
Advertising—Newspapers	Sales & Marketing	Media
Advertising—Outdoor	Sales & Marketing	Outdoor
Advertising—Publications	Sales & Marketing	Media
Advertising—Radio & TV	Sales & Marketing	Media
Advertising—Recruiting	A&G	Human Resources
Advertising Agency Fees	Sales & Marketing	Agency Fees
Afghans, Guestroom	Rooms	Operating Supplies
Aftershave Lotion	Rooms	Guest Supplies
Air Conditioner Filters	POM	HVAC Equip.
Air Deodorizing Accessories/Systems	Mult. Depts.	Operating Supplies
Air Filters	POM	HVAC Equip.
Air Freshener	Mult. Depts.	Cleaning Supplies
Air-Cooling Systems Repairs	POM	HVAC Equip.
Airfare	Mult. Depts.	Travel—Other
Airline Tickets	Mult. Depts.	Travel—Other
Airport Van Maintenance	Rooms	Guest Transportation
Alarm Systems	POM	Life/Safety
Alarms, Smoke	POM	Life/Safety
Alcohol (Cleaning)	Mult. Depts.	Cleaning Supplies
Alert Device for Hearing-Impaired	POM	Life/Safety
All-Purpose Cleaner	Mult. Depts.	Cleaning Supplies
Aluminum Foil	Food	Paper & Plastics
Aluminum Foil, Employee Cafeteria	Empl. Caf.	Paper & Plastics
Aluminum Trays	Food	China
Aluminum Trays, Employee Cafeteria	Empl. Caf.	China
Amenities, Gifts	Mult. Depts.	Comp. Services & Gifts
Amenities, Guest	Rooms	Guest Supplies
Amenity Baskets/Containers (Not Reusable)	Rooms	Guest Supplies
Amenity Baskets/Containers (Reusable)	Rooms	Operating Supplies
Ammonia	Mult. Depts.	Cleaning Supplies
Answering Machines	Mult. Depts.	Operating Supplies
Antacid (for Use by Guests in Rooms)	Rooms	Guest Supplies
Anti-Fatigue Mats	Mult. Depts.	Operating Supplies
Aprons, Uniform	Mult. Depts.	Uniforms
Aquarium, Guestroom or Lobby	Rooms	Operating Supplies
Aquarium Supplies, Guestroom or Lobby	Rooms	Operating Supplies
Armored Transport Fee	A&G	Security

Item Name	Department/Schedule	Account Name
Artificial Plant Cleaner	Mult. Depts.	Cleaning Supplies
Artwork	Mult. Depts.	Operating Supplies
Ash Cans	Mult. Depts.	Operating Supplies
Ash Trays	Mult. Depts.	Operating Supplies
Ash Trays, Aluminum, Glass	Food or Beverage	China
Aspirin (for Use by Guests in Rooms)	Rooms	Guest Supplies
Association Dues—Marketing Employees	Sales & Marketing	Dues & Subscriptions
Attorney's Fees for Collections	A&G	Credit & Collections
Attorney's Fees Other than Collections	A&G	Legal Services
Attorney's Fees/Expenses, Real Estate Taxes	R/POT/I	Real Estate Taxes
Audiovisual Equipment Rent (Charged to Customer)	Food or Beverage	Audiovisual Cost
Audit Fees, Public Accountants	A&G	Audit Charges
Auto Fuel Costs (Guest Transport)	Rooms	Guest Transportation
Auto Lease (Non-Capital) for General Manager	A&G	Transportation
Auto Supplies Used by Property	POM	Operating Supplies
Auto/Truck Repair—Property Use	POM	Elec. & Mech.
Awards, Employees	A&G	Human Resources
Awning Repairs	POM	Building
Bad Debt Allowance	A&G	Prov. for Doubtful Accts.
Baggage Tags (Gratis)	Rooms	Guest Supplies
Bags—Beverage Glass Covers, Guestroom	Rooms	Operating Supplies
Bags, Paper Leftover	Food	Paper & Plastics
Bags, Pastry	Food	Utensils
Baked Goods	Food	Cost of Food Sales
Ball Washers, Golf Course	Golf/Pro Shop	Operating Supplies
Band-Aids	Mult. Depts.	Operating Supplies
Bank Checks, Charges	A&G	Bank Charges
Bank Exchange on Checks and Currency	A&G	Bank Charges
Banners, Golf Tournament	Golf/Pro Shop	Tournament Expenses
Bar Mats	Beverage	Operating Supplies
Barter/Contra Agreement	Sales & Marketing	Media
Baskets, Amenity	Rooms	Operating Supplies
Baskets, Urinal	Mult. Depts.	Operating Supplies
Baskets, Waste Liners	Mult. Depts.	Operating Supplies
Baskets, Welcome	Rooms	Comp. Services & Gifts
Baskets, Wine (for Gratis Presentations)—Not Reusable	Mult. Depts.	Comp. Services & Gifts
Baskets, Wine (for Gratis Presentations)—Reusable	Mult. Depts.	Operating Supplies

Item Name	Department/ Schedule	Account Name
Bath Gel	Rooms	Guest Supplies
Bath Salts	Rooms	Guest Supplies
Bath Sheets	Rooms	Guest Supplies
Bath Soap	Rooms	Guest Supplies
Bath Tissue	Rooms	Guest Supplies
Bath Towels (All Sizes)	Rooms	Linen
Bathing Cap	Rooms	Guest Supplies
Bathing Suits, Disposable	Rooms	Guest Supplies
Bathmats	Rooms	Linen
Bathroom Cleaner	Mult. Depts.	Cleaning Supplies
Bathroom Scale	Rooms	Operating Supplies
Bathroom Throw Rugs	Rooms	Linen
Bathtub Safety Mats	Rooms	Operating Supplies
Bathtub Safety Strips	Rooms	Operating Supplies
Batteries	Mult. Depts.	Operating Supplies
Beaters	Food	Utensils
Bed Pads	Rooms	Linen
Bed Ruffles	Rooms	Linen
Bed Skirts	Rooms	Linen
Bedspreads	Rooms	Linen
Bedsprings Repair	POM	Furniture & Equip.
Beeper Rental	Mult. Depts.	Equip. Rental
Beer	Beverage	Cost of Beverage Sales
Beer Coil Cleaning (Outside Service)	Beverage	Contract Services
Beverage Lists	Beverage	Menus & Beverage Lists
Billboards	Sales & Marketing	Outdoor
Billing Statements/Invoices	A&G	Printing & Stationery
Binder Clips	Mult. Depts.	Operating Supplies
Binders	Mult. Depts.	Operating Supplies
Binding System Accessories	A&G	Printing & Stationery
Blackout Drapes	Rooms	Operating Supplies
Blanket Covers	Rooms	Linen
Blankets, Guestroom	Rooms	Linen
Blankets, Health Club/Spa	Health Club/Spa	Linen
Bleach	Mult. Depts.	Cleaning Supplies
Bleach Packets	Mult. Depts.	Cleaning Supplies
Blenders, Bar	Beverage	Utensils
Blinds Repair	POM	Building
Blouses, Uniform	Mult. Depts.	Uniforms
Body Lotion	Rooms	Guest Supplies
Boiler Repairs	POM	HVAC Equip.

Item Name	Department/ Schedule	Account Name
Boiler Room Supplies	POM	Operating Supplies
Book Matches (Guest)	Mult. Depts.	Operating Supplies
Books, Golf (for Sale)	Golf/Pro Shop ...	Cost of Merch. Sales
Books, In-Room Guest Reading	Rooms	Operating Supplies
Books, Outlet Reservations Log	Food	Operating Supplies
Books, Technical	A&G	Operating Supplies
Books, Technical	Mult. Depts.	Training
Booths, Trade Shows	Sales & Marketing	Trade Shows
Boots, Uniform	Mult. Depts.	Uniforms
Bottle Openers	Beverage	Utensils
Bottle Openers, Guestroom	Rooms	Operating Supplies
Bottle Warmers	Rooms	Operating Supplies
Bottled Water (Gratis in Rooms)	Rooms	Guest Supplies
Bowls, Employee Cafeteria	Empl. Caf.	China
Bowls, Mixing/Preparation (All Sizes & Materials)	Food	China
Bowls, Serving (All Sizes & Materials)	Food	China
Boxes, Carry Out	Food	Paper & Plastics
Boxes, Pastry	Food	Paper & Plastics
Braille Signs	Rooms	Operating Supplies
Brochures, Sales/Marketing	Sales & Marketing	Media
Brooms	Mult. Depts.	Cleaning Supplies
Brushes, Cleaning	Mult. Depts.	Cleaning Supplies
Buckets, Mop	Mult. Depts.	Cleaning Supplies
Bug Traps	Mult. Depts.	Cleaning Supplies
Building Lease, Base	R/POT/I	Land & Buildings
Building Lease, Participating (Based on Operating Results)	R/POT/I	Land & Buildings
Building Repairs	POM	Building
Bumpers, Bed	Rooms	Linen
Bumpers, Crib	Rooms	Linen
Bunting	Rooms	Linen
Business Cards	Mult. Depts.	Printing & Stationery
Business Licenses, General	A&G	Licenses & Permits
Business Taxes, State/County/City	R/POT/I	B/TO Taxes
Butane Fuel	Food	Kitchen Fuel
Butter Dishes (All Materials)	Food	China
Buttons (for Use by Guests in Rooms)	Rooms	Guest Supplies
Cable Guide Cover	Rooms	Printing & Stationery
Cable Television Service	Rooms	Cable/Satellite Television

Item Name	Department/ Schedule	Account Name
Caddy Service	Golf/Pro Shop	Contract Services
Calculators	Mult. Depts.	Operating Supplies
Calendars and Diaries	Mult. Depts.	Operating Supplies
Call Accounting System Lease (Non-Capital)	R/POT/I	IS Equip.
Call Accounting System Software Lease (Non-Capital)	R/POT/I	IS Equip.
Cameras, Security	A&G	Security
Can Openers	Food	Utensils
Can Openers	Rooms	Operating Supplies
Candle Holders, Tabletop	Food	Utensils
Candles	Mult. Depts.	Operating Supplies
Candlesticks	Mult. Depts.	Operating Supplies
Candy (Gratis)	Rooms	Guest Supplies
Candy Dishes, Guestroom (Gratis Candy for Customers)	Rooms	Operating Supplies
Canned Food	Food	Cost of Food Sales
Canopies, Bed	Rooms	Operating Supplies
Cappuccino Machines	Rooms	Operating Supplies
Caps, Uniform	Mult. Depts.	Uniforms
Car Mileage Reimbursement	Mult. Depts.	Travel—Other
Car Rental	Mult. Depts.	Travel—Other
Car Washing (Rooms Vans, Carts, Limos)	Rooms	Guest Transportation
Carafes	Beverage	Glassware
Carafes, Guestroom	Rooms	Operating Supplies
Cardboard Boxes	Food	Paper & Plastics
Carpet Cleaner Chemical	Mult. Depts.	Cleaning Supplies
Carpet Cleaner Equipment	Rooms	Cleaning Supplies
Carpet Cleaning Services	Mult. Depts.	Contract Services
Carpet Cleaning Supplies	Mult. Depts.	Cleaning Supplies
Carpet Repairs	POM	Floor Covering
Carpet Shampoo	Mult. Depts.	Cleaning Supplies
Carpet Shampoo Machines	Mult. Depts.	Cleaning Supplies
Carpet Sweepers	Mult. Depts.	Cleaning Supplies
Carpet/Rug Cleaning (Outside Service)	Mult. Depts.	Contract Services
Carry Out Containers	Food	Paper & Plastics
Cart Name Plates, Golf Tournament	Golf/Pro Shop	Tournament Expenses
Carts, Fuel Costs (Guest Transport)	Rooms	Guest Transportation
Carts, Housekeeper	Rooms	Operating Supplies
Carts, Laundry	Rooms	Operating Supplies
Cash Boxes	A&G	Operating Supplies

Item Name	Department/ Schedule	Account Name
Cash Overage & Shortage	A&G	Cash Overages/Shortages
Cashier Envelopes	Mult. Depts.	Operating Supplies
Cashier Forms	Mult. Depts.	Operating Supplies
Casseroles	Food	China
CD ROM, Writable	Mult. Depts.	Operating Supplies
Ceiling Fan Repairs	POM	HVAC Equip.
Ceiling Repairs	POM	Building
Cellophane Tape	Mult. Depts.	Printing & Stationery
Cellophane Wrap	Food	Operating Supplies
Cellular Phone Charges	Mult. Depts.	Telecommunications
Cellular Phones/Supplies	Mult. Depts.	Telecommunications
Central Plant Costs	POM	HVAC Equip.
Chafing Dishes	Food	Utensils
Chamois	Mult. Depts.	Cleaning Supplies
Charcoal, Cooking	Food	Kitchen Fuel
Charge Vouchers	Mult. Depts.	Printing & Stationery
Charitable Contributions	A&G	Donations
Check Presenters	Food or Beverage	Operating Supplies
Check Verification	A&G	Credit & Collection
Check Writer Machines	A&G	Operating Supplies
Check/Folio/Statement Presentation Folders	Mult. Depts.	Printing & Stationery
Check-In Folders	Rooms	Printing & Stationery
Check-Out Folders	Rooms	Printing & Stationery
Check-Out Notices	Rooms	Printing & Stationery
Checks, Bank	A&G	Printing & Stationery
Cheese Baskets (Gratis)	Mult. Depts.	Comp. Services & Gifts
Chef Hats	Food	Paper & Plastics
Chemicals, Cleaning	Mult. Depts.	Cleaning Supplies
Chemicals, Cooling Tower	POM	HVAC Equip.
Chemicals, Fire Extinguishers	POM	Life/Safety
Chemicals, Laundry	House Laundry	Laundry Supplies
China	Food	China
China Rental	Food	China
China, Employee Cafeteria	Empl. Caf.	China
China, Guestroom	Rooms	Operating Supplies
Christmas Gifts for Employees	A&G	Human Resources
Cigar Cost	Food or Beverage	Misc. Cost of Other Rev.
Claim Settlement Costs, Contract Disputes	A&G	Settlement Costs
Claim Settlement Costs, EEOC	A&G	Settlement Costs
Claim Settlement Costs, Non-Insured	A&G	Settlement Costs
Cleaner, Bathroom	Mult. Depts.	Cleaning Supplies

Item Name	Department/ Schedule	Account Name
Cleaner, Concrete (Parking Garage)	Parking Garage ..	Cleaning Supplies
Cleaner, Tile	Mult. Depts.	Cleaning Supplies
Cleaning Beer Coils (Outside Service)	Beverage	Contract Services
Cleaning Chemicals	Mult. Depts.	Cleaning Supplies
Cleaning Compounds	Mult. Depts.	Cleaning Supplies
Cleaning Fluids	Mult. Depts.	Cleaning Supplies
Cleaning Rags	Mult. Depts.	Cleaning Supplies
Cleaning Sponges	Mult. Depts.	Cleaning Supplies
Cleansers (Non-Dishwashing)	Mult. Depts.	Cleaning Supplies
Cleansing Powder	Mult. Depts.	Cleaning Supplies
Clinic, Employees'	A&G	Human Resources
Clipboards	Mult. Depts.	Operating Supplies
Clipping Services	Sales & Marketing	Contract Services
Clock Radios for Guestrooms	Rooms	Operating Supplies
Clock/DVD Players for Guestrooms	Rooms	Operating Supplies
Clocks for Guestrooms	Rooms	Operating Supplies
Closet Rod	Rooms	Operating Supplies
Closet Sachets	Rooms	Operating Supplies
Clothes Brushes	Rooms	Operating Supplies
Clothing, Golf (for Sale)	Golf/Pro Shop ...	Cost of Clothing Sales
Cloths, Cleaning	Mult. Depts.	Cleaning Supplies
CO_2 for Soft Drink Mix	Food	Cost of Food Sales
Coasters	Rooms	Operating Supplies
Coats, Uniform	Mult. Depts.	Uniforms
Cocktail Picks	Beverage	Paper & Plastics
Coffee	Food	Cost of Food Sales
Coffee Filters	Food	Paper & Plastics
Coffee Filters	Rooms	Guest Supplies
Coffee Filters, Employee Cafeteria	Empl. Caf.	Paper & Plastics
Coffee for Use by Guests in Rooms	Rooms	Guest Supplies
Coffee Mugs	Rooms	Operating Supplies
Coffee Pots for Use by Guests in Rooms	Rooms	Operating Supplies
Coffee Pots (Glass, Plastic, Silver)	Food	China
Coffee Pots, Employee Cafeteria	Empl. Caf.	China
Coffee Urn	Food	Utensils
Coffee Urn Repairs	POM	Kitchen Equip.
Cogeneration of Water	Utility Costs	Water
Coin Drawers	Mult. Depts.	Operating Supplies
Coin Handling Equipment	A&G	Operating Supplies
Coin Wrappers	A&G	Operating Supplies
Coin/Currency Bag Seals	A&G	Operating Supplies

Item Name	Department/ Schedule	Account Name
Coin/Currency Equipment	A&G	Operating Supplies
Colanders	Food	Utensils
Collateral, Selling	Sales & Marketing	Collateral Material
Collection Fees	A&G	Credit & Collection
Combs	Rooms	Guest Supplies
Comforters	Rooms	Linen
Comment Card Processing (Outside Service)	Mult. Depts.	Contract Services
Comment Cards	Mult. Depts.	Printing & Stationery
Commissions, Meeting Planners	Rooms	Comms./Rebates—Group
Commissions, Rental Agents	A&G	Professional Fees
Commissions, Travel Agent (Food & Beverage)	Rooms	Commissions
Commissions, Travel Agent (Rooms)	Rooms	Commissions
Complimentary Beverages	Mult. Depts.	Comp. Services & Gifts
Complimentary Food	Mult. Depts.	Comp. Services & Gifts
Complimentary Parking	Mult. Depts.	Comp. Services & Gifts
Computer Books	A&G	Operating Supplies
Computer Discs	Mult. Depts.	Operating Supplies
Computer Forms, Commercial	Mult. Depts.	Printing & Stationery
Computer Forms, Printed	Mult. Depts.	Printing & Stationery
Computer Hardware Lease (Non-Capital)	R/POT/I	IS Equip.
Computer Manuals, Commercial	A&G	Information Systems
Computer Manuals, Printed	A&G	Information Systems
Computer Monitors	A&G	Information Systems
Computer Monitors, Guestrooms	Rooms	Operating Supplies
Computer Network Maintenance	A&G	Information Systems
Computer Printer Paper	A&G	Operating Supplies
Computer Printer Paper	Mult. Depts.	Printing & Stationery
Computer Rental (Temporary-Accounting, Human Resources)	A&G	Equip. Rental
Computer Software, Commercial Applications	A&G	Information Systems
Computer Software Lease (Non-Capital)	R/POT/I	IS Equip.
Computer Supplies and Accessories	A&G	Information Systems
Computer Training Manuals	Mult. Depts.	Training
Conditioner, Hair	Rooms	Guest Supplies
Consultant Fees	Mult. Depts.	Contract Services
Consultant Fees, Market Research	Sales & Marketing	Outside Services
Consultant Fees, Professional	A&G	Professional Fees
Consultant Fees, Property Taxes	R/POT/I	Real Estate Taxes
Containers, Amenity	Rooms	Operating Supplies
Contract Cleaning, Awning	Mult. Depts.	Contract Services

Item Name	Department/ Schedule	Account Name
Contract Cleaning, Floors	Mult. Depts.	Contract Services
Contract Cleaning, Fumigation	Mult. Depts.	Contract Services
Contract Cleaning, Kitchen Hoods	Food	Contract Services
Contract Cleaning, Windows	Mult. Depts.	Contract Services
Contract Exterminating	POM	Contract Services
Convention Bureau	Sales & Marketing	Dues & Subscriptions
Cookie Cutters	Food	Utensils
Cookie Wrappings, Guestroom	Rooms	Guest Supplies
Cookies, Guestroom	Rooms	Guest Supplies
Cooking Utensils	Food	Utensils
Cooking Utensils, Employee Cafeteria	Empl. Caf.	Utensils
Cooling System Repairs	POM	HVAC Equip.
Cooling Tower Repairs	POM	HVAC Equip.
Cooperative Marketing Costs—National/ Regional	Sales & Marketing	Franchise/Affiliation Ad.
Copier Lease (Non-Capital)	R/POT/I	Other Property & Equip.
Copier Rental/Lease	Mult. Depts.	Equip. Rental
Copier Toner	Mult. Depts.	Operating Supplies
Copy Paper	Mult. Depts.	Operating Supplies
Copying Service	Mult. Depts.	Printing & Stationery
Cords	Rooms	Operating Supplies
Cords, Drapery	Rooms	Operating Supplies
Corkscrews	Beverage	Utensils
Corkscrews for Use by Guests in Rooms	Rooms	Operating Supplies
Corporate Sales/Marketing Support	Sales & Marketing	Corp. Office Reimb.
Correction Fluid/Tape	A&G	Operating Supplies
Cosmetics	Rooms	Guest Supplies
Cots	Rooms	Operating Supplies
Cotton Balls	Rooms	Operating Supplies
Court Fees	A&G	Legal Services
Covers, Toilet Seats	Rooms	Operating Supplies
CPR Kits	Mult. Depts.	Operating Supplies
CPU Stands	A&G	Operating Supplies
Creamer Packets	Rooms	Guest Supplies
Creamers	Food	China
Creams, Body/Face (for Sale in Health Club/ Spa)	Health Club/Spa	Cost of Merch. Sales
Creams, Body/Face (Health Club/Spa)	Health Club/Spa	Health & Beauty Products
Creams, Body/Face (Rooms)	Rooms	Guest Supplies
Credit Application Forms	A&G	Printing & Stationery

Item Name	Department/ Schedule	Account Name
Credit Card Commissions	A&G	Credit Card Commissions
Credit Card Invoices	A&G	Printing & Stationery
Credit Reports	A&G	Credit & Collection
Credit Service Expense	A&G	Credit & Collection
Crib Bumper Pads	Rooms	Operating Supplies
Crib Covers	Rooms	Operating Supplies
Crib Mattresses	Rooms	Operating Supplies
Cribs	Rooms	Operating Supplies
Crocks (All Materials)	Food	China
Cups, China, for Use by Guests in Rooms	Rooms	Operating Supplies
Cups, Disposable, for Use by Guests in Rooms	Rooms	Guest Supplies
Cups, Drinking (Non-Coffee, All Sizes & Materials)	Food	Glassware
Cups, Employee Cafeteria	Empl. Caf.	Glassware
Cups, Paper/Plastic	Food	Paper & Plastics
Cups, Paper/Plastic, Employee Cafeteria	Empl. Caf.	Paper & Plastics
Cups/Saucers, Cappuccino	Food	China
Cups/Saucers, Coffee	Food	China
Cups/Saucers, Espresso	Food	China
Currency Bill Straps	A&G	Operating Supplies
Curtain Holdbacks	Mult. Depts.	Operating Supplies
Curtain Hooks	Mult. Depts.	Operating Supplies
Curtain Repairs	POM	Building
Curtain Rods	Mult. Depts.	Operating Supplies
Curtain Stackbacks	Mult. Depts.	Operating Supplies
Curtains	Mult. Depts.	Operating Supplies
Curtains, Dry Cleaning	Mult. Depts.	Laundry & Dry Cleaning
Customer Parking Paid to Third Party	Parking Garage	Contract Services
Customer Research, Outside Service	Sales & Marketing	Outside Services
Customer Survey, Outside Service	Sales & Marketing	Outside Services
Cut Flowers	Mult. Depts.	Decorations
Cutting Boards	Food	Utensils
Daily Reports	A&G	Printing & Stationery
Dairy Products	Food	Cost of Food Sales
Damaged Articles, Guest	A&G	Loss & Damage
Data Binders and Accessories	Mult. Depts.	Operating Supplies
Data Cartridges and Tapes	A&G	Information Systems
Data Processing Supplies	A&G	Information Systems
Data Systems and Storage Files	Mult. Depts.	Operating Supplies
Database Marketing Expense	Sales & Marketing	Direct Mail

Item Name	Department/ Schedule	Account Name
Decorations, Holiday & Special Occasions	Mult. Depts.	Decorations
Defibrillators	Mult. Depts.	Operating Supplies
Degreaser	Mult. Depts.	Cleaning Supplies
Dental Floss	Rooms	Guest Supplies
Dental Kit	Rooms	Guest Supplies
Deodorant	Rooms	Guest Supplies
Deodorizers	Rooms	Cleaning Supplies
Desalinization of Water	Utility Costs	Water
Desk Accessories	Mult. Depts.	Operating Supplies
Desk Caddies	Mult. Depts.	Operating Supplies
Desk Pad Holders	Mult. Depts.	Operating Supplies
Desk Pads	Mult. Depts.	Operating Supplies
Detective Service	A&G	Security
Detergent for Use by Guests in Rooms	Rooms	Guest Supplies
Detergent, House Laundry	House Laundry	Cleaning Supplies
Detergents (Dish)	Food	Dishwashing Supplies
Direct Mail Expenses, Outside Service	Sales & Marketing	Outside Services
Directory Advertising	Sales & Marketing	Media
Dish Drainer, Guestroom	Rooms	Operating Supplies
Dish Soap for Use by Guests in Rooms	Rooms	Guest Supplies
Dishcloths, Guestroom	Rooms	Operating Supplies
Dishes for Use by Guests in Rooms	Rooms	Operating Supplies
Dishwasher Repairs	POM	Kitchen Equip.
Dishwasher Soap for Use by Guests in Rooms	Rooms	Guest Supplies
Dishwashing Soaps and Rinsing Agents	Food	Dishwashing Supplies
Dishwashing Soaps and Rinsing Agents, Employee Cafeteria	Empl. Caf.	Dishwashing Supplies
Disinfectants	Mult. Depts.	Cleaning Supplies
Diskettes	A&G	Operating Supplies
Dispenser, Bath Tissue	Rooms	Operating Supplies
Dispensers, Lotion	Rooms	Operating Supplies
Dispensers, Soap	Rooms	Operating Supplies
Do Not Disturb Cards	Rooms	Operating Supplies
Document Destruction Fees	A&G	Contract Services
Doilies, Guestroom	Rooms	Operating Supplies
Doilies, Paper	Food	Paper & Plastics
Donations, Charitable	A&G	Donations
Door Viewer	Rooms	Operating Supplies
Doormats	Rooms	Operating Supplies
Doorstop	Rooms	Operating Supplies

Item Name	Department/ Schedule	Account Name
Double-Stick Tape	Mult. Depts.	Operating Supplies
Doubtful Accounts Provision	A&G	Prov. for Doubtful Accts.
Drain System Repairs	POM	Plumbing
Draperies, Dry Cleaning	Mult. Depts.	Laundry & Dry Cleaning
Drapery Baton	Mult. Depts.	Operating Supplies
Drapery Cords	Mult. Depts.	Operating Supplies
Drapery Liners	Mult. Depts.	Operating Supplies
Drapery Repairs	POM	Building
Drapes	Mult. Depts.	Operating Supplies
Drapes, Blackout	Mult. Depts.	Operating Supplies
Dresses, Uniform	Mult. Depts.	Uniforms
Drug Testing of Employees	A&G	Human Resources
Dry Cleaning Bags for Use by Guests in Rooms	Rooms	Guest Supplies
Dry Cleaning Costs, Non-Guest (In-House Laundry)	Mult. Depts.	Laundry & Dry Cleaning
Dry Cleaning Services, Non-Guest (Outside Laundry)	Mult. Depts.	Laundry & Dry Cleaning
Dry Goods (Flour, Pasta, etc.)	Food	Cost of Food Sales
Dry Ice	Food	Ice
Dry Ice, Employee Cafeteria	Empl. Caf.	Ice
Dryers, Hair	Rooms	Operating Supplies
Duct Tape	Mult. Depts.	Operating Supplies
Dues, Hotel Associations (Marketing)	Sales & Marketing	Dues & Subscriptions
Dues, Hotel Associations (Non-Marketing)	A&G	Dues & Subscriptions
Dues, Professional Associations (Marketing)	Sales & Marketing	Dues & Subscriptions
Dues, Professional Associations (Non-Marketing)	A&G	Dues & Subscriptions
Dumpster Charges	POM	Waste Removal
Dust Cloths	Mult. Depts.	Cleaning Supplies
Dust Mops	Mult. Depts.	Cleaning Supplies
Dust Pan Brushes	Mult. Depts.	Cleaning Supplies
Dust Pans	Mult. Depts.	Cleaning Supplies
Dusters	Mult. Depts.	Cleaning Supplies
Dusting Mitts	Mult. Depts.	Cleaning Supplies
Duvet Covers	Rooms	Linen
Duvets	Rooms	Linen
DVD Player, Guestrooms	Rooms	Operating Supplies
Easels (Charged to Customer)	Food	Misc. Cost of Other Rev.
Educational Activities for Employees	Mult. Depts.	Training
Educational Assistance	Mult. Depts.	Training
Educational Books/Pamphlets for Employees	Mult. Depts.	Training

Item Name	Department/Schedule	Account Name
Eggs	Food	Cost of Food Sales
Electric Bulbs	POM	Light Bulbs
Electric Sub-Meters Maintenance	POM	Elec. & Mech.
Electric Supplies	POM	Elec. & Mech.
Electrical Adapters	Mult. Depts.	Operating Supplies
Electrical Hookup (Charged to Customer)	Food or Beverage	Misc. Cost of Other Rev.
Electrical Repairs	POM	Elec. & Mech.
Electrical Tape	POM	Operating Supplies
Electricity	Utilities	Electricity
Elevator Repairs	POM	Elevators & Escalators
Elixers, Health Club/Spa	Health Club/Spa	Health & Beauty Products
Elixers, Health Club/Spa (for Sale)	Health Club/Spa	Cost of Merch. Sales
Emergency Exit Instruction Card	Rooms	Operating Supplies
Emergency Exit Signs	POM	Life/Safety
Emery Boards	Rooms	Guest Supplies
Employee Meal Food Cost Credit	Food	Cost of Food Sales
Employee Pins	Mult. Depts.	Operating Supplies
Entertainment Outside, Employee	Mult. Depts.	Travel—Meals & Enter.
Entertainment, Employee	A&G	Human Resources
Envelopes	Mult. Depts.	Printing & Stationery
Envelopes, Cashier	Mult. Depts.	Printing & Stationery
Erasers	Mult. Depts.	Operating Supplies
Escalator Repairs	POM	Elevators & Escalators
Espresso Maker for Use by Guests in Rooms	Rooms	Operating Supplies
Espresso Pods for Use by Guests in Rooms	Rooms	Guest Supplies
Ethernet Cables	A&G	Information Systems
Exchange on Bank Checks and Currency	A&G	Bank Charges
Exit Signs	POM	Life/Safety
Express Delivery Charges	A&G	P&ODC
Express Mail/UPS (Marketing)	Sales & Marketing	P&ODC
Express Mail/UPS (Non-Marketing)	A&G	P&ODC
Extension Cords	Mult. Depts.	Operating Supplies
Extermination Service	POM	Contract Services
Fabric Conditioner	House Laundry	Laundry Supplies
Fabric Softener	House Laundry	Laundry Supplies
Fabric Softener Packets	House Laundry	Laundry Supplies
Face Cloths, Health Club/Spa	Health Club/Spa	Linen
Facial Tissue	Rooms	Guest Supplies
Facial Tissue Box Cover	Rooms	Operating Supplies

Item Name	Department/ Schedule	Account Name
Familiarization (FAM) Tour Expenses	Sales & Marketing	Fam (Familiarization) Trips
Fans, Paper (for Use by Guests in Rooms)	Rooms	Guest Supplies
Fans, Portable	Mult. Depts.	Operating Supplies
Fax Machine Supplies and Accessories	A&G	Operating Supplies
Feather Duster	Mult. Depts.	Cleaning Supplies
Fees, Attorney, for Collections	A&G	Credit & Collection
Fees, Attorney, Other than Collections	A&G	Legal Services
Fees, Audit, Public Accountants	A&G	Professional Fees
Fees, Collection	A&G	Credit & Collection
Fees, Court	A&G	Legal Services
Fees, Instructor/Speaker (Training)	Mult. Depts.	Training
Fees, Legal	A&G	Legal Services
Fees, Medical	A&G	Human Resources
Fees, Notary	A&G	Audit Charges
Fees, Stock Transfer Agents	A&G	Professional Fees
Fees, Transfer	A&G	Professional Fees
Fees, Trustees (Handling Bond, etc.)	A&G	Professional Fees
Fences & Bridges Maintenance	Golf/Pro Shop ...	Grounds M&L
Fertilizer	POM	Grounds M&L
Fertilizers, Golf Course	Golf/Pro Shop ...	Grounds M&L
File Folders	Mult. Depts.	Operating Supplies
Film Purchase and Developing	Mult. Depts.	Operating Supplies
Filter Paper	Food	Paper & Plastics
Filters, Air Conditioning	POM	HVAC Equip.
Filters, Coffee	Rooms	Guest Supplies
Filters, Heating	POM	HVAC Equip.
Filters, Vacuum	Mult. Depts.	Cleaning Supplies
Fines (Health, Safety, etc.)	Mult. Depts.	Miscellaneous
Fingernail File	Rooms	Guest Supplies
Fire Alarm Service	POM	Life/Safety
Fire Axes	POM	Life/Safety
Fire Bucket Sand	POM	Life/Safety
Fire Extinguisher	POM	Life/Safety
Fire Extinguisher Chemicals	POM	Life/Safety
Fire-Starter Packets for Use by Guests in Rooms .	Rooms	Guest Supplies
Fireplace Lighter	Mult. Depts.	Operating Supplies
Fireplace Screen	Mult. Depts.	Operating Supplies
Fireplace Tools	Mult. Depts.	Operating Supplies
Firewood	Mult. Depts.	Operating Supplies

Item Name	Department/ Schedule	Account Name
First Aid Kits/Supplies	Mult. Depts.	Operating Supplies
Fish	Food	Cost of Food Sales
Flag Pins, Golf	Golf/Pro Shop	Operating Supplies
Flags	Mult. Depts.	Operating Supplies
Flashlights	Mult. Depts.	Operating Supplies
Flatware (Includes Silver, Stainless)	Food	Flatware
Flatware Cleaner	Food	Dishwashing Supplies
Flatware for Use by Guests in Rooms	Rooms	Operating Supplies
Flatware Rental	Food	Flatware
Flip Charts (Charged to Customers)	Food	Misc. Cost of Other Rev.
Floor Plans	Mult. Depts.	Printing & Stationery
Floor Polish	Mult. Depts.	Cleaning Supplies
Floor Refinishing	POM	Floor Covering
Floor Soap	Mult. Depts.	Cleaning Supplies
Floor Wax	Mult. Depts.	Cleaning Supplies
Floral Arrangements	Mult. Depts.	Decorations
Flower Purchases	POM	Grounds M&L
Flower Vases, Glass (Tabletop)	Food	Decorations
Flowers (Tabletop)	Food	Decorations
Flowers, Artificial	Mult. Depts.	Decorations
Flowers, Banquet Tables	Food	Decorations
Flowers, Fresh	Mult. Depts.	Decorations
Flowers, Golf Course	Golf/Pro Shop	Grounds M&L
Fluorescent Light Bulbs	POM	Light Bulbs
Fly Strips	Mult. Depts.	Cleaning Supplies
Fly Swatters	Mult. Depts.	Cleaning Supplies
Foam Insulated Cups	Food	Paper & Plastics
Foil Wrapping	Food	Paper & Plastics
Folios	Rooms	Printing & Stationery
Food Processor	Food	Utensils
Food Warmer Fuel	Food	Kitchen Fuel
Food Warmer Fuel, Employee Cafeteria	Empl. Caf.	Kitchen Fuel
Food, Employee Cafeteria	Empl. Caf.	Cost of Food
Forks, Kitchen	Food	Utensils
Forms, General	Mult. Depts.	Printing & Stationery
Forms, Guest Questionnaire	Mult. Depts.	Printing & Stationery
Forms, Guest Suggestion	Mult. Depts.	Printing & Stationery
Forms, Payroll and Tax	A&G	Printing & Stationery
Forms, Printed	Mult. Depts.	Printing & Stationery
Fountain Pens for Use by Guests in Rooms	Rooms	Guest Supplies
Frames, Art	Mult. Depts.	Operating Supplies

Item Name	Department/ Schedule	Account Name
Franchise Fee (Chain Royalty)	Sales & Marketing	Franchise Fees
Freight & Shipping Charged to Banquet Customer	Food	Misc. Cost of Other Rev.
Freight Charges (Marketing)	Sales & Marketing	P&ODC
Freight Charges (Non-Marketing)	A&G	P&ODC
Frequent Flyer Programs	Sales & Marketing	Loyalty Progs./Aff. Fees
Frequent Guest Programs	Sales & Marketing	Loyalty Progs./Aff. Fees
Fruit	Food	Cost of Food Sales
Fruit Baskets Gratis to Customers	Mult. Depts.	Comp. Services & Gifts
Fuel Costs, Auto (Guest Transport)	Rooms	Guest Transportation
Fuel Costs, Cart (Guest Transport)	Rooms	Guest Transportation
Fuel for Cooking, Employee Cafeteria	Empl. Caf.	Kitchen Fuel
Fuel, Kitchen	Food	Kitchen Fuel
Fumigation	POM	Contract Services
Fumigators, Kitchen/Restaurant	Food	Contract Services
Furniture Polish	Mult. Depts.	Cleaning Supplies
Furniture Refinishing	POM	Furniture & Equip.
Furniture Repairs	POM	Furniture & Equip.
Furniture Wax	Mult. Depts.	Cleaning Supplies
Garage Licenses	Parking Garage ..	Licenses & Permits
Garbage Bags	Mult. Depts.	Operating Supplies
Garbage Can Liners	Mult. Depts.	Operating Supplies
Garbage Cans	Mult. Depts.	Operating Supplies
Gas for Cooking	Food	Kitchen Fuel
Gas for Cooking, Employee Cafeteria	Empl. Caf.	Kitchen Fuel
Gas for Utilities	Utility Costs	Gas
Gasoline, Motor Vehicles (Company and Employee Use)	Mult. Depts.	Operating Supplies
Gasoline and Lubricants, Golf Cart	Golf/Pro Shop . . .	Gasoline & Lubricants
Gasoline and Lubricants, Mowers (Golf Course) .	Golf/Pro Shop . . .	Gasoline & Lubricants
Gasoline and Lubricants, Tractors/Trucks (Golf Course)	Golf/Pro Shop . . .	Gasoline & Lubricants
Gasoline for Food Delivery Vehicle	Food	Operating Supplies
Generator Rentals (Property Power Back-Up) . . .	POM	Equip. Rental
Generator Repairs	POM	Elec. & Mech.
Geothermal Power	Utility Costs	Other Fuels
Gideon Bibles	Rooms	Operating Supplies
Gifts to Customers	Mult. Depts.	Comp. Services & Gifts
Glass Bags	Rooms	Operating Supplies
Glass Bowls	Food	China

Item Name	Department/ Schedule	Account Name
Glass Cleaner	Mult. Depts.	Cleaning Supplies
Glass Covers	Rooms	Operating Supplies
Glass Dishes	Food	China
Glass Racks	Food	Operating Supplies
Glasses, Drinking (Alcoholic Beverage/All Sizes & Materials)	Beverage	Glassware
Glasses, Drinking (Non-Alcoholic/All Sizes & Materials)	Food	Glassware
Glassware (All Types) for Use by Guests in Rooms	Rooms	Operating Supplies
Glassware Rental	Food	Glassware
Glassware, Employee Cafeteria	Empl. Caf.	Glassware
Gloves, Golf (for Sale)	Golf/Pro Shop	Cost of Merch. Sales
Gloves, Rubber	Mult. Depts.	Cleaning Supplies
Glue	Mult. Depts.	Operating Supplies
Goldfish	Mult. Depts.	Operating Supplies
Golf Bags (for Rental)	Golf/Pro Shop	Operating Supplies
Golf Bags (for Sale)	Golf/Pro Shop	Cost of Merch. Sales
Golf Balls (for Sale)	Golf/Pro Shop	Cost of Merch. Sales
Golf Balls (Practice Range)	Golf/Pro Shop	Operating Supplies
Golf Cart Batteries	Golf/Pro Shop	Golf Cart Batteries/Elec.
Golf Cart Rental	Golf/Pro Shop	Equip. Rental
Golf Cart Repairs & Maintenance	Golf/Pro Shop	Golf Cart Repairs & Maint.
Golf Clubs (for Rental)	Golf/Pro Shop	Operating Supplies
Golf Clubs (for Sale)	Golf/Pro Shop	Cost of Merch. Sales
Gratis Food, Bar	Beverage	Comp. Services & Gifts
Gross Receipt Taxes Not Paid by Customers, State/County/City	R/POT/I	B/TO Taxes
Guest Checks	Food or Beverage	Printing & Stationery
Guest Comment Cards	Mult. Depts.	Printing & Stationery
Guest Guide	Rooms	Printing & Stationery
Guest Loyalty Programs	Sales & Marketing	Loyalty Progs./Aff. Fees
Guest Questionnaire Forms	Mult. Depts.	Printing & Stationery
Guest Relocation Due to Lack of Room Availability	Rooms	Guest Relocation
Guest Suggestion Forms	Mult. Depts.	Printing & Stationery
Guest Transportation Service Contracts	Rooms	Guest Transportation
Gum Remover	Mult. Depts.	Cleaning Supplies
Gym Equipment (Non-Capital)	Health Club/Spa	Athletic Supplies

Item Name	Department/ Schedule	Account Name
Hair Dryers	Rooms	Operating Supplies
Hair Nets for Food Service Employees	Food	Operating Supplies
Hair Nets for Use by Guests in Rooms	Rooms	Guest Supplies
Hair Pins for Use by Guests in Rooms	Rooms	Guest Supplies
Hair Spray for Use by Guests in Rooms	Rooms	Guest Supplies
Hairbrushes for Use by Guests in Rooms	Rooms	Guest Supplies
Hamper, Laundry	House Laundry	Operating Supplies
Hand Lotion	Rooms	Guest Supplies
Hand Sanitizer	Rooms	Guest Supplies
Hand Soap for Use by Guests in Rooms	Rooms	Guest Supplies
Hand Towels	Rooms	Linen
Hangers (All Types)	Rooms	Operating Supplies
Hats, Uniform	Mult. Depts.	Uniforms
Hazardous Materials Remediation	POM	Life/Safety
HBO	Rooms	Cable/Satellite Television
Health Permits	Food or Beverage	Licenses & Permits
Heat Pump Repairs	POM	HVAC Equip.
Heating System Repairs	POM	HVAC Equip.
Help Wanted Ads	A&G	Human Resources
High Chairs	Mult. Depts.	Operating Supplies
Hole Punch	Mult. Depts.	Operating Supplies
Hooks, Coat	Mult. Depts.	Operating Supplies
Hooks, Door	Mult. Depts.	Operating Supplies
Hot Chocolate Packets for Use by Guests in Rooms	Rooms	Guest Supplies
Hotel Association Dues (Marketing)	Sales & Marketing	Dues & Subscriptions
Hotel Association Dues (Non-Marketing)	A&G	Dues & Subscriptions
Hotel Maps	Rooms	Printing & Stationery
Hotel Sales & Marketing Association Dues	Sales & Marketing	Dues & Subscriptions
Housekeeper Carts	Rooms	Operating Supplies
Housekeeping Reports	Rooms	Printing & Stationery
Housing, Employee	A&G	Human Resources
Humidifier	Rooms	Operating Supplies
Ice Buckets and Liners	Rooms	Operating Supplies
Ice Buckets and Liners	Food or Beverage	Operating Supplies
Ice Carvings/Sculpture	Food	Decorations
Ice Consumption	Food or Beverage	Ice
Ice Tongs	Food	Utensils
Ice Tongs for Use by Guests in Rooms	Rooms	Operating Supplies
Inflatable Beds	Rooms	Operating Supplies

Item Name	Department/ Schedule	Account Name
In-House Video, Welcome Channel	Sales & Marketing	Media
Ink	Mult. Depts.	Operating Supplies
Ink Cartridges	Mult. Depts.	Operating Supplies
Innkeepers Liability Card Frames	Rooms	Operating Supplies
Innkeepers Liability Cards	Rooms	Printing & Stationery
In-Room Guest Account Services (Check-Out) ...	Rooms	Contract Services
Insecticides	Mult. Depts.	Cleaning Supplies
Insecticides, Golf Course	Golf/Pro Shop ...	Grounds M&L
Inspection Fees, Boilers	POM	Licenses & Permits
Inspection Fees, Elevators	POM	Licenses & Permits
Inspection Fees, Escalators	POM	Licenses & Permits
Inspection Fees for Licensing	Mult. Depts.	Licenses & Permits
Inspection Fees, Life/Safety System	POM	Licenses & Permits
Instructor Fees, Training	Mult. Depts.	Training
Insurance Deductibles, Liability/Burglary, Theft, Umbrella	R/POT/I	Liability
Insurance Deductibles, Property	R/POT/I	Building & Contents
Insurance Expenses, Boiler Explosion	R/POT/I	Building & Contents
Insurance Expenses, Building	R/POT/I	Building & Contents
Insurance Expenses, Burglary	R/POT/I	Liability
Insurance Expenses, Business Interruption	R/POT/I	Building & Contents
Insurance Expenses, Earthquake	R/POT/I	Building & Contents
Insurance Expenses, Fire	R/POT/I	Building & Contents
Insurance Expenses, Furnishings and Equipment	R/POT/I	Building & Contents
Insurance Expenses, Guest Liability	R/POT/I	Liability
Insurance Expenses, Liability	R/POT/I	Liability
Insurance Expenses, Property	R/POT/I	Building & Contents
Insurance Expenses, Theft	R/POT/I	Liability
Insurance Expenses, Tornado	R/POT/I	Building & Contents
Insurance Expenses, Umbrella	R/POT/I	Liability
Insurance Expenses, Weather	R/POT/I	Building & Contents
Internal Audit Expense	A&G	Audit Charges
Internal Audit Fees (Chain Properties)	A&G	Audit Charges
Internet Access Costs	Telecom.	Costs of Internet Service
Internet Advertising	Sales & Marketing	Media
Internet Connection Fees	Mult. Depts.	Telecommunications
Internet Telephone Charges (Staff)	Mult. Depts.	Telecommunications
Internet Web Page, Reservations	Rooms	Reservations
Interview Expenses	A&G	Human Resources
Investigation of Employees	A&G	Human Resources

Item Name	Department/ Schedule	Account Name
Iron	Rooms	Operating Supplies
Ironing Board Covers	Rooms	Operating Supplies
Ironing Board Holders	Rooms	Operating Supplies
Ironing Boards	Rooms	Operating Supplies
Irrigation System Repairs	POM	Grounds M&L
Jackets, Uniform	Mult. Depts.	Uniforms
Jumpers, Uniform	Mult. Depts.	Uniforms
Key Blank	POM	Building
Key Cards	Rooms	Operating Supplies
Key Chain Coil	Mult. Depts.	Operating Supplies
Key Chain Reel	Mult. Depts.	Operating Supplies
Key Lock Box	Mult. Depts.	Operating Supplies
Key Rings	Mult. Depts.	Operating Supplies
Key Tags	Mult. Depts.	Operating Supplies
Keyboard Drawers	Mult. Depts.	Operating Supplies
Keyboards, Computer	A&G	Information Systems
Keys	POM	Building
Keys, Safe Deposit Box	Rooms	Operating Supplies
Kitchen Equipment Repairs	POM	Kitchen Equip.
Kitchen Hood Cleaning	Food	Contract Services
Kitchen Refrigeration Repair	POM	Kitchen Equip.
Knife Sharpening	Food	Contract Services
Knives, Kitchen	Food	Utensils
Label Maker	Mult. Depts.	Operating Supplies
Label Maker Supplies	Mult. Depts.	Operating Supplies
Ladles, Kitchen	Food	Utensils
Lamp Finials	POM	Furniture & Equip.
Lamp Repairs	POM	Furniture & Equip.
Lamp Shades	Mult. Depts.	Operating Supplies
Land Lease	R/POT/I	Land & Buildings
Landscaping Service (Indoor and Outdoor)	POM	Grounds M&L
Laptop Computers	A&G	Information Systems
Laundry Bags (Cloth) for Use by Guests in Rooms	Rooms	Operating Supplies
Laundry Bags (Disposable) for Use by Guests in Rooms	Rooms	Guest Supplies
Laundry Carts	House Laundry	Operating Supplies
Laundry Chemicals	House Laundry	Laundry Supplies
Laundry Costs, Non-Guest (In-House Laundry)	Mult. Depts.	Laundry & Dry Cleaning
Laundry, Dryer Repairs	POM	Laundry Equip.

Item Name	Department/ Schedule	Account Name
Laundry, Hamper	House Laundry	Operating Supplies
Laundry, Ironer Repairs	POM	Laundry Equip.
Laundry Services, Non-Guest (Outside Laundry)	Mult. Depts.	Laundry & Dry Cleaning
Laundry, Sheet Folder Repairs	POM	Laundry Equip.
Laundry Soap	House Laundry	Laundry Supplies
Laundry Soap Packets	House Laundry	Laundry Supplies
Laundry Tags	House Laundry	Operating Supplies
Laundry, Washer Repairs	POM	Laundry Equip.
Legal Fees/Expenses for Collections	A&G	Credit & Collections
Legal Fees/Expenses Other than Collections	A&G	Legal Services
Legal Fees/Expenses, Real Estate Taxes	R/POT/I	Real Estate Taxes
Lemon Oil	Mult. Depts.	Cleaning Supplies
Letters for Bulletin/Sign Boards	A&G	Operating Supplies
Licenses, Beverage	Beverage	Licenses & Permits
Licenses, Cabaret	Beverage	Licenses & Permits
Licenses, Checkrooms	Food or Beverage	Licenses & Permits
Licenses, Elevators	POM	Licenses & Permits
Licenses, Engineering	POM	Licenses & Permits
Licenses, Health Permit	Food or Beverage	Licenses & Permits
Licenses, Locksmith	POM	Licenses & Permits
Licenses, Music Copyright	Food or Beverage	Licenses & Permits
Licenses, Temporary Space Liquor	Beverage	Licenses & Permits
Light Fixture Repairs	POM	Elec. & Mech.
Limousine Services, Guest (No Charge)	Rooms	Guest Transportation
Limousine, Employee Use	A&G	Transportation
Line for Computer/Fax/Modem	Mult. Depts.	Telecommunications
Linen Cleaning (All Types)	Food	Laundry & Dry Cleaning
Linen Napkins	Food	Linen
Linen Rental	Mult. Depts.	Linen
Linen Rental (All Types)	Food	Linen
Linen Tablecloth	Food	Linen
Linen, Employee Cafeteria	Empl. Caf.	Linen
Liners, Drapery	Mult. Depts.	Operating Supplies
Liners, Paper	Food	Paper & Plastics
Lint Brush	Mult. Depts.	Cleaning Supplies
Lint Remover	Mult. Depts.	Cleaning Supplies
Liquid Soap for Use by Guests in Rooms	Rooms	Guest Supplies
Liquor	Beverage	Cost of Beverage Sales
Literature, Educational for Employees	A&G	Training
Litigation Settlement Costs, Contract Disputes	A&G	Settlement Costs
Litigation Settlement Costs, EEOC	A&G	Settlement Costs

Item Name	Department/ Schedule	Account Name
Litigation Settlement Costs, Non-Insured	A&G	Settlement Costs
Local Call Cost (Departmental)	Mult. Depts.	Telecommunications
Local Call Usage Expense	Telecom.	Cost of Local Calls
Lock Repairs/Service	POM	Building
Lodging of Employees	A&G	Human Resources
Log Books	Mult. Depts.	Operating Supplies
Log Books, Outlet Reservations	Food	Operating Supplies
Long Distance Call Cost (Departmental)	Mult. Depts.	Telecommunications
Long Distance Call Usage Expense	Telecom.	Cost of Long Distance Calls
Lost and Damaged Articles (Guest)	A&G	Loss & Damage
Lost and Found Reports	A&G	Printing & Stationery
Lotions, Health Club/Spa	Health Club/Spa	Health & Beauty Products
Lotions, Health Club/Spa (for Sale)	Health Club/Spa	Cost of Merch. Sales
Luggage Racks	Rooms	Operating Supplies
Luggage Tags for Use by Guests in Rooms	Rooms	Guest Supplies
Lye	Mult. Depts.	Cleaning Supplies
Machine Stands	A&G	Operating Supplies
Magazine Advertising	Sales & Marketing	Media
Magazine Subscriptions	Mult. Depts.	Dues & Subscriptions
Magazines for Use by Guests in Rooms	Rooms	Guest Supplies
Magazines, Golf (for Sale)	Golf/Pro Shop	Cost of Merch. Sales
Magazines, Golf (for Staff Use)	Golf/Pro Shop	Dues & Subscriptions
Magazines, Trade (Marketing)	Sales & Marketing	Dues & Subscriptions
Magazines, Trade (Non-Marketing)	A&G	Dues & Subscriptions
Mail Bags	A&G	Operating Supplies
Mail Chute Rentals	A&G	Operating Supplies
Mailing Lists	Sales & Marketing	Direct Mail
Maintenance Contracts, Electric Signs	POM	Elec. & Mech.
Maintenance Contracts, Elevators	POM	Elevators & Escalators
Maintenance Contracts, Escalators	POM	Elevators & Escalators
Maintenance Contracts, Office Equipment	POM	Elec. & Mech.
Maintenance Request Forms	POM	Printing & Stationery
Makeup Mirror	Rooms	Operating Supplies
Makeup Remover for Use by Guests in Rooms	Rooms	Guest Supplies
Management Company Expenses (Travel, Entertainment, etc.)	Mult. Depts.	Corp. Office Reimb.
Management Fee, Fixed	Mgt. Fees	Management Fees
Management Fee, Incentive	Mgt. Fees	Management Fees
Management Fee, Percentage of Revenue/Profit	Mgt. Fees	Management Fees

Item Name	Department/Schedule	Account Name
Management Fee, Specific Department	Mult. Depts.	Management Fees
Mangle Belts	POM	Laundry Equip.
Manuals, Instructional	Mult. Depts.	Training
Manuals, Service (Instructional Materials)	POM	Operating Supplies
Manuals, Training	Mult. Depts.	Training
Maps	Rooms	Printing & Stationery
Markers (Flip Chart)	Food	Operating Supplies
Marketing Service Fees	Sales & Marketing	Outside Sales Rep.
Marking Ink	Mult. Depts.	Operating Supplies
Matches for Customer Use	Mult. Depts.	Operating Supplies
Mats, Floor	POM	Operating Supplies
Mats, Floor	Mult. Depts.	Operating Supplies
Mats, Rubber	POM	Operating Supplies
Mats, Rubber (Bar)	Beverage	Operating Supplies
Mattress Cover	Rooms	Linen
Mattress, Crib	Rooms	Operating Supplies
Mattress Pad	Rooms	Linen
Mattress Protectors	Rooms	Operating Supplies
Mattress Repair	POM	Furniture & Equip.
Meals, Business Expense	Mult. Depts.	Travel—Meals & Enter.
Meals, Employees (Cost of Food)	Empl. Caf.	Cost of Food
Meals, Entertainment	Sales & Marketing	Travel—Meals & Enter.
Meals and Entertainment, Outside	Mult. Depts.	Travel—Meals & Enter.
Meals, Musicians and Entertainers	Food or Beverage	Music & Enter.
Meat	Food	Cost of Food Sales
Media, Magazines	Sales & Marketing	Media
Media, Newspapers	Sales & Marketing	Media
Media, Other	Sales & Marketing	Media
Media, TV	Sales & Marketing	Media
Medical Supplies and Drugs for Employees	A&G	Human Resources
Meeting Planner Surveys (Outside Service)	Sales & Marketing	Contract Services
Membership Dues, Associations (Marketing)	Sales & Marketing	Dues & Subscriptions
Membership Dues, Associations (Non-Marketing)	A&G	Dues & Subscriptions
Membership Fees, Professional Organizations	Mult. Depts.	Dues & Subscriptions
Memo Pads	Mult. Depts.	Operating Supplies
Menu Covers (Food or Beverage)	Food or Beverage	Menus & Beverage Lists
Menu Design (Food or Beverage)	Food or Beverage	Menus & Beverage Lists
Menu Printing (Food or Beverage)	Food or Beverage	Menus & Beverage Lists
Microfiche Supplies	A&G	Operating Supplies

Item Name	Department/ Schedule	Account Name
Microwave, Guestroom	Rooms	Operating Supplies
Mileage Reimbursement	Mult. Depts.	Travel—Other
Mini-Blinds	Mult. Depts.	Operating Supplies
Mints, Guest (Restaurant)	Food	Comp. Services & Gifts
Mixers for Alcoholic Beverages	Beverage	Cost of Beverage Sales
Mixing Bowls	Food	Utensils
Mixing Cans, Bar	Beverage	Utensils
Modem Lines	A&G	Information Systems
Modems	A&G	Information Systems
Molds	Food	Utensils
Mop Buckets	Mult. Depts.	Cleaning Supplies
Mop Handles	Mult. Depts.	Cleaning Supplies
Mop Wringers	Mult. Depts.	Cleaning Supplies
Mops	Mult. Depts.	Cleaning Supplies
Motor Repairs	POM	Elec. & Mech.
Mouse, Computer	Mult. Depts.	Operating Supplies
Mouse Pads	Mult. Depts.	Operating Supplies
Mouse Traps	Rooms	Operating Supplies
Mouthwash for Use by Guests in Rooms	Rooms	Guest Supplies
Mowers, Tractors, and Trucks Maintenance—Golf	Golf/Pro Shop	Grounds M&L
Mugs, Coffee, for Use by Guests in Rooms	Rooms	Operating Supplies
Music, Health Club/Spa	Health Club/Spa	Ambience
Music Licenses	Food or Beverage	Licenses & Permits
Music, Live Musicians	Food or Beverage	Music & Enter.
Music, Mechanical	Food or Beverage	Music & Enter.
Music on Hold Service	Telecom.	Contract Services
Nail Polish Remover for Use by Guests in Rooms	Rooms	Guest Supplies
Name Badges	Mult. Depts.	Operating Supplies
Napkins (Paper/Cloth) for Use by Guests in Rooms	Rooms	Operating Supplies
Napkins, Cocktail	Beverage	Paper & Plastics
Napkins, Linen	Food	Linen
Napkins, Paper	Food	Paper & Plastics
Newsletter, House (for Employees)	A&G	Human Resources
Newsletters	Sales & Marketing	Direct Mail
Newspaper Bags for Use by Guests in Rooms	Rooms	Guest Supplies
Newspapers for Use by Guests in Rooms	Rooms	Guest Supplies
Night Lights	Rooms	Operating Supplies
Notary Fees	A&G	Professional Fees
Notary Fees, Collection of Accounts	A&G	Credit & Collection

Item Name	Department/ Schedule	Account Name
Office Supplies, General	Mult. Depts.	Operating Supplies
Oil (for Utility Use)	Utility Costs	Oil
Openers, Can	Food	Utensils
Orientation Expenses	Mult. Depts.	Training
Outdoor Advertising	Sales & Marketing	Outdoor
Outlet Safety Plugs	Mult. Depts.	Operating Supplies
Overages & Shortages, Cash	A&G	Cash Overages & Shortages
Overalls, Uniform	Mult. Depts.	Uniforms
Overnight Delivery (Marketing)	Sales & Marketing	P&ODC
Overnight Delivery (Non-Marketing)	A&G	P&ODC
Owners Expenses (Travel, Entertainment, etc.)	A&G	Corp. Office Reimb.
Oxalic Acid	Mult. Depts.	Cleaning Supplies
Packing Tape	Mult. Depts.	Operating Supplies
Pager Rental	Mult. Depts.	Telecommunications
Pagers	Mult. Depts.	Telecommunications
Pails	Mult. Depts.	Cleaning Supplies
Pain Relievers	Mult. Depts.	Operating Supplies
Paint	POM	Painting & Decorating
Paint Brushes/Rollers	POM	Painting & Decorating
Paint Sprayer Rental	POM	Equip. Rental
Paint Thinner	POM	Painting & Decorating
Painting, Contracted	POM	Painting & Decorating
Pamphlets, Educational or Instructional (for Employees)	Mult. Depts.	Training
Pans, Baking, Broiling, Frying	Food	Utensils
Pants, Uniform	Mult. Depts.	Uniforms
Paper Clips	Mult. Depts.	Operating Supplies
Paper Liners	Mult. Depts.	Operating Supplies
Paper Plates/Cups/Napkins/Tablecloths	Food	Paper & Plastics
Paper Plates/Cups/Napkins/Tablecloths, Employee Cafeteria	Empl. Caf.	Paper & Plastics
Paper Towel Holders, Guestroom	Rooms	Operating Supplies
Paper Towels, Guestroom	Rooms	Operating Supplies
Paper Tray Liners, Rooms	Rooms	Operating Supplies
Paper, Copier/Printer	Mult. Depts.	Operating Supplies
Parchment	Mult. Depts.	Operating Supplies
Parking, Gate Tickets	Parking Garage	Printing & Stationery
Parking, Gratis F&B Guest	Food or Beverage	Comp. Services & Gifts
Parking, Permit Cards	Mult. Depts.	Printing & Stationery

Item Name	Department/ Schedule	Account Name
Parking, Violation Stickers	Mult. Depts.	Printing & Stationery
Paste	Mult. Depts.	Operating Supplies
Payroll Processing Fees	A&G	Payroll Processing
Payroll, 401(k) Costs	Mult. Depts.	Employee Benefits
Payroll, Bonus Pay (Discretionary)	Mult. Depts.	Supplemental Pay
Payroll, Bonus Pay (Performance-Based)	Mult. Depts.	Bonus & Incentives
Payroll, Child Care, Employee	Mult. Depts.	Employee Benefits
Payroll, City Head Tax	Mult. Depts.	Payroll Taxes
Payroll, Disability Pay	Mult. Depts.	Employee Benefits
Payroll, Employee Functions	A&G	Salaries & Wages
Payroll, Federal Unemployment Tax	Mult. Depts.	Payroll Taxes
Payroll, FICA Tax	Mult. Depts.	Payroll Taxes
Payroll, Health & Dental Insurance	Mult. Depts.	Employee Benefits
Payroll, Holiday Pay	Mult. Depts.	Supplemental Pay
Payroll, Hourly Wages	Mult. Depts.	Salaries & Wages
Payroll, Incentive Pay (Discretionary)	Mult. Depts.	Supplemental Pay
Payroll, Incentive Pay (Performance-Based)	Mult. Depts.	Bonus & Incentives
Payroll, Jury Duty Pay	Mult. Depts.	Supplemental Pay
Payroll, Leased labor	Mult. Depts.	Salaries & Wages
Payroll, Life Insurance	Mult. Depts.	Employee Benefits
Payroll, Long-Term Disability	Mult. Depts.	Employee Benefits
Payroll, Meals (Cost Allocation from Employee Cafeteria)	Mult. Depts.	Employee Benefits
Payroll, Paid Time Off	Mult. Depts.	Supplemental Pay
Payroll, Pension Costs	Mult. Depts.	Employee Benefits
Payroll, Profit Sharing	Mult. Depts.	Employee Benefits
Payroll, Relocation Pay	Mult. Depts.	Supplemental Pay
Payroll, Salaried Wages	Mult. Depts.	Salaries & Wages
Payroll, Severance Pay	Mult. Depts.	Supplemental Pay
Payroll, Sick Pay	Mult. Depts.	Supplemental Pay
Payroll, State Disability Insurance	Mult. Depts.	Payroll Taxes
Payroll, State Unemployment Tax	Mult. Depts.	Payroll Taxes
Payroll, Union Benefits (All)	Mult. Depts.	Employee Benefits
Payroll, Vacation Pay	Mult. Depts.	Supplemental Pay
Payroll, Workers' Compensation Insurance	Mult. Depts.	Employee Benefits
Pencil Holders	Mult. Depts.	Operating Supplies
Pencil Sharpeners	Mult. Depts.	Operating Supplies
Pencils	Mult. Depts.	Operating Supplies
Pens	Mult. Depts.	Operating Supplies
Personal Computer, Lease (Non-Capital)	R/POT/I	IS Equip.

Item Name	Department/ Schedule	Account Name
Personal Property Tax Refunds (Contra), State/ County/City	R/POT/I	Personal Property Taxes
Personal Property Taxes, State/County/City	R/POT/I	Personal Property Taxes
Personnel Forms, General	A&G	Human Resources
Pest Control, Golf Course	Golf/Pro Shop	Contract Services
Pest Control, Services	POM	Contract Services
Pest Control, Supplies (In-House Use)	POM	Engineering Supplies
Petty Cash Forms	A&G	Printing & Stationery
Phone Books for Guestrooms	Rooms	Operating Supplies
Physician's Fees, Employees (Non–Workers' Compensation)	A&G	Human Resources
Physician's Fees, Employees (Workers' Compensation)	Mult. Depts.	Employee Benefits
Piano Rental (Lounge/Restaurant Entertainment)	Food or Beverage	Music & Enter.
Piano Tuning	Food or Beverage	Contract Services
Pillow Cases	Rooms	Linen
Pillow Mints	Rooms	Guest Supplies
Pillow Shams	Rooms	Linen
Pillows, Down, Foam, Polyester, Neck, Decorative Throw	Rooms	Linen
Pins, Employee	Mult. Depts.	Operating Supplies
Pins, Push	Mult. Depts.	Operating Supplies
Pins, Safety	Mult. Depts.	Operating Supplies
Pins, Stick	Mult. Depts.	Operating Supplies
Pins, Straight	Mult. Depts.	Operating Supplies
Pitchers, Guestrooms	Rooms	Operating Supplies
Pitchers, Water	Food	China
Placards	Mult. Depts.	Operating Supplies
Placemats, Guestrooms	Rooms	Operating Supplies
Plant Purchases (Indoor and Outdoor)	POM	Grounds M&L
Plant Rentals	POM	Grounds M&L
Plant Services (Watering, etc.)	POM	Contract Services
Plants	Mult. Depts.	Operating Supplies
Plants and Shrubs, Golf Course	Golf/Pro Shop	Grounds M&L
Plaster Repairs	POM	Building
Plastic Flatware	Food	Paper & Plastics
Plastic Flatware, Employee Cafeteria	Empl. Caf.	Paper & Plastics
Plastic Food Storage Containers	Food	Paper & Plastics
Plastic Spray Bottles	Mult. Depts.	Cleaning Supplies
Plastic Wrap	Food	Paper & Plastics

Item Name	Department/Schedule	Account Name
Plate Cover, Dome	Food	Utensils
Plates, All Sizes & Materials (Except Paper/Plastic)	Food	China
Plates, All Sizes & Materials (Except Paper/Plastic), Employee Cafeteria	Empl. Caf.	China
Plates, Paper/Plastic	Food	Paper & Plastics
Plates, Paper/Plastic, Employee Cafeteria	Empl. Caf.	Paper & Plastics
Platform Lift/Cherry Picker Rental	POM	Equip. Rental
Platters, Serving	Food	China
Playing Cards for Use by Guests in Rooms	Rooms	Guest Supplies
Playpens	Rooms	Operating Supplies
Plumbing Fixture Repairs	POM	Plumbing
Plungers, Toilet	Rooms	Operating Supplies
PMS Hardware Lease (Non-Capital)	R/POT/I	IS Equip.
PMS Software Lease (Non-Capital)	R/POT/I	IS Equip.
PMS System Maintenance	A&G	Information Systems
Pocket Thermometers	Food	Utensils
Polish	Mult. Depts.	Cleaning Supplies
Portable Fans	Mult. Depts.	Operating Supplies
Portable Sanitary Facilities, Golf Tournament	Golf/Pro Shop	Tournament Expenses
Portable Steam Cleaners	Mult. Depts.	Operating Supplies
POS Hardware Lease (Non-Capital)	R/POT/I	IS Equip.
POS Promotional Materials	Sales & Marketing	In-House Graphics
POS Software Lease (Non-Capital)	R/POT/I	IS Equip.
POS Supplies	Food or Beverage	Printing & Stationery
POS System Maintenance	A&G	Information Systems
Post Cards for Use by Guests in Rooms	Rooms	Guest Supplies
Post Office Box Rental	A&G	P&ODC
Postage for Promotional Mailings	Sales & Marketing	Direct Mail
Postage (Marketing)	Sales & Marketing	P&ODC
Postage (Non-Marketing)	A&G	P&ODC
Postage Meter Rentals (Marketing)	Sales & Marketing	P&ODC
Postage Meter Rentals (Non-Marketing)	A&G	P&ODC
Poster Board	Mult. Depts.	Printing & Stationery
Posters, Safety	A&G	Human Resources
Post-it Notes	Mult. Depts.	Printing & Stationery
Potholder Mitt, Guestroom	Rooms	Operating Supplies
Potholder, Guestroom	Rooms	Operating Supplies
Pots	Food	Utensils
Pour Spouts, Liquor	Beverage	Utensils

Item Name	Department/ Schedule	Account Name
Presentation Binders	A&G	Operating Supplies
Presto Logs, Guestroom	Rooms	Operating Supplies
Printed Forms	Mult. Depts.	Printing & Stationery
Printer Paper	Mult. Depts.	Printing & Stationery
Printer Supplies and Accessories	Mult. Depts.	Operating Supplies
Printing Calculator	Mult. Depts.	Operating Supplies
Prizes, Employee	A&G	Human Resources
Prizes, Golf Tournament	Golf/Pro Shop	Tournament Expenses
Production, Magazines	Sales & Marketing	Media
Production, Newspapers	Sales & Marketing	Media
Production, Other	Sales & Marketing	Media
Production, TV	Sales & Marketing	Media
Professional Dues (Marketing)	Sales & Marketing	Dues & Subscriptions
Professional Dues (Non-Marketing)	A&G	Dues & Subscriptions
Professional Fees	A&G	Professional Fees
Professional Services, Contract Golf Pro	Golf/Pro Shop	Professional Fees
Professional Services, Contract Groundskeepers	Golf/Pro Shop	Professional Fees
Promotional Vouchers	Sales & Marketing	Promotion
Propane, Cooking & Preparation	Food	Kitchen Fuel
Propane, Utility Use	Utility Costs	Other Fuels
Props, Banquets	Food or Beverage	Operating Supplies
Protective Service	A&G	Security
Provision for Doubtful Accounts	A&G	Prov. for Doubtful Accts.
Public Address System Repairs	POM	Elec. & Mech.
Public Area Cleaning Service, Lobby/Guestroom Corridors	Rooms	Contract Services
Public Area Cleaning Service, Restaurant/Banquet Foyers	Food or Beverage	Contract Services
Public Relations Service Fees	Sales & Marketing	Outside Sales Rep.
Public Restroom Cleaning Service	Food or Beverage	Contract Services
Publications, House (for Employees)	Mult. Depts.	Training
Pull Carts, Golf (for Rental)	Golf/Pro Shop	Operating Supplies
Pull Carts, Golf (for Sale)	Golf/Pro Shop	Cost of Merch. Sales
Pump Repairs	POM	Elec. & Mech.
Purchasing Service Fees	Mult. Depts.	Contract Services
Q-Tips	Mult. Depts.	Operating Supplies
Quilt	Rooms	Linen
Quilt Rack	Rooms	Operating Supplies
Radio Communications	Mult. Depts.	Telecommunications
Radios, Guestroom	Rooms	Operating Supplies

Item Name	Department/ Schedule	Account Name
Rags, Cleaning	Mult. Depts.	Cleaning Supplies
Ramekins (All Materials)	Food	China
Razors for Use by Guests in Rooms	Rooms	Guest Supplies
Real Property Tax Refunds (Contra), State/ County/City	R/POT/I	Real Estate Taxes
Real Property Taxes, State/County/City	R/POT/I	Real Estate Taxes
Record Books	Mult. Depts.	Operating Supplies
Recorders, Mini/Micro Cassette and Accessories	Mult. Depts.	Operating Supplies
Recycle Bins	Mult. Depts.	Operating Supplies
Reference Checking, Employee	A&G	Human Resources
Referral Program	Sales & Marketing	Loyalty Progs./Aff. Fees
Refrigeration Supplies (HVAC)	POM	HVAC Equip.
Refrigerator Repairs, Kitchen	POM	Kitchen Equip.
Registered Cable/Telex Address	Sales & Marketing	Telecommunications
Rent, Temporary Parking Space	Parking Garage	Rent
Rentals, Linen	Mult. Depts.	Linen
Rentals, Piano (Lounge/Restaurant Entertainment)	Food or Beverage	Music & Enter.
Rentals, Table (Banquet Not Charged to Customer)	Food	Banquet Expense
Rentals, Truck (Food Delivery)	Food	Equip. Rental
Repairs and Maintenance, Golf Cart Paths	Golf/Pro Shop	Grounds M&L
Repairs and Maintenance, Golf Half-Way House/ Restrooms	POM	Building
Repairs and Maintenance, Golf Storage Areas	POM	Building
Repairs, Uniforms	Mult. Depts.	Uniforms
Replacement of Window Glass	POM	Building
Report Covers	A&G	Operating Supplies
Reports	Mult. Depts.	Operating Supplies
Representation Firms, Convention	Sales & Marketing	Contract Services
Reseeding Golf Course	Golf/Pro Shop	Grounds M&L
Reservation Books	Food	Operating Supplies
Reservation Fees (Chain Assessment)	Rooms	Reservations
Reservation Fees (GDS)	Rooms	Reservations
Reservation Telephone Expense	Rooms	Reservations
Reservation Web Site Building and Maintenance	Rooms	Reservations
Ribbons, Typewriter, Calculator, Cash Register	Mult. Depts.	Operating Supplies
Ring Binders	A&G	Operating Supplies
Robes	Rooms	Linen
Robes, Health Club/Spa	Health Club/Spa	Linen

Item Name	Department/Schedule	Account Name
Rollaway Beds	Rooms	Operating Supplies
Roller Shades	Mult. Depts.	Operating Supplies
Roman Shades	Mult. Depts.	Operating Supplies
Room Attendant Reports	Rooms	Printing & Stationery
Room Charges, Travel	Mult. Depts.	Travel—Other
Room Costs, Musicians and Entertainers	Food or Beverage	Music & Enter.
Room Directories	Rooms	Printing & Stationery
Room Directory Binders	Rooms	Printing & Stationery
Room Rack Forms	Rooms	Printing & Stationery
Room Service Breakfast Card	Rooms	Printing & Stationery
Royalties for Use of Third-Party Brand Name	Mult. Depts.	Royalty Fees
Rubber Bands	Mult. Depts.	Operating Supplies
Rubber Boots, Kitchen	Food	Operating Supplies
Rubber Cement	Mult. Depts.	Operating Supplies
Rubber Gloves	Mult. Depts.	Cleaning Supplies
Rubber Sheets	Rooms	Linen
Rubber Stamps	Mult. Depts.	Operating Supplies
Rubber Tub Mat	Rooms	Operating Supplies
Rug Cleaners	Mult. Depts.	Cleaning Supplies
Rug Cleaning Services	Mult. Depts.	Contract Services
Rugs, Bathroom	Rooms	Linen
Rugs, Throw	Mult. Depts.	Operating Supplies
Rulers	Mult. Depts.	Operating Supplies
Safe Deposit Box Keys	Rooms	Operating Supplies
Safe Deposit Box Rentals (Off-Site)	A&G	Security
Safe Deposit Record Cards	Rooms	Printing & Stationery
Safety Glasses	Mult. Depts.	Operating Supplies
Safety Pins	Mult. Depts.	Operating Supplies
Safety Posters	Mult. Depts.	Training
Salad Bowls	Food	China
Sales and Occupancy Taxes Not Paid by Customers	R/POT/I	B/TO Taxes
Salt and Pepper Shakers	Food	China
Sand, Cinders, and Top Dressing, Golf Course	Golf/Pro Shop	Grounds M&L
Sand, Fire Buckets	POM	Life/Safety
Sanitary Pads/Tampons	Rooms	Guest Supplies
Satellite Television Service	Rooms	Cable/Satellite Television
Sauce Boats (All Materials)	Food	China
Saucers, Coffee	Food	China

Item Name	Department/ Schedule	Account Name
Scissors	Mult. Depts.	Operating Supplies
Scissors, Kitchen	Food	Utensils
Scoreboard Rental, Golf Tournament	Golf/Pro Shop	Tournament Expenses
Scorecards, Golf	Golf/Pro Shop	Printing & Stationery
Scotch Tape	Mult. Depts.	Operating Supplies
Scouring Pads	Food	Dishwashing Supplies
Scrapers, Cleaning	Mult. Depts.	Cleaning Supplies
Scrapers, Dish	Food	Dishwashing Supplies
Screen Repairs	POM	Building
Scrub Brushes	Mult. Depts.	Cleaning Supplies
Security, Contracted	A&G	Security
Security, Golf Tournament	Golf/Pro Shop	Tournament Expenses
Seeds, Golf Course	Golf/Pro Shop	Grounds M&L
Service Bureau Maintenance	Sales & Marketing	Outside Sales Rep.
Service Manuals (Employee)	Mult. Depts.	Training
Serving Spoons for Use by Guests in Rooms	Rooms	Guest Supplies
Serving Utensils	Food	Flatware
Sewer	Utilities	Sewer
Sewing Kits for Use by Guests in Rooms	Rooms	Guest Supplies
Shakers, Bar	Beverage	Utensils
Shampoo, Carpet	Mult. Depts.	Cleaning Supplies
Shampoo for Use by Guests in Rooms	Rooms	Guest Supplies
Shams	Rooms	Linen
Shaving Cream/Gel for Use by Guests in Rooms	Rooms	Guest Supplies
Shaving Mirror, Guestroom	Rooms	Operating Supplies
Sheers	Rooms	Operating Supplies
Sheet Music	Food or Beverage	Music & Enter.
Sheets, Fitted	Rooms	Linen
Sheets, Flat	Rooms	Linen
Sheets, Health Club/Spa	Health Club/Spa	Linen
Shelf Paper	Mult. Depts.	Operating Supplies
Shipping Supplies	Mult. Depts.	Operating Supplies
Shipping Tags	Mult. Depts.	Operating Supplies
Shirts, Uniforms	Mult. Depts.	Uniforms
Shoe Brushes for Use by Guests in Rooms	Rooms	Guest Supplies
Shoe Mitts for Use by Guests in Rooms	Rooms	Guest Supplies
Shoe Polish for Use by Guests in Rooms	Rooms	Guest Supplies
Shoes, Golf (for Rent)	Golf/Pro Shop	Operating Supplies
Shoes, Golf (for Sale)	Golf/Pro Shop	Cost of Merch. Sales
Shoes, Uniform	Mult. Depts.	Uniforms
Shopping Service	Mult. Depts.	Contract Services

Item Name	Department/ Schedule	Account Name
Shortages and Overages, Cash	A&G	Cash Overages/Shortages
Shorts, Uniform	Mult. Depts.	Uniforms
Shot Glasses, Bar	Beverage	Glassware
Shovels	POM	Engineering Supplies
Shovels, Snow	POM	Grounds M&L
Shower Caps for Use by Guests in Rooms	Rooms	Guest Supplies
Shower Curtain Liners	Rooms	Operating Supplies
Shower Curtain Rings	Rooms	Operating Supplies
Shower Curtains	Rooms	Operating Supplies
Shower Slippers	Rooms	Operating Supplies
Shutter Repair	POM	Building
Signage, Golf Maintenance	Golf/Pro Shop	Grounds M&L
Signs and Banners	Mult. Depts.	Operating Supplies
Signs, Directional	POM	Building
Silver Polish	Food	Dishwashing Supplies
Silverware, Employee Cafeteria	Empl. Caf.	Flatware
Silverware for Use by Guests in Rooms	Rooms	Guest Supplies
Skirts, Uniform	Mult. Depts.	Uniforms
Slippers for Use by Guests in Rooms	Rooms	Operating Supplies
Slippers, Health Club/Spa	Health Club/Spa	Linen
Smocks, Uniform	Mult. Depts.	Uniforms
Smoke Alarms	POM	Life/Safety
Smoking Urn Sand Stamp	Mult. Depts.	Operating Supplies
Snacks, Health Club/Spa (Gratis)	Health Club/Spa	Comp. Services & Gifts
Sneeze Guards	Food	Operating Supplies
Snow Removal Service	POM	Grounds M&L
Soap and Soap Dishes, Guestroom	Rooms	Cleaning Supplies
Soap Scum Remover, Guestroom	Rooms	Cleaning Supplies
Soaps, Cleaning	Mult. Depts.	Cleaning Supplies
Social Activities, Employees	A&G	Human Resources
Socks, Uniform	Mult. Depts.	Uniforms
Soda for Use by Guests in Rooms	Rooms	Guest Supplies
Soft Drink Syrup or Premix	Food	Cost of Food Sales
Software Application Upgrades	A&G	Information Systems
Software, Golf Tournament	Golf/Pro Shop	Tournament Expenses
Solar Power	Utility Costs	Other Fuels
Souffle Dishes (All Materials)	Food	China
Sound System Repairs	POM	Elec. & Mech.
Spa Products	Health Club/Spa	Health & Beauty Products
Spa Products (for Sale)	Health Club/Spa	Cost of Merch. Sales
Spatulas, Kitchen	Food	Utensils

Item Name	Department/ Schedule	Account Name
Speaker Fees, Training	Mult. Depts.	Training
Speakers, Stereo, Guestroom	Rooms	Operating Supplies
Sponges	Mult. Depts.	Cleaning Supplies
Sponges, Dishwashing	Food	Dishwashing Supplies
Spoons for Use by Guests in Rooms	Rooms	Operating Supplies
Spoons, Mixing	Food	Utensils
Sports Activities & Equipment, Employees	A&G	Human Resources
Spray Bottle	Mult. Depts.	Cleaning Supplies
Squeegees	Mult. Depts.	Cleaning Supplies
Stain Remover	Mult. Depts.	Cleaning Supplies
Stain Remover Packets	Mult. Depts.	Cleaning Supplies
Stain Spotter	Mult. Depts.	Cleaning Supplies
Stainless Steel Cleaner	Mult. Depts.	Cleaning Supplies
Stairway Repairs	POM	Building
Stamp Pads	Mult. Depts.	Operating Supplies
Stamp Pads (Ink)	Mult. Depts.	Operating Supplies
Stamps, Reservations	Rooms	Reservations
Stamps, Rubber	Mult. Depts.	Operating Supplies
Staplers/Staples	Mult. Depts.	Operating Supplies
Starch	House Laundry	Laundry Supplies
Stationery	Mult. Depts.	Printing & Stationery
Stationery for Use by Guests in Rooms	Rooms	Guest Supplies
Stationery Portfolio	Rooms	Operating Supplies
Steak Markers	Food	Operating Supplies
Steam for Utility Use	Utilities	Steam
Steel Wool	Food	Dishwashing Supplies
Stencils	Mult. Depts.	Operating Supplies
Sterno for Food Warming	Food	Kitchen Fuel
Stir Sticks, Cocktail	Beverage	Paper & Plastics
Stir Sticks for Use by Guests in Rooms	Rooms	Guest Supplies
Stirrers, Beverage	Beverage	Utensils
Stock Pot Repairs	POM	Kitchen Equip.
Stock Transfer Agents, Fees	A&G	Professional Fees
Stoppers, Bottle (Bar)	Beverage	Utensils
Stoppers, Sink	POM	Plumbing
Stoppers, Tubs	POM	Plumbing
Storage Files	A&G	Operating Supplies
Storage of Equipment/Records (Off-Site)	A&G	Contract Services
Strainers, Bar	Beverage	Utensils
Strainers, Guestroom	Rooms	Operating Supplies
Straws, Cocktail	Beverage	Paper & Plastics

Item Name	Department/ Schedule	Account Name
Straws, Soft Drink	Food	Paper & Plastics
Styrofoam Cups	Food	Paper & Plastics
Subscriptions, Trade (Marketing)	Sales & Marketing	Dues & Subscriptions
Subscriptions, Trade (Non-Marketing)	A&G	Dues & Subscriptions
Sugar Caddy, Guestroom	Rooms	Operating Supplies
Sugar Holders	Food	China
Sugar Packets for Use by Guests in Rooms	Rooms	Guest Supplies
Suggestion Awards, Employees	A&G	Human Resources
Suits, Uniform	Mult. Depts.	Uniforms
Surge Protectors	Mult. Depts.	Operating Supplies
Sweetener Packets for Use by Guests in Rooms	Rooms	Guest Supplies
Swimming Pool/Spa Accessories	POM	Swimming Pool
Swimmimg Pool/Spa Chemicals	POM	Swimming Pool
Swimming Pool/Spa Maintenance	POM	Swimming Pool
Swimming Pool/Spa Repairs	POM	Swimming Pool
Swimsuit Bags for Use by Guests in Rooms	Rooms	Guest Supplies
Switchboard Repairs	Telecom.	Contract Services
Swizzle Sticks for Use by Guests in Rooms	Rooms	Guest Supplies
Table Cover Repair/Replacement	POM	Elec. & Mech.
Table Pads	Food	Operating Supplies
Table Pads, Guestroom	Rooms	Operating Supplies
Table Protectors, Guestroom	Rooms	Operating Supplies
Table Rental (Banquet Not Charged to Customer)	Food	Banquet Expense
Table Runners, Linen	Food	Linen
Table Skirts, Linen	Food	Linen
Table Tent Cards, Guestroom	Rooms	Operating Supplies
Table Tents	Food or Beverage	Printing & Stationery
Table-Top Repair/Replacement—Glass	POM	Furniture & Equip.
Table Undercloth, Linen	Food	Linen
Tablecloths, Guestroom	Rooms	Operating Supplies
Tablecloths, Linen	Food	Linen
Tablecloths, Paper/Plastic	Food	Paper & Plastics
Tags, Baggage (Gratis)	Rooms	Guest Supplies
Tank Toilet Floats	POM	Plumbing
Tape	POM	Operating Supplies
Tape, Adhesive	Mult. Depts.	Operating Supplies
Tape, Carpet	POM	Floor Covering
Tape, Cellophane	Mult. Depts.	Operating Supplies
Tape Holder	Mult. Depts.	Operating Supplies
Tape, Masking	POM	Operating Supplies
Tape, Painter	POM	Painting & Decorating

Item Name	Department/ Schedule	Account Name
Tape Recorders	A&G	Operating Supplies
Tape, Scotch	Mult. Depts.	Printing & Stationery
Tape Transcribers	A&G	Operating Supplies
Taxes on Utilities (All Utilities)	Utility Costs	Utility Taxes
Taxi Fare	Mult. Depts.	Travel—Other
Tea Bags for Use by Guests in Rooms	Rooms	Guest Supplies
Teapots and Lids (All Materials)	Food	China
Teapots, Guestroom	Rooms	Operating Supplies
Technical Books, Employee Use	Mult. Depts.	Training
Technical Books, Maintenance	POM	Operating Supplies
Telecommunications Equipment Maintenance	A&G	Information Systems
Telephone Accessories, General	Mult. Depts.	Telecommunications
Telephone Charges	Mult. Depts.	Telecommunications
Telephone Cords	Telecom.	Operating Supplies
Telephone Directories for Departmental Use	Sales & Marketing	Operating Supplies
Telephone Directories for Guestrooms	Rooms	Operating Supplies
Telephone Directory Advertising	Sales & Marketing	Media
Telephone Directory Covers and Holders	Mult. Depts.	Operating Supplies
Telephone Face Plate	Telecom.	Operating Supplies
Telephone Hardware Lease (Non-Capital)	R/POT/I	Telecom. Equip.
Telephone Headsets	Telecom.	Operating Supplies
Telephone Local Trunk Costs	Telecom.	Cost of Local Calls
Telephone Long Distance Trunk Costs	Telecom.	Cost of Long Distance Calls
Telephone Message Cards	Rooms	Printing & Stationery
Telephone Message Pads	Rooms	Guest Supplies
Telephone Software Lease (Non-Capital)	R/POT/I	Telecom. Equip.
Telephone Switch Lease (Non-Capital)	R/POT/I	Telecom. Equip.
Television	Mult. Depts.	Operating Supplies
Television Remote	Rooms	Operating Supplies
Television Repairs	POM	Furniture & Equip.
Tent Rental for Parties/Banquets (Not Charged to Customer)	Food	Banquet Expense
Thread for Use by Guests in Rooms	Rooms	Guest Supplies
Throw, Guestroom	Rooms	Operating Supplies
Ties, Uniform	Mult. Depts.	Uniforms
Tile Cleaner	Mult. Depts.	Cleaning Supplies
Tile Repairs (Floor)	POM	Floor Covering
Tissue Box Covers, Guestroom	Rooms	Operating Supplies
Tissue for Use by Guests in Rooms	Rooms	Guest Supplies

Item Name	Department/ Schedule	Account Name
Tobacco Cost	Food	Misc. Cost of Other Rev.
Toilet Brushes	Mult. Depts.	Cleaning Supplies
Toilet Seat Covers	Rooms	Guest Supplies
Toilet Tissue	Rooms	Guest Supplies
Tolls, Highway	Mult. Depts.	Travel—Other
Toner (for Copier)	A&G	Operating Supplies
Tongs, Cooking	Food	Utensils
Tongs, Serving	Food	Flatware
Tonics, Health Club/Spa	Health Club/Spa	Health & Beauty Products
Tonics, Health Club/Spa (for Sale)	Health Club/Spa	Cost of Merch. Sales
Tools	POM	Engineering Supplies
Toothbrush Holders, Guestroom	Rooms	Operating Supplies
Toothbrushes for Use by Guests in Rooms	Rooms	Guest Supplies
Toothpaste for Use by Guests in Rooms	Rooms	Guest Supplies
Toothpicks	Food	Paper & Plastics
Toothpicks for Use by Guests in Rooms	Rooms	Guest Supplies
Topsoil for Golf Course	Golf/Pro Shop	Grounds M&L
Total Quality Management	A&G	Human Resources
Towelettes for Use by Guests in Rooms	Rooms	Guest Supplies
Towels, Bar	Beverage	Linen
Towels, Bar (Guestroom)	Rooms	Linen
Towels, Bath (All Sizes)	Rooms	Linen
Towels, Cleaning Rags	Mult. Depts.	Cleaning Supplies
Towels, Hand	Rooms	Linen
Towels, Health Club/Spa	Health Club/Spa	Linen
Towels, Paper	Mult. Depts.	Cleaning Supplies
Toys for Use by Guests in Rooms	Rooms	Operating Supplies
Trade Publications Subscriptions (Marketing)	Sales & Marketing	Dues & Subscriptions
Trade Publications Subscriptions (Non-Marketing)	A&G	Dues & Subscriptions
Trade Publications, Repair/Maintenance	POM	Dues & Subscriptions
Trade Show Booth Construction	Sales & Marketing	Trade Shows
Trade Show Promotional Items	Sales & Marketing	Trade Shows
Training Program Costs	Mult. Depts.	Training
Training, Travel	Mult. Depts.	Training
Transfer Fees, Licenses	Mult. Depts.	Licenses & Permits
Transportation Charged to Customer, Banquets	Food	Misc. Cost of Other Rev.
Transportation of Employees	A&G	Transportation
Trash Can Liners	Mult. Depts.	Operating Supplies
Trash Cans	Mult. Depts.	Operating Supplies

Item Name	Department/ Schedule	Account Name
Trash Compactor Lease (Non-Capital)	R/POT/I	Other Property & Equip.
Trash Receptacles	Mult. Depts.	Operating Supplies
Travel Expenses (Food/Beverage)	Mult. Depts.	Travel—Meals & Enter.
Travel Expenses (Non–Food/Beverage)	Mult. Depts.	Travel—Other
Travel Meals	Mult. Depts.	Travel—Meals & Enter.
Tray Jacks	Food	Operating Supplies
Tray Liners	Food	Operating Supplies
Trays (All Materials), Employee Cafeteria	Empl. Caf.	Operating Supplies
Trays, Guestroom	Rooms	Operating Supplies
Trays, Serving (All Materials)	Food	Operating Supplies
Tree Purchases	POM	Grounds M&L
Tree Removal & Trimming Service, Golf Course	Golf/Pro Shop	Contract Services
Tree Rentals	POM	Grounds M&L
Trigger Sprayer Bottles	Mult. Depts.	Cleaning Supplies
Trousers, Uniform	Mult. Depts.	Uniforms
Truck Rental (Food Delivery)	Food	Equip. Rental
T-Shirts, Uniform	Mult. Depts.	Uniforms
Tubes, Pastry	Food	Utensils
Tumblers, Guestroom	Rooms	Operating Supplies
TV Guides, Guestroom	Rooms	Operating Supplies
Tweezers for Use by Guests in Rooms	Rooms	Guest Supplies
Two-Way Radios	Mult. Depts.	Telecommunications
Umbrellas	Mult. Depts.	Operating Supplies
Uncollectible Accounts Provision	A&G	Prov. for Doubtful Accts.
Underinsured Losses, Liability	R/POT/I	Liability
Underinsured Losses, Property	R/POT/I	Building & Contents
Uniforms, Cleaning	Mult. Depts.	Uniform Laundry
Uniforms, Cleaning Allowance	Mult. Depts.	Uniform Laundry
Uniforms, Repair	Mult. Depts.	Uniforms
Upholstery Cleaner	Mult. Depts.	Cleaning Supplies
Upholstery Repair	POM	Furniture & Equip.
Urinal Baskets	Mult. Depts.	Operating Supplies
Utensils, Employee Cafeteria	Empl. Caf.	Utensils
Utensils, Kitchen	Food	Utensils
Utensils, Serving	Food	Flatware
Vacuum Accessories	Mult. Depts.	Cleaning Supplies
Vacuum Belts	Mult. Depts.	Cleaning Supplies
Vacuum Cleaner Accessories	Mult. Depts.	Cleaning Supplies
Vacuum Cleaners	Mult. Depts.	Cleaning Supplies
Vacuum Filters	Mult. Depts.	Cleaning Supplies
Vacuums, Canister	Mult. Depts.	Cleaning Supplies

Item Name	Department/Schedule	Account Name
Vacuums, Portable	Mult. Depts.	Cleaning Supplies
Vacuums, Upright	Mult. Depts.	Cleaning Supplies
Valences/Swags	POM	Building
Vases (Tabletop)	Food	Operating Supplies
VCR, Guestroom	Rooms	Cable/Satellite Television
Vegetables	Food	Cost of Food Sales
Vehicle Lease (Non-Capital)	R/POT/I	Other Property & Equip.
Venetian Blinds Repairs	POM	Building
Video Camera	Mult. Depts.	Operating Supplies
Video Check-Out Service	Rooms	Contract Services
Video Comment Card Service	Rooms	Contract Services
Videotapes, Training/Safety	Mult. Depts.	Training
Vinyl Wall Covering	POM	Painting & Decorating
VIP Guest Gifts	Mult. Depts.	Comp. Services & Gifts
Visual Planners	Mult. Depts.	Operating Supplies
Vouchers, Pettty Cash	A&G	Printing & Stationery
Walks, Relocation of Guest Due to Lack of Room Availability	Rooms	Guest Relocation
Wallpaper	POM	Painting & Decorating
Want Ads (Help Wanted)	A&G	Human Resources
Wash Cloths	Rooms	Linen
Waste Baskets	Mult. Depts.	Operating Supplies
Waste Receptacles	Mult. Depts.	Operating Supplies
Waste, Garbage, Refuse, Rubbish, Ash Removal	POM	Waste Removal
Wastewater Surcharge	Utility Costs	Sewer
Water	Utility Costs	Water
Water and Drainage Systems Maintenance, Golf Course	Golf/Pro Shop	Irrigation
Water Conservation Cards	Rooms	Printing & Stationery
Water Controllers, Computerized Water Systems, Golf Course	Golf/Pro Shop	Irrigation
Water Pitchers, Guestroom	Rooms	Operating Supplies
Water Usage, Golf Course	Golf/Pro Shop	Water
Waxed Paper	Food	Paper & Plastics
Waxes	Mult. Depts.	Cleaning Supplies
Wax, Floor	Mult. Depts.	Cleaning Supplies
Web Site Development	Sales & Marketing	E-Commerce
Welcome Baskets, Guestroom	Rooms	Comp. Services & Gifts
Wet Floor Signs	Mult. Depts.	Operating Supplies
Wind Power	Utility Costs	Other Fuels

Item Name	Department/ Schedule	Account Name
Window Cleaning Services	Mult. Depts.	Contract Services
Window Locks	POM	Building
Window Shade Repairs	POM	Building
Wine	Beverage	Cost of Beverage Sales
Wine Cellar Supplies	Beverage	Operating Supplies
Wine Lists	Beverage	Menus & Beverage Lists
Wire Whips	Food	Utensils
Wireless Cards	A&G	Information Systems
Woolite Packets	Mult. Depts.	Cleaning Supplies
Wrapping Paper	Mult. Depts.	Operating Supplies
Writing Supplies	Mult. Depts.	Operating Supplies

Expense Dictionary
Section Two: Sorted by Department/Schedule and Account Name

Department/ Schedule	Account Name	Item Name
Mult. Depts.	Bonus & Incentives	Bonus Pay (Performance-Based)
Mult. Depts.	Bonus & Incentives	Incentive Pay (Performance-Based)
Mult. Depts.	Cleaning Supplies	Acids
Mult. Depts.	Cleaning Supplies	Air Freshener
Mult. Depts.	Cleaning Supplies	Alcohol (Cleaning)
Mult. Depts.	Cleaning Supplies	All-Purpose Cleaner
Mult. Depts.	Cleaning Supplies	Ammonia
Mult. Depts.	Cleaning Supplies	Artificial Plant Cleaner
Mult. Depts.	Cleaning Supplies	Bathroom Cleaner
Mult. Depts.	Cleaning Supplies	Bleach
Mult. Depts.	Cleaning Supplies	Bleach Packets
Mult. Depts.	Cleaning Supplies	Brooms
Mult. Depts.	Cleaning Supplies	Brushes
Mult. Depts.	Cleaning Supplies	Buckets, Mop
Mult. Depts.	Cleaning Supplies	Bug Traps
Mult. Depts.	Cleaning Supplies	Carpet Cleaner Chemical
Mult. Depts.	Cleaning Supplies	Carpet Cleaning Supplies
Mult. Depts.	Cleaning Supplies	Carpet Shampoo
Mult. Depts.	Cleaning Supplies	Carpet Shampoo Machines
Mult. Depts.	Cleaning Supplies	Carpet Sweepers
Mult. Depts.	Cleaning Supplies	Chamois
Mult. Depts.	Cleaning Supplies	Cleaning Chemicals
Mult. Depts.	Cleaning Supplies	Cleaning Cloths, Compounds, Fluids, Rags, Sponges
Mult. Depts.	Cleaning Supplies	Cleansers (Non-Dishwashing)
Mult. Depts.	Cleaning Supplies	Cleansing Powder
Mult. Depts.	Cleaning Supplies	Degreaser
Mult. Depts.	Cleaning Supplies	Disinfectants
Mult. Depts.	Cleaning Supplies	Dust Cloths
Mult. Depts.	Cleaning Supplies	Dust Mop
Mult. Depts.	Cleaning Supplies	Dusters
Mult. Depts.	Cleaning Supplies	Dusting Mitts
Mult. Depts.	Cleaning Supplies	Dustpan Brushes
Mult. Depts.	Cleaning Supplies	Dustpans
Mult. Depts.	Cleaning Supplies	Feather Duster
Mult. Depts.	Cleaning Supplies	Filters, Vacuum

Department/ Schedule	Account Name	Item Name
Mult. Depts.	Cleaning Supplies	Floor Polish
Mult. Depts.	Cleaning Supplies	Floor Soap
Mult. Depts.	Cleaning Supplies	Floor Wax
Mult. Depts.	Cleaning Supplies	Fly Strips
Mult. Depts.	Cleaning Supplies	Fly Swatters
Mult. Depts.	Cleaning Supplies	Furniture Polish
Mult. Depts.	Cleaning Supplies	Furniture Wax
Mult. Depts.	Cleaning Supplies	Glass Cleaner
Mult. Depts.	Cleaning Supplies	Gloves, Rubber
Mult. Depts.	Cleaning Supplies	Gum Remover
Mult. Depts.	Cleaning Supplies	Insecticides
Mult. Depts.	Cleaning Supplies	Lemon Oil
Mult. Depts.	Cleaning Supplies	Lint Brush
Mult. Depts.	Cleaning Supplies	Lint Remover
Mult. Depts.	Cleaning Supplies	Lye
Mult. Depts.	Cleaning Supplies	Mop Buckets
Mult. Depts.	Cleaning Supplies	Mop Handles
Mult. Depts.	Cleaning Supplies	Mop Wringers
Mult. Depts.	Cleaning Supplies	Mops
Mult. Depts.	Cleaning Supplies	Oxalic Acid
Mult. Depts.	Cleaning Supplies	Pails
Mult. Depts.	Cleaning Supplies	Plastic Spray Bottles
Mult. Depts.	Cleaning Supplies	Polish
Mult. Depts.	Cleaning Supplies	Rags, Cleaning
Mult. Depts.	Cleaning Supplies	Rubber Gloves
Mult. Depts.	Cleaning Supplies	Rug Cleaners
Mult. Depts.	Cleaning Supplies	Scrapers, Cleaning
Mult. Depts.	Cleaning Supplies	Scrub Brushes
Mult. Depts.	Cleaning Supplies	Shampoo, Carpet
Mult. Depts.	Cleaning Supplies	Soaps, Cleaning
Mult. Depts.	Cleaning Supplies	Sponges
Mult. Depts.	Cleaning Supplies	Spray Bottle
Mult. Depts.	Cleaning Supplies	Squeegees
Mult. Depts.	Cleaning Supplies	Stain Remover
Mult. Depts.	Cleaning Supplies	Stain Remover Packets
Mult. Depts.	Cleaning Supplies	Stain Spotter
Mult. Depts.	Cleaning Supplies	Stainless Steel Cleaner
Mult. Depts.	Cleaning Supplies	Tile Cleaner
Mult. Depts.	Cleaning Supplies	Toilet Brushes
Mult. Depts.	Cleaning Supplies	Towels, Cleaning Rags
Mult. Depts.	Cleaning Supplies	Towels, Paper

Department/ Schedule	Account Name	Item Name
Mult. Depts.	Cleaning Supplies	Trigger Sprayer Bottles
Mult. Depts.	Cleaning Supplies	Upholstery Cleaner
Mult. Depts.	Cleaning Supplies	Vacuum Accessories
Mult. Depts.	Cleaning Supplies	Vacuum Belts
Mult. Depts.	Cleaning Supplies	Vacuum Cleaner Accessories
Mult. Depts.	Cleaning Supplies	Vacuum Cleaners
Mult. Depts.	Cleaning Supplies	Vacuum Filters
Mult. Depts.	Cleaning Supplies	Vacuums—Canister, Portable, Upright
Mult. Depts.	Cleaning Supplies	Waxes
Mult. Depts.	Cleaning Supplies	Woolite Packets
Mult. Depts.	Comp. Services/Gifts	Amenities, Gifts
Mult. Depts.	Comp. Services/Gifts	Baskets, Wine (for Gratis Presentations)—Not Reusable
Mult. Depts.	Comp. Services/Gifts	Cheese Baskets, Gratis
Mult. Depts.	Comp. Services/Gifts	Complimentary Beverage
Mult. Depts.	Comp. Services/Gifts	Complimentary Food
Mult. Depts.	Comp. Services/Gifts	Complimentary Parking
Mult. Depts.	Comp. Services/Gifts	Fruit Baskets Gratis to Customers
Mult. Depts.	Comp. Services/Gifts	Gifts to Customers
Mult. Depts.	Comp. Services/Gifts	VIP Guest Gifts
Mult. Depts.	Contract Services	Carpet Cleaning Services
Mult. Depts.	Contract Services	Carpet/Rug Cleaning (Outside Service)
Mult. Depts.	Contract Services	Comment Card Processing (Outside Service)
Mult. Depts.	Contract Services	Consultant Fees
Mult. Depts.	Contract Services	Contract Cleaning—Awning, Floors, Fumigation, Windows
Mult. Depts.	Contract Services	Purchasing Service Fees
Mult. Depts.	Contract Services	Rug Cleaning Services
Mult. Depts.	Contract Services	Shopping Service
Mult. Depts.	Contract Services	Window Cleaning Services
Mult. Depts.	Corp. Office Reimb.	Management Company Expenses (Travel, Entertainment, etc.)
Mult. Depts.	Decorations	Cut Flowers
Mult. Depts.	Decorations	Decorations, Holiday and Special Occasion
Mult. Depts.	Decorations	Floral Arrangements
Mult. Depts.	Decorations	Flowers, Fresh and Artificial
Mult. Depts.	Dues & Subscriptions	Magazine Subscriptions
Mult. Depts.	Dues & Subscriptions	Membership Fees—Professional Organizations
Mult. Depts.	Employee Benefits	Payroll—401(k) Costs
Mult. Depts.	Employee Benefits	Payroll—Child Care, Employee

Department/ Schedule	Account Name	Item Name
Mult. Depts.	Employee Benefits	Payroll—Disability Pay
Mult. Depts.	Employee Benefits	Payroll—Health and Dental Insurance
Mult. Depts.	Employee Benefits	Payroll—Life Insurance
Mult. Depts.	Employee Benefits	Payroll—Long-Term Disability
Mult. Depts.	Employee Benefits	Payroll—Meals (Cost Allocation from Employee Cafeteria)
Mult. Depts.	Employee Benefits	Payroll—Pension Costs
Mult. Depts.	Employee Benefits	Payroll—Profit Sharing
Mult. Depts.	Employee Benefits	Payroll—Union Benefits (All)
Mult. Depts.	Employee Benefits	Payroll—Workers' Compensation Insurance
Mult. Depts.	Employee Benefits	Physician's Fees, Employees (Workers' Compensation)
Mult. Depts.	Equip. Rental	Beeper Rental
Mult. Depts.	Equip. Rental	Copier Rental/Lease
Mult. Depts.	Laundry & Dry Cleaning	Curtains, Dry Cleaning
Mult. Depts.	Laundry & Dry Cleaning	Draperies, Dry Cleaning
Mult. Depts.	Laundry & Dry Cleaning	Dry Cleaning Costs, Non-Guest (In-House Laundry)
Mult. Depts.	Laundry & Dry Cleaning	Dry Cleaning Services, Non-Guest (Outside Laundry)
Mult. Depts.	Laundry & Dry Cleaning	Laundry Costs, Non-Guest (In-House Laundry)
Mult. Depts.	Laundry & Dry Cleaning	Laundry Services, Non-Guest (Outside Laundry)
Mult. Depts.	Licenses & Permits	Inspection Fees for Licensing
Mult. Depts.	Licenses & Permits	Transfer Fees, Licenses
Mult. Depts.	Linen	Linen Rental
Mult. Depts.	Management Fees	Management Fee—Specific Department
Mult. Depts.	Miscellaneous	Fines (Health, Safety, etc.)
Mult. Depts.	Operating Supplies	Adapter Plug, Electrical
Mult. Depts.	Operating Supplies	Adding Machine Tape
Mult. Depts.	Operating Supplies	Adding Machines
Mult. Depts.	Operating Supplies	Adhesive Tape
Mult. Depts.	Operating Supplies	Air Deodorizing Accessories/Systems
Mult. Depts.	Operating Supplies	Answering Machines
Mult. Depts.	Operating Supplies	Anti-Fatigue Mats
Mult. Depts.	Operating Supplies	Artwork
Mult. Depts.	Operating Supplies	Ash Cans
Mult. Depts.	Operating Supplies	Ashtrays
Mult. Depts.	Operating Supplies	Band-Aids
Mult. Depts.	Operating Supplies	Baskets, Urinal
Mult. Depts.	Operating Supplies	Baskets, Waste Liners

Department/ Schedule	Account Name	Item Name
Mult. Depts.	Operating Supplies	Baskets, Wine (for Gratis Presentations)— Reusable
Mult. Depts.	Operating Supplies	Batteries
Mult. Depts.	Operating Supplies	Binder Clips
Mult. Depts.	Operating Supplies	Binders
Mult. Depts.	Operating Supplies	Book Matches (Guest)
Mult. Depts.	Operating Supplies	Calculators
Mult. Depts.	Operating Supplies	Calendars and Diaries
Mult. Depts.	Operating Supplies	Candles
Mult. Depts.	Operating Supplies	Candlesticks
Mult. Depts.	Operating Supplies	Cashier Envelopes
Mult. Depts.	Operating Supplies	Cashier Forms
Mult. Depts.	Operating Supplies	CD ROM, Writable
Mult. Depts.	Operating Supplies	Cellophane Tape
Mult. Depts.	Operating Supplies	Clipboards
Mult. Depts.	Operating Supplies	Coin Drawers
Mult. Depts.	Operating Supplies	Computer Discs
Mult. Depts.	Operating Supplies	Copier Paper
Mult. Depts.	Operating Supplies	Copier Toner
Mult. Depts.	Operating Supplies	CPR Kits
Mult. Depts.	Operating Supplies	Curtain Holdbacks
Mult. Depts.	Operating Supplies	Curtain Hooks
Mult. Depts.	Operating Supplies	Curtain Rods
Mult. Depts.	Operating Supplies	Curtain Stackbacks
Mult. Depts.	Operating Supplies	Curtains
Mult. Depts.	Operating Supplies	Data Binders and Accessories
Mult. Depts.	Operating Supplies	Data Systems and Storage Files
Mult. Depts.	Operating Supplies	Defibrillator
Mult. Depts.	Operating Supplies	Desk Accessories
Mult. Depts.	Operating Supplies	Desk Caddies
Mult. Depts.	Operating Supplies	Desk Pad and Holder
Mult. Depts.	Operating Supplies	Double-Stick Tape
Mult. Depts.	Operating Supplies	Drapery Baton
Mult. Depts.	Operating Supplies	Drapery Cords
Mult. Depts.	Operating Supplies	Drapery Liners
Mult. Depts.	Operating Supplies	Drapes
Mult. Depts.	Operating Supplies	Drapes, Blackout
Mult. Depts.	Operating Supplies	Duct Tape
Mult. Depts.	Operating Supplies	Electrical Adapters
Mult. Depts.	Operating Supplies	Employee Pins

Department/ Schedule	Account Name	Item Name
Mult. Depts.	Operating Supplies	Erasers
Mult. Depts.	Operating Supplies	Extension Cords
Mult. Depts.	Operating Supplies	Fans, Portable
Mult. Depts.	Operating Supplies	File Folders
Mult. Depts.	Operating Supplies	Film, Camera
Mult. Depts.	Operating Supplies	Fireplace Lighter
Mult. Depts.	Operating Supplies	Fireplace Screen
Mult. Depts.	Operating Supplies	Fireplace Tools
Mult. Depts.	Operating Supplies	Firewood
Mult. Depts.	Operating Supplies	First Aid Kits/Supplies
Mult. Depts.	Operating Supplies	Flags
Mult. Depts.	Operating Supplies	Flashlights
Mult. Depts.	Operating Supplies	Frames, Art
Mult. Depts.	Operating Supplies	Garbage Bags
Mult. Depts.	Operating Supplies	Garbage Can Liners
Mult. Depts.	Operating Supplies	Garbage Cans
Mult. Depts.	Operating Supplies	Gasoline—Motor Vehicles (Company and Employee Use)
Mult. Depts.	Operating Supplies	Glue
Mult. Depts.	Operating Supplies	Goldfish
Mult. Depts.	Operating Supplies	High Chairs
Mult. Depts.	Operating Supplies	Hole Punch
Mult. Depts.	Operating Supplies	Hooks, Coat
Mult. Depts.	Operating Supplies	Hooks, Door
Mult. Depts.	Operating Supplies	Ink
Mult. Depts.	Operating Supplies	Ink Cartridges
Mult. Depts.	Operating Supplies	Key Chain Coils
Mult. Depts.	Operating Supplies	Key Chain Reels
Mult. Depts.	Operating Supplies	Key Lock Box
Mult. Depts.	Operating Supplies	Key Rings
Mult. Depts.	Operating Supplies	Key Tags
Mult. Depts.	Operating Supplies	Keyboard Drawers
Mult. Depts.	Operating Supplies	Label Maker
Mult. Depts.	Operating Supplies	Label Maker Supplies
Mult. Depts.	Operating Supplies	Lampshades
Mult. Depts.	Operating Supplies	Liners, Drapery
Mult. Depts.	Operating Supplies	Log Books
Mult. Depts.	Operating Supplies	Marking Ink
Mult. Depts.	Operating Supplies	Matches, Customer Use
Mult. Depts.	Operating Supplies	Mats, Floor

Department/ Schedule	Account Name	Item Name
Mult. Depts.	Operating Supplies	Memo Pads
Mult. Depts.	Operating Supplies	Mini-Blinds
Mult. Depts.	Operating Supplies	Mouse, Computer
Mult. Depts.	Operating Supplies	Mouse Pads
Mult. Depts.	Operating Supplies	Name Badges
Mult. Depts.	Operating Supplies	Office Supplies, General
Mult. Depts.	Operating Supplies	Outlet Safety Plugs
Mult. Depts.	Operating Supplies	Packing Tape
Mult. Depts.	Operating Supplies	Pain Relievers
Mult. Depts.	Operating Supplies	Paper Clips
Mult. Depts.	Operating Supplies	Paper, Copier
Mult. Depts.	Operating Supplies	Paper Liners
Mult. Depts.	Operating Supplies	Parchment
Mult. Depts.	Operating Supplies	Paste
Mult. Depts.	Operating Supplies	Pencil Holders
Mult. Depts.	Operating Supplies	Pencil Sharpeners
Mult. Depts.	Operating Supplies	Pencils
Mult. Depts.	Operating Supplies	Pens
Mult. Depts.	Operating Supplies	Pins—Employee, Safety, Stick, Straight
Mult. Depts.	Operating Supplies	Placards
Mult. Depts.	Operating Supplies	Plants
Mult. Depts.	Operating Supplies	Portable Fans
Mult. Depts.	Operating Supplies	Portable Steam Cleaners
Mult. Depts.	Operating Supplies	Poster Board
Mult. Depts.	Operating Supplies	Post-it Notes
Mult. Depts.	Operating Supplies	Printer Supplies and Accessories
Mult. Depts.	Operating Supplies	Printing Calculator
Mult. Depts.	Operating Supplies	Q-Tips
Mult. Depts.	Operating Supplies	Record Books
Mult. Depts.	Operating Supplies	Recorders, Mini/Micro Cassette and Accessories
Mult. Depts.	Operating Supplies	Recycle Bins
Mult. Depts.	Operating Supplies	Reports
Mult. Depts.	Operating Supplies	Ribbons—Typewriter, Calculator, Cash Register
Mult. Depts.	Operating Supplies	Roller Shades
Mult. Depts.	Operating Supplies	Roman Shades
Mult. Depts.	Operating Supplies	Rubber Bands
Mult. Depts.	Operating Supplies	Rubber Cement
Mult. Depts.	Operating Supplies	Rubber Stamps
Mult. Depts.	Operating Supplies	Rugs, Throw
Mult. Depts.	Operating Supplies	Rulers
Mult. Depts.	Operating Supplies	Safety Glasses

Department/ Schedule	Account Name	Item Name
Mult. Depts.	Operating Supplies	Safety Pins
Mult. Depts.	Operating Supplies	Scissors
Mult. Depts.	Operating Supplies	Shelf Paper
Mult. Depts.	Operating Supplies	Shipping Supplies
Mult. Depts.	Operating Supplies	Shipping Tags
Mult. Depts.	Operating Supplies	Signs and Banners
Mult. Depts.	Operating Supplies	Smoking Urn Sand Stamp
Mult. Depts.	Operating Supplies	Stamp Pads
Mult. Depts.	Operating Supplies	Stamp Pads (Ink)
Mult. Depts.	Operating Supplies	Stamps, Rubber
Mult. Depts.	Operating Supplies	Staplers
Mult. Depts.	Operating Supplies	Staples
Mult. Depts.	Operating Supplies	Stencils
Mult. Depts.	Operating Supplies	Surge Protectors
Mult. Depts.	Operating Supplies	Tape, Adhesive
Mult. Depts.	Operating Supplies	Tape Holder
Mult. Depts.	Operating Supplies	Tape, Scotch
Mult. Depts.	Operating Supplies	Telephone Directory Covers and Holders
Mult. Depts.	Operating Supplies	Television
Mult. Depts.	Operating Supplies	Trash Can Liners
Mult. Depts.	Operating Supplies	Trash Cans/Receptacles
Mult. Depts.	Operating Supplies	Umbrellas
Mult. Depts.	Operating Supplies	Urinal Baskets
Mult. Depts.	Operating Supplies	Video Camera
Mult. Depts.	Operating Supplies	Visual Planners
Mult. Depts.	Operating Supplies	Waste Baskets
Mult. Depts.	Operating Supplies	Waste Receptacles
Mult. Depts.	Operating Supplies	Wastebaskets (Employee)
Mult. Depts.	Operating Supplies	Wet Floor Signs
Mult. Depts.	Operating Supplies	Wrapping Paper
Mult. Depts.	Operating Supplies	Writing Supplies
Mult. Depts.	Payroll Taxes	City Head Tax
Mult. Depts.	Payroll Taxes	Federal Unemployment Tax
Mult. Depts.	Payroll Taxes	FICA Tax
Mult. Depts.	Payroll Taxes	State Disability Insurance
Mult. Depts.	Payroll Taxes	State Unemployment Tax
Mult. Depts.	Printing & Stationery . . .	Business Cards
Mult. Depts.	Printing & Stationery . . .	Charge Vouchers
Mult. Depts.	Printing & Stationery . . .	Check/Folio/Statement Presentation Folders
Mult. Depts.	Printing & Stationery . . .	Comment Cards
Mult. Depts.	Printing & Stationery . . .	Computer Forms—Commercial, Printed

Department/Schedule	Account Name	Item Name
Mult. Depts.	Printing & Stationery	Computer Printer Paper
Mult. Depts.	Printing & Stationery	Copying Service
Mult. Depts.	Printing & Stationery	Envelopes
Mult. Depts.	Printing & Stationery	Envelopes—Cashier
Mult. Depts.	Printing & Stationery	Floor Plans
Mult. Depts.	Printing & Stationery	Forms, General
Mult. Depts.	Printing & Stationery	Forms, Printed
Mult. Depts.	Printing & Stationery	Guest Comment Cards
Mult. Depts.	Printing & Stationery	Guest Questionnaire Forms
Mult. Depts.	Printing & Stationery	Guest Suggestion Forms
Mult. Depts.	Printing & Stationery	Parking Permit Cards
Mult. Depts.	Printing & Stationery	Parking Violation Stickers
Mult. Depts.	Printing & Stationery	Printed Forms
Mult. Depts.	Printing & Stationery	Printer Paper
Mult. Depts.	Printing & Stationery	Stationery
Mult. Depts.	Royalty Fees	Royalties for Use of Third-Party Brand Name
Mult. Depts.	Salaries & Wages	Hourly Wages
Mult. Depts.	Salaries & Wages	Leased Labor
Mult. Depts.	Salaries & Wages	Salaried Wages
Mult. Depts.	Supplemental Pay	Bonus Pay (Discretionary)
Mult. Depts.	Supplemental Pay	Holiday Pay
Mult. Depts.	Supplemental Pay	Incentive Pay (Discretionary)
Mult. Depts.	Supplemental Pay	Jury Duty Pay
Mult. Depts.	Supplemental Pay	Paid Time Off
Mult. Depts.	Supplemental Pay	Relocation Pay
Mult. Depts.	Supplemental Pay	Severance Pay
Mult. Depts.	Supplemental Pay	Sick Pay
Mult. Depts.	Supplemental Pay	Vacation Pay
Mult. Depts.	Telecom.	Cellular Phones/Supplies/Charges
Mult. Depts.	Telecom.	Internet Connection Fees
Mult. Depts.	Telecom.	Internet Telephone Charges (Staff)
Mult. Depts.	Telecom.	Line, Computer/Fax/Modem
Mult. Depts.	Telecom.	Local Call Cost (Departmental)
Mult. Depts.	Telecom.	Long Distance Call Cost (Departmental)
Mult. Depts.	Telecom.	Pager Rental
Mult. Depts.	Telecom.	Pagers
Mult. Depts.	Telecom.	Radio Communications
Mult. Depts.	Telecom.	Telephone Accessories, General
Mult. Depts.	Telecom.	Telephone Charges
Mult. Depts.	Telecom.	Two-Way Radios
Mult. Depts.	Training	Books, Technical

Department/ Schedule	Account Name	Item Name
Mult. Depts.	Training	Computer Training Manuals
Mult. Depts.	Training	Educational Activities for Employees
Mult. Depts.	Training	Educational Assistance
Mult. Depts.	Training	Educational Books/Pamphlets for Employees
Mult. Depts.	Training	Instructor Fees, Training
Mult. Depts.	Training	Manuals, Instructional/Training
Mult. Depts.	Training	Orientation Expenses
Mult. Depts.	Training	Pamphlets, Educational/Instructional (for Employees)
Mult. Depts.	Training	Publications, House (for Employees)
Mult. Depts.	Training	Safety Posters
Mult. Depts.	Training	Service Manuals (Employee)
Mult. Depts.	Training	Speaker Fees, Training
Mult. Depts.	Training	Training Program Costs
Mult. Depts.	Training	Training, Travel
Mult. Depts.	Training	Videotapes, Training/Safety
Mult. Depts.	Travel—Meals & Enter.	Entertainment, Outside—Employee
Mult. Depts.	Travel—Meals & Enter.	Meals, Business Expense
Mult. Depts.	Travel—Meals & Enter.	Meals and Entertainment, Outside
Mult. Depts.	Travel—Meals & Enter.	Travel Expenses (Food/Beverage)
Mult. Depts.	Travel—Meals & Enter.	Travel Meals
Mult. Depts.	Travel—Other	Airfare
Mult. Depts.	Travel—Other	Car Rental
Mult. Depts.	Travel—Other	Mileage Reimbursement
Mult. Depts.	Travel—Other	Room Charges, Travel
Mult. Depts.	Travel—Other	Taxi Fare
Mult. Depts.	Travel—Other	Tolls, Highway
Mult. Depts.	Travel—Other	Travel Expenses (Non–Food/Beverage)
Mult. Depts.	Uniform Laundry	Uniform Cleaning
Mult. Depts.	Uniform Laundry	Uniform Cleaning Allowance
Mult. Depts.	Uniforms	Aprons
Mult. Depts.	Uniforms	Blouses
Mult. Depts.	Uniforms	Boots
Mult. Depts.	Uniforms	Caps
Mult. Depts.	Uniforms	Coats
Mult. Depts.	Uniforms	Dresses
Mult. Depts.	Uniforms	Hats
Mult. Depts.	Uniforms	Jackets
Mult. Depts.	Uniforms	Jumpers
Mult. Depts.	Uniforms	Overalls

Department/ Schedule	Account Name	Item Name
Mult. Depts.	Uniforms	Pants
Mult. Depts.	Uniforms	Repairs, Uniforms
Mult. Depts.	Uniforms	Shirts
Mult. Depts.	Uniforms	Shoes
Mult. Depts.	Uniforms	Shorts
Mult. Depts.	Uniforms	Skirts
Mult. Depts.	Uniforms	Smocks
Mult. Depts.	Uniforms	Socks
Mult. Depts.	Uniforms	Suits
Mult. Depts.	Uniforms	Ties
Mult. Depts.	Uniforms	Trousers
Mult. Depts.	Uniforms	T-Shirts
Mult. Depts.	Uniforms	Uniforms Repair
A&G	Audit Charges	Audit Fees, Public Accountants
A&G	Audit Charges	Fees, Notary
A&G	Audit Charges	Internal Audit Expense
A&G	Audit Charges	Internal Audit Fees (Chain Properties)
A&G	Bank Charges	Bank Checks, Charges
A&G	Bank Charges	Exchange on Bank Checks and Currency
A&G	Cash Overages/Shortages	Cash Overages and Shortages
A&G	Cent. Acct. Charges	Accounting Fees—Centralized (Management Company)
A&G	Cent. Acct. Charges	Accounting Fees—Centralized (Owner)
A&G	Contract Services	Accountant's Fees (Replacing Hotel Employees)
A&G	Contract Services	Document Destruction Fees
A&G	Contract Services	Storage of Equipment/Records (Off-Site)
A&G	Corp. Office Reimb.	Owners Expenses (Travel, Entertainment, etc.)
A&G	Credit & Collection	Check Verification
A&G	Credit & Collection	Collection Fees
A&G	Credit & Collection	Credit Reports
A&G	Credit & Collection	Credit Service Expense
A&G	Credit & Collection	Fees, Attorney, for Collections
A&G	Credit & Collection	Fees, Collection
A&G	Credit & Collection	Legal Fees/Expenses for Collections
A&G	Credit & Collection	Notary Fees, Collection of Accounts
A&G	Credit Card Comm.	Credit Card Commissions
A&G	Donations	Charitable Contributions
A&G	Dues & Subscriptions . . .	Dues—Hotel Associations (Non-Marketing)
A&G	Dues & Subscriptions . . .	Dues—Professional Associations (Non-Marketing)

Department/ Schedule	Account Name	Item Name
A&G	Dues & Subscriptions	Hotel Association Dues (Non-Marketing)
A&G	Dues & Subscriptions	Magazines—Trade (Non-Marketing)
A&G	Dues & Subscriptions	Membership Dues—Associations (Non-Marketing)
A&G	Dues & Subscriptions	Professional Dues (Non-Marketing)
A&G	Dues & Subscriptions	Subscriptions—Trade (Non-Marketing)
A&G	Equip. Rental	Computer Rental (Temporary-Accounting, Human Resources)
A&G	Human Resources	Advertising—Recruiting
A&G	Human Resources	Awards—Employees
A&G	Human Resources	Christmas Gifts—Employees
A&G	Human Resources	Clinic—Employees
A&G	Human Resources	Drug Testing of Employees
A&G	Human Resources	Entertainment, Employee
A&G	Human Resources	Fees, Medical
A&G	Human Resources	Help Wanted Ads
A&G	Human Resources	Housing, Employee
A&G	Human Resources	Interview Expenses
A&G	Human Resources	Investigation of Employees
A&G	Human Resources	Lodging of Employees
A&G	Human Resources	Medical Supplies for Employees
A&G	Human Resources	Medical Supplies and Drugs for Employees
A&G	Human Resources	Newsletter—House (for Employees)
A&G	Human Resources	Personnel Forms, General
A&G	Human Resources	Physician's Fees—Employees (Non–Workers' Compensation)
A&G	Human Resources	Posters, Safety
A&G	Human Resources	Prizes, Employee
A&G	Human Resources	Reference Checking, Employee
A&G	Human Resources	Social Activities, Employees
A&G	Human Resources	Sports Activities and Equipment, Employees
A&G	Human Resources	Suggestion Awards, Employees
A&G	Human Resources	Total Quality Management
A&G	Human Resources	Want Ads (Help Wanted)
A&G	Information Systems	Computer Manuals, Commercial
A&G	Information Systems	Computer Manuals, Printed
A&G	Information Systems	Computer Monitors
A&G	Information Systems	Computer Network Maintenance
A&G	Information Systems	Computer Software—Commercial Applications
A&G	Information Systems	Computer Supplies and Accessories

Department/ Schedule	Account Name	Item Name
A&G	Information Systems	Data Cartridges and Tapes
A&G	Information Systems	Data Processing Supplies
A&G	Information Systems	Ethernet Cables
A&G	Information Systems	Keyboards, Computer
A&G	Information Systems	Laptop Computers
A&G	Information Systems	Modem Lines
A&G	Information Systems	Modems
A&G	Information Systems	PMS System Maintenance
A&G	Information Systems	POS System Maintenance
A&G	Information Systems	Software Application Upgrades
A&G	Information Systems	Telecommunications Equipment Maintenance
A&G	Information Systems	Wireless Cards
A&G	Legal Services	Court/Legal Fees—Other than Collections
A&G	Licenses & Permits	Business Licenses, General
A&G	Loss & Damage	Lost and Damaged Articles—Guest
A&G	Operating Supplies	Books, Technical
A&G	Operating Supplies	Cash Boxes
A&G	Operating Supplies	Cashier Envelopes
A&G	Operating Supplies	Check Writer Machines
A&G	Operating Supplies	Coin Handling Equipment
A&G	Operating Supplies	Coin Wrappers
A&G	Operating Supplies	Coin/Currency Bag Seals
A&G	Operating Supplies	Coin/Currency Equipment
A&G	Operating Supplies	Computer Books
A&G	Operating Supplies	Computer Printer Paper
A&G	Operating Supplies	Correction Fluid/Tape
A&G	Operating Supplies	CPU Stands
A&G	Operating Supplies	Currency Bill Straps
A&G	Operating Supplies	Desk Pads (Employee)
A&G	Operating Supplies	Diskettes
A&G	Operating Supplies	Fax Machine Supplies and Accessories
A&G	Operating Supplies	Film Purchase and Developing
A&G	Operating Supplies	Letters for Bulletin/Sign Boards
A&G	Operating Supplies	Machine Stands
A&G	Operating Supplies	Mail Bags
A&G	Operating Supplies	Mail Chute Rentals
A&G	Operating Supplies	Microfiche Supplies
A&G	Operating Supplies	Presentation Binders
A&G	Operating Supplies	Report Covers
A&G	Operating Supplies	Ring Binders
A&G	Operating Supplies	Storage Files

Department/ Schedule	Account Name	Item Name
A&G	Operating Supplies	Tape Recorders
A&G	Operating Supplies	Tape Transcribers
A&G	Operating Supplies	Toner for Copiers
A&G	Payroll Processing	Payroll Processing Fees
A&G	P&ODC	Express Delivery Charges
A&G	P&ODC	Express Mail/UPS (Non-Marketing)
A&G	P&ODC	Freight Charges (Non-Marketing)
A&G	P&ODC	Overnight Delivery (Non-Marketing)
A&G	P&ODC	Post Office Box Rental
A&G	P&ODC	Postage (Non-Marketing)
A&G	P&ODC	Postage Meter Rentals (Non-Marketing)
A&G	Printing & Stationery	Billing Statements/Invoices
A&G	Printing & Stationery	Binding System Accessories
A&G	Printing & Stationery	Checks, Bank
A&G	Printing & Stationery	Credit Application Forms
A&G	Printing & Stationery	Credit Card Invoices
A&G	Printing & Stationery	Daily Reports
A&G	Printing & Stationery	Forms, Payroll and Tax
A&G	Printing & Stationery	Lost and Found Reports
A&G	Printing & Stationery	Petty Cash Forms
A&G	Printing & Stationery	Vouchers, Petty Cash
A&G	Professional Fees	Accountant's Fees, Consulting
A&G	Professional Fees	Commissions, Rental Agents
A&G	Professional Fees	Consultant Fees, Professional
A&G	Professional Fees	Fees, Audit—Public Accountants
A&G	Professional Fees	Fees, Stock Transfer Agents
A&G	Professional Fees	Fees, Transfer
A&G	Professional Fees	Fees, Trustees (Handling Bond, etc.)
A&G	Professional Fees	Notary Fees
A&G	Professional Fees	Professional Fees
A&G	Professional Fees	Stock Transfer Agents, Fees
A&G	Prov. for Doubtful Accts.	Bad Debt Allowance
A&G	Prov. for Doubtful Accts.	Provision for Doubtful Accounts
A&G	Prov. for Doubtful Accts.	Uncollectible Accounts
A&G	Salaries & Wages	Payroll—Employee Functions
A&G	Security	Armored Transport Fee
A&G	Security	Cameras, Security
A&G	Security	Detective Service
A&G	Security	Protective Service
A&G	Security	Safe Deposit Box Rentals (Off-Site)
A&G	Security	Security—Contracted

Department/Schedule	Account Name	Item Name
A&G	Settlement Costs	Claim/Litigation Settlement Costs, Contract Disputes
A&G	Settlement Costs	Claim/Litigation Settlement Costs, EEOC
A&G	Settlement Costs	Claim/Litigation Settlement Costs, Non-Insured
A&G	Training	Literature—Educational for Employees
A&G	Transportation	Auto Lease (Non-Capital) for General Manager
A&G	Transportation	Limousine—Employee Use
A&G	Transportation	Transportation of Employees
Beverage	Comp. Services/Gifts	Gratis Food—Bar
Beverage	Contract Services	Beer Coil Cleaning (Outside Service)
Beverage	Cost of Bev. Sales	Beer
Beverage	Cost of Bev. Sales	Liquor
Beverage	Cost of Bev. Sales	Mixers for Alcoholic Beverages
Beverage	Cost of Bev. Sales	Wine
Beverage	Glassware	Carafes
Beverage	Glassware	Glasses—Drinking (Alcoholic Beverage/All Sizes and Materials)
Beverage	Glassware	Shot Glasses—Bar
Beverage	Licenses & Permits	Licenses—Beverage
Beverage	Licenses & Permits	Licenses—Cabaret
Beverage	Licenses & Permits	Licenses—Temporary Space Liquor
Beverage	Linen	Towels, Bar
Beverage	Menus & Bev. Lists	Beverage Lists
Beverage	Menus & Bev. Lists	Wine Lists
Beverage	Operating Supplies	Bar Mats
Beverage	Operating Supplies	Ice Buckets
Beverage	Operating Supplies	Mats, Rubber (Bar)
Beverage	Operating Supplies	Wine Cellar Supplies
Beverage	Paper & Plastics	Cocktail Picks
Beverage	Paper & Plastics	Napkins, Cocktail
Beverage	Paper & Plastics	Stir Sticks, Cocktail
Beverage	Paper & Plastics	Straws, Cocktail
Beverage	Utensils	Blenders, Bar
Beverage	Utensils	Bottle Openers
Beverage	Utensils	Corkscrews
Beverage	Utensils	Mixing Cans, Bar
Beverage	Utensils	Pour Spouts, Liquor
Beverage	Utensils	Shakers, Bar
Beverage	Utensils	Stirrers, Beverage
Beverage	Utensils	Stoppers, Bottle—Bar

Department/ Schedule	Account Name	Item Name
Beverage	Utensils	Strainer, Bar
Empl. Caf.	China	Aluminum Trays, Employee Cafeteria
Empl. Caf.	China	Bowls, Employee Cafeteria
Empl. Caf.	China	China, Employee Cafeteria
Empl. Caf.	China	Coffee Pots, Employee Cafeteria
Empl. Caf.	China	Plates (Except Paper/Plastic), Employee Cafeteria
Empl. Caf.	Cost of Food	Meals, Employees
Empl. Caf.	Dishwashing Supplies ..	Dishwashing Soaps and Rinsing Agents, Employee Cafeteria
Empl. Caf.	Flatware	Flatware, Silverware, Employee Cafeteria
Empl. Caf.	Glassware	Glassware, Employee Cafeteria
Empl. Caf.	Ice	Dry Ice, Employee Cafeteria
Empl. Caf.	Kitchen Fuel	Food Warmer Fuel, Employee Cafeteria
Empl. Caf.	Kitchen Fuel	Fuel for Cooking, Employee Cafeteria
Empl. Caf.	Linen	Linen, Employee Cafeteria
Empl. Caf.	Operating Supplies	Trays (All Materials), Employee Cafeteria
Empl. Caf.	Paper & Plastics	Aluminum Foil, Employee Cafeteria
Empl. Caf.	Paper & Plastics	Coffee Filters, Employee Cafeteria
Empl. Caf.	Paper & Plastics	Cups, Paper/Plastic, Employee Cafeteria
Empl. Caf.	Paper & Plastics	Paper Plates/Cups/Napkins/Tablecloths, Employee Cafeteria
Empl. Caf.	Paper & Plastics	Plastic Flatware, Employee Cafeteria
Empl. Caf.	Paper & Plastics	Plates, Paper/Plastic, Employee Cafeteria
Empl. Caf.	Utensils	Utensils, Employee Cafeteria
Food	Banquet Expense	Table Rental (Banquet Not Charged to Customer)
Food	China	Aluminum Trays
Food	China	Bowls, Mixing/Preparation (All Sizes and Materials)
Food	China	Bowls, Serving (All Sizes and Materials)
Food	China	Butter Dishes (All Materials)
Food	China	Casseroles
Food	China	China
Food	China	China Rental
Food	China	Coffee Pots—Glass, Plastic, Silver
Food	China	Creamers
Food	China	Crocks (All Materials)
Food	China	Cups/Saucers, Cappuccino
Food	China	Cups/Saucers, Coffee
Food	China	Cups/Saucers, Espresso

Department/ Schedule	Account Name	Item Name
Food	China	Glass Bowls
Food	China	Glass Dishes
Food	China	Pitchers, Water
Food	China	Plates, All Sizes and Materials (Except Paper/ Plastic)
Food	China	Platters, Serving
Food	China	Ramekins (All Materials)
Food	China	Salad Bowls
Food	China	Salt and Pepper Shakers
Food	China	Sauce Boats (All Materials)
Food	China	Saucers, Coffee
Food	China	Souffle Dishes (All Materials)
Food	China	Sugar Holders
Food	China	Teapots and Lids (All Materials)
Food	Comp. Services/Gifts	Mints, Guest (Restaurant)
Food	Contract Services	Fumigators—Kitchen/Restaurant
Food	Contract Services	Kitchen Hood Cleaning
Food	Contract Services	Knife Sharpening
Food	Cost of Food Sales	Baked Goods
Food	Cost of Food Sales	Canned Food
Food	Cost of Food Sales	CO_2 for Soft Drink Mix
Food	Cost of Food Sales	Coffee
Food	Cost of Food Sales	Dairy Products
Food	Cost of Food Sales	Dry Goods (Flour, Pasta, etc.)
Food	Cost of Food Sales	Eggs
Food	Cost of Food Sales	Employee Meal Food Cost Credit
Food	Cost of Food Sales	Fish
Food	Cost of Food Sales	Fruit
Food	Cost of Food Sales	Meat
Food	Cost of Food Sales	Soft Drink Syrup or Premix
Food	Cost of Food Sales	Vegetables
Food	Decorations	Flower Vases, Glass (Tabletop)
Food	Decorations	Flowers (Tabletop)
Food	Decorations	Flowers, Banquet Tables
Food	Decorations	Ice Carvings/Sculpture
Food	Dishwashing Supplies	Dishwashing Soaps/Detergents/Rinsing Agents
Food	Dishwashing Supplies	Flatware Cleaner
Food	Dishwashing Supplies	Scouring Pads
Food	Dishwashing Supplies	Scrapers, Dish
Food	Dishwashing Supplies	Silver Polish

Department/ Schedule	Account Name	Item Name
Food	Dishwashing Supplies	Sponges, Dishwashing
Food	Dishwashing Supplies	Steel Wool
Food	Equip. Rental	Truck Rental (Food Delivery)
Food	Flatware	Flatware (Includes Silver, Stainless)
Food	Flatware	Flatware Rental
Food	Flatware	Serving Utensils (Non-Kitchen)
Food	Flatware	Tongs, Serving (Non-Kitchen)
Food	Flatware	Utensils, Serving (Non-Kitchen)
Food	Glassware	Cups, Drinking (Non-Coffee/All Sizes and Materials)
Food	Glassware	Glasses, Drinking (Non-Alcoholic/All Sizes and Materials)
Food	Glassware	Glassware Rental
Food	Ice	Dry Ice
Food	Kitchen Fuel	Butane Fuel
Food	Kitchen Fuel	Charcoal, Cooking
Food	Kitchen Fuel	Food Warmer Fuel
Food	Kitchen Fuel	Fuel, Kitchen
Food	Kitchen Fuel	Gas, Cooking
Food	Kitchen Fuel	Propane, Cooking and Preparation
Food	Kitchen Fuel	Sterno—Food Warming
Food	Laundry & Dry Cleaning	Linen Cleaning (All Types)
Food	Linen	Linen Napkins
Food	Linen	Linen Rental (All Types)
Food	Linen	Linen Tablecloth
Food	Linen	Table Runners, Linen
Food	Linen	Table Skirts, Linen
Food	Linen	Table Undercloth, Linen
Food	Misc. Cost of Other Rev.	Easels (Charged to Customer)
Food	Misc. Cost of Other Rev.	Flip Charts (Charged to Customers)
Food	Misc. Cost of Other Rev.	Freight and Shipping Charged to Banquet Customer
Food	Misc. Cost of Other Rev.	Tobacco Cost
Food	Misc. Cost of Other Rev.	Transportation Charged to Customer—Banquets
Food	Operating Supplies	Books—Outlet Reservations Log
Food	Operating Supplies	Cellophane Wrap
Food	Operating Supplies	Gas for Food Delivery Vehicle
Food	Operating Supplies	Glass Racks
Food	Operating Supplies	Hair Nets (Food Service Employee)
Food	Operating Supplies	Log Books, Outlet Reservations

Department/ Schedule	Account Name	Item Name
Food	Operating Supplies	Markers (Flip Chart)
Food	Operating Supplies	Reservation Books
Food	Operating Supplies	Rubber Boots, Kitchen
Food	Operating Supplies	Sneeze Guards
Food	Operating Supplies	Steak Markers
Food	Operating Supplies	Table Pads
Food	Operating Supplies	Tray Jacks
Food	Operating Supplies	Tray Liners
Food	Operating Supplies	Trays, Serving (All Materials)
Food	Operating Supplies	Vases (Tabletop)
Food	Paper & Plastics	Aluminum Foil
Food	Paper & Plastics	Bags, Paper Leftover
Food	Paper & Plastics	Boxes, Carry Out
Food	Paper & Plastics	Boxes, Pastry
Food	Paper & Plastics	Cardboard Boxes
Food	Paper & Plastics	Carry Out Containers
Food	Paper & Plastics	Chef Hats
Food	Paper & Plastics	Coffee Filters
Food	Paper & Plastics	Cups, Paper/Plastic
Food	Paper & Plastics	Doilies, Paper
Food	Paper & Plastics	Filter Paper
Food	Paper & Plastics	Foam Insulated Cups
Food	Paper & Plastics	Foil Wrapping
Food	Paper & Plastics	Liners, Paper
Food	Paper & Plastics	Paper Plates/Cups/Napkins/Tablecloths
Food	Paper & Plastics	Plastic Flatware
Food	Paper & Plastics	Plastic Food Storage Containers
Food	Paper & Plastics	Plastic Wrap
Food	Paper & Plastics	Plates, Paper/Plastic
Food	Paper & Plastics	Straws, Soft Drink
Food	Paper & Plastics	Styrofoam Cups
Food	Paper & Plastics	Tablecloths, Paper/Plastic
Food	Paper & Plastics	Toothpicks
Food	Paper & Plastics	Waxed Paper
Food	Utensils	Bags, Pastry
Food	Utensils	Beaters
Food	Utensils	Can Openers
Food	Utensils	Candle Holders, Tabletop
Food	Utensils	Chaffing Dishes
Food	Utensils	Coffee Urn
Food	Utensils	Colanders

Department/ Schedule	Account Name	Item Name
Food	Utensils	Cookie Cutters
Food	Utensils	Cooking Utensils
Food	Utensils	Cutting Boards
Food	Utensils	Food Processor
Food	Utensils	Forks, Kitchen
Food	Utensils	Ice Tongs
Food	Utensils	Knives, Kitchen
Food	Utensils	Ladles, Kitchen
Food	Utensils	Mixing Bowls
Food	Utensils	Molds
Food	Utensils	Openers, Can
Food	Utensils	Pans, Baking, Broiling, Frying
Food	Utensils	Plate Cover, Dome
Food	Utensils	Pocket Thermometers
Food	Utensils	Pots
Food	Utensils	Scissors, Kitchen
Food	Utensils	Spatulas, Kitchen
Food	Utensils	Spoons, Mixing
Food	Utensils	Tongs, Cooking
Food	Utensils	Tubes, Pastry
Food	Utensils	Utensils, Kitchen
Food	Utensils	Wire Whips
Food or Bev.	Audiovisual Cost	Audiovisual Equipment Rent (Charged to Customer)
Food or Bev.	China	Ash Trays, Aluminum, Glass
Food or Bev.	Comp. Services & Gifts . .	Customer Amenities (Newspapers, etc.)
Food or Bev.	Comp. Services & Gifts . .	Parking, Gratis—F&B Guest
Food or Bev.	Contract Services	Piano Tuning
Food or Bev.	Contract Services	Public Area Cleaning Service—Restaurant/ Banquet Foyers
Food or Bev.	Contract Services	Public Restroom Cleaning Service
Food or Bev.	Ice	Ice Consumption
Food or Bev.	Licenses & Permits	Health Permits
Food or Bev.	Licenses & Permits	Licenses, Checkrooms
Food or Bev.	Licenses & Permits	Licenses, Health Permit
Food or Bev.	Licenses & Permits	Licenses, Music Copyright
Food or Bev.	Licenses & Permits	Music Licenses
Food or Bev.	Menus & Bev. Lists	Menu Covers (Food or Beverage)
Food or Bev.	Menus & Bev. Lists	Menu Design (Food or Beverage)
Food or Bev.	Menus & Bev. Lists	Menu Printing (Food or Beverage)

Department/ Schedule	Account Name	Item Name
Food or Bev.	Misc. Cost of Other Rev.	Cigar Cost
Food or Bev.	Misc. Cost of Other Rev.	Electrical Hookup (Charged to Customer)
Food or Bev.	Music & Enter.	Meals, Musicians and Entertainers
Food or Bev.	Music & Enter.	Music—Live Musicians
Food or Bev.	Music & Enter.	Music—Mechanical
Food or Bev.	Music & Enter.	Piano Rental (Lounge/Restaurant Entertainment)
Food or Bev.	Music & Enter.	Room Costs, Musicians and Entertainers
Food or Bev.	Music & Enter.	Sheet Music
Food or Bev.	Operating Supplies	Check Presenters
Food or Bev.	Operating Supplies	Props, Banquets
Food or Bev.	Printing & Stationery	Guest Checks
Food or Bev.	Printing & Stationery	POS Supplies
Food or Bev.	Printing & Stationery	Table Tents
Golf/Pro Shop	Contract Services	Caddy Service
Golf/Pro Shop	Contract Services	Pest Control, Golf Course
Golf/Pro Shop	Contract Services	Tree Removal and Trimming Service, Golf Course
Golf/Pro Shop	Cost of Clothing Sales	Clothing, Golf (for Sale)
Golf/Pro Shop	Cost of Merch. Sales	Books, Golf (for Sale)
Golf/Pro Shop	Cost of Merch. Sales	Gloves, Golf (for Sale)
Golf/Pro Shop	Cost of Merch. Sales	Golf Bags (for Sale)
Golf/Pro Shop	Cost of Merch. Sales	Golf Balls (for Sale)
Golf/Pro Shop	Cost of Merch. Sales	Golf Clubs (for Sale)
Golf/Pro Shop	Cost of Merch. Sales	Magazines, Golf (for Sale)
Golf/Pro Shop	Cost of Merch. Sales	Pull-Carts, Golf (for Sale)
Golf/Pro Shop	Cost of Merch. Sales	Shoes, Golf (for Sale)
Golf/Pro Shop	Dues & Subscriptions	Magazines, Golf (for Staff Use)
Golf/Pro Shop	Equip. Rental	Golf Cart Rental
Golf/Pro Shop	Gasoline & Lubricants	Gasoline and Lubricants, Golf Cart
Golf/Pro Shop	Golf Cart Batteries/Elec.	Golf Cart Batteries
Golf/Pro Shop	Golf Cart R&M	Golf Cart Repairs and Maintenance
Golf/Pro Shop	Grounds M&L	Fences and Bridges Maintenance
Golf/Pro Shop	Grounds M&L	Fertilizers, Golf Course
Golf/Pro Shop	Grounds M&L	Flowers, Golf Course
Golf/Pro Shop	Grounds M&L	Insecticides, Golf Course
Golf/Pro Shop	Grounds M&L	Mowers, Tractors, and Trucks Maintenance
Golf/Pro Shop	Grounds M&L	Plants and Shrubs, Golf Course
Golf/Pro Shop	Grounds M&L	Repairs and Maintenance, Golf Cart Paths
Golf/Pro Shop	Grounds M&L	Reseeding Golf Course
Golf/Pro Shop	Grounds M&L	Sand, Cinders, and Top Dressing, Golf Course
Golf/Pro Shop	Grounds M&L	Seeds, Golf Course
Golf/Pro Shop	Grounds M&L	Signage, Golf Maintenance

Department/ Schedule	Account Name	Item Name
Golf/Pro Shop . . .	Grounds M&L	Topsoil, Golf Course
Golf/Pro Shop . . .	Irrigation	Water and Drainage Systems Maintenance
Golf/Pro Shop . . .	Irrigation	Water Controllers and Computerized Water Systems
Golf/Pro Shop . . .	Operating Supplies	Ball Washers, Golf Course
Golf/Pro Shop . . .	Operating Supplies	Flag Pins, Golf
Golf/Pro Shop . . .	Operating Supplies	Golf Bags (for Rental)
Golf/Pro Shop . . .	Operating Supplies	Golf Balls (Practice Range)
Golf/Pro Shop . . .	Operating Supplies	Golf Clubs (for Rental)
Golf/Pro Shop . . .	Operating Supplies	Pull-Carts, Golf (for Rental)
Golf/Pro Shop . . .	Operating Supplies	Shoes, Golf (for Rental)
Golf/Pro Shop . . .	Printing & Stationery . . .	Scorecards
Golf/Pro Shop . . .	Professional Fees	Professional Services, Contract Golf Pro
Golf/Pro Shop . . .	Professional Fees	Professional Services, Contract Groundskeepers
Golf/Pro Shop . . .	Tournament Expenses . . .	Banners, Golf Tournament
Golf/Pro Shop . . .	Tournament Expenses . . .	Cart Name Plates, Golf Tournament
Golf/Pro Shop . . .	Tournament Expenses . . .	Portable Sanitary Facilities, Golf Tournament
Golf/Pro Shop . . .	Tournament Expenses . . .	Prizes, Golf Tournament
Golf/Pro Shop . . .	Tournament Expenses . . .	Scoreboard Rental, Golf Tournament
Golf/Pro Shop . . .	Tournament Expenses . . .	Security, Golf Tournament
Golf/Pro Shop . . .	Tournament Expenses . . .	Software, Golf Tournament
Golf/Pro Shop . . .	Water	Water Usage—Golf Course
Health Club/Spa .	Ambience	Music, Health Club/Spa
Health Club/Spa .	Athletic Supplies	Gym Equipment (Non-Capital)
Health Club/Spa .	Comp. Services/Gifts . . .	Snacks, Health Club/Spa (Gratis)
Health Club/Spa .	Cost of Merch. Sales	Creams, Body/Face (for Sale)
Health Club/Spa .	Cost of Merch. Sales	Elixers (for Sale)
Health Club/Spa .	Cost of Merch. Sales	Lotions (for Sale)
Health Club/Spa .	Cost of Merch. Sales	Spa Products (for Sale)
Health Club/Spa .	Cost of Merch. Sales	Tonics (for Sale)
Health Club/Spa .	Health & Beauty Prod. . .	Creams, Body/Face
Health Club/Spa .	Health & Beauty Prod. . .	Elixers
Health Club/Spa .	Health & Beauty Prod. . .	Lotions
Health Club/Spa .	Health & Beauty Prod. . .	Spa Products
Health Club/Spa .	Health & Beauty Prod. . .	Tonics
Health Club/Spa .	Linen	Blankets
Health Club/Spa .	Linen	Face Cloths
Health Club/Spa .	Linen	Robes
Health Club/Spa .	Linen	Sheets
Health Club/Spa .	Linen	Slippers

Department/ Schedule	Account Name	Item Name
Health Club/Spa .	Linen	Towels
House Laundry . .	Cleaning Supplies	Detergent
House Laundry . .	Cleaning Supplies	Stain Remover
House Laundry . .	Laundry Supplies	Chemicals, Laundry
House Laundry . .	Laundry Supplies	Fabric Conditioner
House Laundry . .	Laundry Supplies	Fabric Softener
House Laundry . .	Laundry Supplies	Fabric Softener Packets
House Laundry . .	Laundry Supplies	Laundry Chemicals
House Laundry . .	Laundry Supplies	Laundry Soap
House Laundry . .	Laundry Supplies	Laundry Soap Packets
House Laundry . .	Laundry Supplies	Starch
House Laundry . .	Operating Supplies	Laundry Carts
House Laundry . .	Operating Supplies	Laundry Hampers
House Laundry . .	Operating Supplies	Laundry Tags
Mgt. Fees	Management Fees	Management Fee, Fixed
Mgt. Fees	Management Fees	Management Fee, Incentive
Mgt. Fees	Management Fees	Management Fee, Percentage of Revenue/Profit
Parking Garage . .	Cleaning Supplies	Cleaner, Concrete (Parking Garage)
Parking Garage . .	Contract Services	Customer Parking Paid to Third-Party
Parking Garage . .	Licenses & Permits	Garage Licenses
Parking Garage . .	Printing & Stationery . . .	Parking Gate Tickets
Parking Garage . .	Rent	Rent—Temporary Parking Space
POM	Building	Awning Repairs
POM	Building	Blinds Repair
POM	Building	Building Repairs
POM	Building	Ceiling Repairs
POM	Building	Curtain Repairs
POM	Building	Drapery Repairs
POM	Building	Key Blanks and Keys
POM	Building	Lock Repairs/Service
POM	Building	Plaster Repairs
POM	Building	Repairs and Maintenance, Half-Way House/ Restrooms (Golf)
POM	Building	Repairs and Maintenance, Storage Areas (Golf)
POM	Building	Replacement of Window Glass
POM	Building	Screen Repairs
POM	Building	Shutter Repair
POM	Building	Signs, Directional
POM	Building	Stairway Repairs
POM	Building	Valences/Swags

Department/ Schedule	Account Name	Item Name
POM	Building	Venetian Blinds Repairs
POM	Building	Window Locks
POM	Building	Window Shade Repairs
POM	Contract Services	Extermination Services
POM	Contract Services	Fumigation
POM	Contract Services	Pest Control Services
POM	Contract Services	Plant Services (Watering, etc.)
POM	Elec. & Mech.	Auto/Truck Repair—Property Use
POM	Elec. & Mech.	Electric Sub-Meters Maintenance
POM	Elec. & Mech.	Electric Supplies
POM	Elec. & Mech.	Electrical Repairs
POM	Elec. & Mech.	Generator Repairs
POM	Elec. & Mech.	Light Fixture Repairs
POM	Elec. & Mech.	Maintenance Contracts—Electric Signs, Office Equipment
POM	Elec. & Mech.	Motor Repairs
POM	Elec. & Mech.	Public Address System Repairs
POM	Elec. & Mech.	Pump Repairs
POM	Elec. & Mech.	Sound System Repairs
POM	Elec. & Mech.	Table Cover Repair/Replacement
POM	Elevators & Escalators	Elevator and Escalator Repairs
POM	Elevators & Escalators	Maintenance Contracts, Elevators and Escalators
POM	Engineering Supplies	Pest Control Supplies (In-House Use)
POM	Engineering Supplies	Shovels
POM	Engineering Supplies	Tools
POM	Equip. Rental	Generator Rentals (Property Power Back-Up)
POM	Equip. Rental	Paint Sprayer Rental
POM	Equip. Rental	Platform Lift/Cherry Picker Rental
POM	Floor Covering	Adhesive, Stair Tread
POM	Floor Covering	Carpet Repairs
POM	Floor Covering	Floor Refinishing
POM	Floor Covering	Tape, Carpet
POM	Floor Covering	Tile Repairs (Floor)
POM	Furniture & Equip.	Bedsprings Repairs
POM	Furniture & Equip.	Furniture Refinishing
POM	Furniture & Equip.	Furniture Repairs
POM	Furniture & Equip.	Lamp Finials
POM	Furniture & Equip.	Lamp Repairs
POM	Furniture & Equip.	Mattress Repair
POM	Furniture & Equip.	Table-Top Repair/Replacement, Glass

Department/ Schedule	Account Name	Item Name
POM	Furniture & Equip.	Television Repairs
POM	Furniture & Equip.	Upholstery Repairs
POM	Grounds M&L	Fertilizer
POM	Grounds M&L	Flower Purchases
POM	Grounds M&L	Irrigation System Repairs
POM	Grounds M&L	Landscaping Service (Indoor and Outdoor)
POM	Grounds M&L	Plant Purchases (Indoor and Outdoor)
POM	Grounds M&L	Plant Rentals
POM	Grounds M&L	Shovels, Snow
POM	Grounds M&L	Snow Removal Service
POM	Grounds M&L	Tree Purchases
POM	Grounds M&L	Tree Rentals
POM	HVAC Equip.	Air Conditioner Filters
POM	HVAC Equip.	Air Filters
POM	HVAC Equip.	Air-Cooling Systems Repairs
POM	HVAC Equip.	Boiler Repairs
POM	HVAC Equip.	Ceiling Fan Repairs
POM	HVAC Equip.	Central Plant Costs
POM	HVAC Equip.	Chemicals, Cooling Tower
POM	HVAC Equip.	Cooling System Repairs
POM	HVAC Equip.	Cooling Tower Repairs
POM	HVAC Equip.	Filters, Air Conditioning/Heating
POM	HVAC Equip.	Heat Pump Repairs
POM	HVAC Equip.	Heating System Repairs
POM	HVAC Equip.	Refrigeration Supplies (HVAC)
POM	Kitchen Equip.	Coffee Urn Repairs
POM	Kitchen Equip.	Dishwasher Repairs
POM	Kitchen Equip.	Kitchen Equipment Repairs
POM	Kitchen Equip.	Refrigerator Repairs, Kitchen
POM	Kitchen Equip.	Stock Pot Repairs
POM	Laundry Equip.	Laundry Dryer Repairs
POM	Laundry Equip.	Laundry Ironer Repairs
POM	Laundry Equip.	Laundry Sheet Folder Repairs
POM	Laundry Equip.	Laundry Washer Repairs
POM	Laundry Equip.	Mangle Belts
POM	Licenses & Permits	Inspection Fees—Boilers, Elevators, Escalators, Life/Safety
POM	Licenses & Permits	Licenses, Elevators
POM	Licenses & Permits	Licenses, Engineering
POM	Licenses & Permits	Licenses, Locksmith

Department/ Schedule	Account Name	Item Name
POM	Life/Safety	Accessibility Sign
POM	Life/Safety	ADA Compliance Items
POM	Life/Safety	Alarm Systems
POM	Life/Safety	Alert Device for Hearing-Impaired
POM	Life/Safety	Chemicals, Fire Extinguishers
POM	Life/Safety	Emergency Exit Signs
POM	Life/Safety	Exit Signs
POM	Life/Safety	Fire Alarm Service
POM	Life/Safety	Fire Axes
POM	Life/Safety	Fire Bucket Sand
POM	Life/Safety	Fire Extinguisher
POM	Life/Safety	Fire Extinguisher Chemicals
POM	Life/Safety	Hazardous Materials Remediation
POM	Life/Safety	Sand, Fire Buckets
POM	Life/Safety	Smoke Alarms
POM	Light Bulbs	Electric Bulbs
POM	Light Bulbs	Fluorescent Light Bulbs
POM	Operating Supplies	Auto Supplies Used by Properties
POM	Operating Supplies	Boiler Room Supplies
POM	Operating Supplies	Duct Tape
POM	Operating Supplies	Electrical Tape
POM	Operating Supplies	Manuals, Service (Instructional Materials)
POM	Operating Supplies	Mats, Floor
POM	Operating Supplies	Mats, Rubber
POM	Operating Supplies	Tape
POM	Operating Supplies	Technical Books, Maintenance
POM	Operating Supplies	Trade Publications, Repair/Maintenance
POM	Painting & Decorating	Paint
POM	Painting & Decorating	Paint Brushes/Rollers
POM	Painting & Decorating	Paint Thinner
POM	Painting & Decorating	Painting, Contracted
POM	Painting & Decorating	Tape, Painters
POM	Painting & Decorating	Vinyl Wall Covering
POM	Painting & Decorating	Wallpaper
POM	Plumbing	Drain System Repairs
POM	Plumbing	Plumbing Fixture Repairs
POM	Plumbing	Stoppers, Sink/Tub
POM	Plumbing	Tank, Toilet Floats
POM	Printing & Stationery	Maintenance Request Forms

Department/ Schedule	Account Name	Item Name
POM	Swimming Pool	Swimming Pool/Spa Accessories/Chemicals/ Maintenance
POM	Swimming Pool	Swimming Pool/Spa Repairs
POM	Waste Removal	Trash Container Charges
POM	Waste Removal	Waste, Garbage, Refuse, Rubbish, Ash Removal
R/POT/I	Building & Contents	Insurance Deductibles, Property
R/POT/I	Building & Contents	Insurance Expenses, Boiler Explosion
R/POT/I	Building & Contents	Insurance Expenses, Business Interruption
R/POT/I	Building & Contents	Insurance Expenses, Earthquake
R/POT/I	Building & Contents	Insurance Expenses, Fire
R/POT/I	Building & Contents	Insurance Expenses, Property
R/POT/I	Building & Contents	Insurance Expenses, Tornado
R/POT/I	Building & Contents	Insurance Expenses, Weather
R/POT/I	Building & Contents	Insurance Expenses, Building
R/POT/I	Building & Contents	Insurance Expenses, Furnishings and Equipment
R/POT/I	Building & Contents	Underinsured Losses, Property
R/POT/I	B/TO Taxes	Business Taxes—State/County/City
R/POT/I	B/TO Taxes	Gross Receipts Taxes Not Paid by Customers— State/County/City
R/POT/I	B/TO Taxes	Sales and Occupancy Taxes Not Paid by Customers
R/POT/I	IS Equip.	Call Accounting System Lease (Non-Capital)
R/POT/I	IS Equip.	Call Accounting System Software Lease (Non- Capital)
R/POT/I	IS Equip.	Computer Hardware Lease (Non-Capital)
R/POT/I	IS Equip.	Computer Software Lease (Non-Capital)
R/POT/I	IS Equip.	Personal Computer Lease (Non-Capital)
R/POT/I	IS Equip.	PMS Hardware Lease (Non-Capital)
R/POT/I	IS Equip.	PMS Software Lease (Non-Capital)
R/POT/I	IS Equip.	POS Hardware Lease (Non-Capital)
R/POT/I	IS Equip.	POS Software Lease (Non-Capital)
R/POT/I	Land & Buildings	Building Lease, Base
R/POT/I	Land & Buildings	Building Lease, Participating (Based on Operating Results)
R/POT/I	Land & Buildings	Land Lease
R/POT/I	Liability	Insurance Deductibles—Liability/Burglary, Theft, Umbrella
R/POT/I	Liability	Insurance Expenses, Burglary
R/POT/I	Liability	Insurance Expenses, Guest Liability
R/POT/I	Liability	Insurance Expenses, Liability

Department/ Schedule	Account Name	Item Name
R/POT/I	Liability	Insurance Expenses, Theft
R/POT/I	Liability	Insurance Expenses, Umbrella
R/POT/I	Liability	Underinsured Losses, Liability
R/POT/I	Other Property & Equip.	Copier Lease (Non-Capital)
R/POT/I	Other Property & Equip.	Trash Compactor Lease (Non-Capital)
R/POT/I	Other Property & Equip.	Vehicle Lease (Non-Capital)
R/POT/I	Personal Property Taxes .	Personal Property Tax Refunds (Contra)—State/ County/City
R/POT/I	Personal Property Taxes .	Personal Property Taxes—State/County/City
R/POT/I	Real Estate Taxes	Attorney's Fees/Expenses, Real Estate Taxes
R/POT/I	Real Estate Taxes	Consultant Fees—Property Taxes
R/POT/I	Real Estate Taxes	Legal Fees/Expenses—Real Estate Taxes
R/POT/I	Real Estate Taxes	Real Property Tax Refunds (Contra)—State/ County/City
R/POT/I	Real Estate Taxes	Real Property Taxes—State/County/City
R/POT/I	Telecom. Equip.	Telephone Hardware Lease (Non-Capital)
R/POT/I	Telecom. Equip.	Telephone Software Lease (Non-Capital)
R/POT/I	Telecom. Equip.	Telephone Switch Lease (Non-Capital)
Rooms	Cable/Satellite TV	Cable Television Service
Rooms	Cable/Satellite TV	HBO
Rooms	Cable/Satellite TV	Satellite Television Service
Rooms	Cable/Satellite TV	VCR, Guestroom
Rooms	Cleaning Supplies	Carpet Cleaner Equipment
Rooms	Cleaning Supplies	Deodorizers
Rooms	Cleaning Supplies	Soap and Soap Dishes, Guestroom
Rooms	Cleaning Supplies	Soap Scum Remover, Guestroom
Rooms	Commissions	Commissions, Travel Agent (Food and Beverage)
Rooms	Commissions	Commissions, Travel Agent (Rooms)
Rooms	Comms./Rebates—Group	Commissions, Meeting Planners
Rooms	Comp. Services/Gifts . . .	Welcome Baskets, Guestroom
Rooms	Contract Services	In-Room Guest Account Services (Check-Out)
Rooms	Contract Services	Public Area Cleaning Service, Lobby/Guestroom Corridors
Rooms	Contract Services	Video Check-Out Service
Rooms	Contract Services	Video Comment Card Service
Rooms	Guest Relocation	Guest Relocation Due to Lack of Room Availability
Rooms	Guest Supplies	Aftershave Lotion
Rooms	Guest Supplies	Amenities, Guest
Rooms	Guest Supplies	Amenity Baskets/Containers (Not Reusable)

Department/ Schedule	Account Name	Item Name
Rooms	Guest Supplies	Antacid (for Use by Guests in Rooms)
Rooms	Guest Supplies	Aspirin (for Use by Guests in Rooms)
Rooms	Guest Supplies	Baggage Tags, Gratis
Rooms	Guest Supplies	Bath Gel
Rooms	Guest Supplies	Bath Salts
Rooms	Guest Supplies	Bath Sheets
Rooms	Guest Supplies	Bath Soap
Rooms	Guest Supplies	Bath Tissue
Rooms	Guest Supplies	Bathing Cap
Rooms	Guest Supplies	Bathing Suits, Disposable
Rooms	Guest Supplies	Body Lotion
Rooms	Guest Supplies	Bottled Water, Gratis in Rooms
Rooms	Guest Supplies	Buttons (for Use by Guests in Rooms)
Rooms	Guest Supplies	Candy (Gratis)
Rooms	Guest Supplies	Coffee Filters
Rooms	Guest Supplies	Coffee (for Use by Guests in Rooms)
Rooms	Guest Supplies	Combs
Rooms	Guest Supplies	Conditioner, Hair
Rooms	Guest Supplies	Cookie Wrappings, Guestroom
Rooms	Guest Supplies	Cookies, Guestroom
Rooms	Guest Supplies	Cosmetics
Rooms	Guest Supplies	Creamer Packets
Rooms	Guest Supplies	Creams, Body/Face (Guestroom)
Rooms	Guest Supplies	Cups, Paper/Plastic/Disposable (Guestroom)
Rooms	Guest Supplies	Dental Floss
Rooms	Guest Supplies	Dental Kit
Rooms	Guest Supplies	Deodorant
Rooms	Guest Supplies	Detergent for Use by Guests in Rooms
Rooms	Guest Supplies	Dish Soap for Use by Guests in Rooms
Rooms	Guest Supplies	Dishwasher Soap for Use by Guests in Rooms
Rooms	Guest Supplies	Dry-Cleaning Bag for Use by Guests in Rooms
Rooms	Guest Supplies	Emery Boards
Rooms	Guest Supplies	Espresso Pods for Use by Guests in Rooms
Rooms	Guest Supplies	Facial Tissue
Rooms	Guest Supplies	Fans, Paper (for Use by Guests in Rooms)
Rooms	Guest Supplies	Filters, Coffee
Rooms	Guest Supplies	Fingernail File
Rooms	Guest Supplies	Fire-Starter Packets for Use by Guests in Rooms
Rooms	Guest Supplies	Hair Nets
Rooms	Guest Supplies	Hair Pins
Rooms	Guest Supplies	Hair Spray

Department/ Schedule	Account Name	Item Name
Rooms	Guest Supplies	Hairbrushes
Rooms	Guest Supplies	Hand Lotion
Rooms	Guest Supplies	Hand Sanitizer
Rooms	Guest Supplies	Hand Soap for Use by Guests in Rooms
Rooms	Guest Supplies	Hot Chocolate Packets for Use by Guests in Rooms
Rooms	Guest Supplies	Laundry Bag (Disposable) for Use by Guests in Rooms
Rooms	Guest Supplies	Liquid Soap for Use by Guests in Rooms
Rooms	Guest Supplies	Luggage Tags for Use by Guests in Rooms
Rooms	Guest Supplies	Magazines for Use by Guests in Rooms
Rooms	Guest Supplies	Makeup Remover for Use by Guests in Rooms
Rooms	Guest Supplies	Mouthwash for Use by Guests in Rooms
Rooms	Guest Supplies	Nail Polish Remover for Use by Guests in Rooms
Rooms	Guest Supplies	Newspaper Bags for Use by Guests in Rooms
Rooms	Guest Supplies	Newspapers for Use by Guests in Rooms
Rooms	Guest Supplies	Pens for Use by Guests in Rooms
Rooms	Guest Supplies	Pillow Mints
Rooms	Guest Supplies	Playing Cards for Use by Guests in Rooms
Rooms	Guest Supplies	Post Cards for Use by Guests in Rooms
Rooms	Guest Supplies	Razors for Use by Guests in Rooms
Rooms	Guest Supplies	Sanitary Pads/Tampons
Rooms	Guest Supplies	Serving Spoons for Use by Guests in Rooms
Rooms	Guest Supplies	Sewing Kits for Use by Guests in Rooms
Rooms	Guest Supplies	Shampoo for Use by Guests in Rooms
Rooms	Guest Supplies	Shaving Cream/Gel for Use by Guests in Rooms
Rooms	Guest Supplies	Shoe Brushes for Use by Guests in Rooms
Rooms	Guest Supplies	Shoe Mitt for Use by Guests in Rooms
Rooms	Guest Supplies	Shoe Polish for Use by Guests in Rooms
Rooms	Guest Supplies	Shower Caps for Use by Guests in Rooms
Rooms	Guest Supplies	Silverware for Use by Guests in Rooms
Rooms	Guest Supplies	Soda for Use by Guests in Rooms
Rooms	Guest Supplies	Stationery for Use by Guests in Rooms
Rooms	Guest Supplies	Stir Sticks for Use by Guests in Rooms
Rooms	Guest Supplies	Sugar Packets
Rooms	Guest Supplies	Sweetener Packets for Use by Guests in Rooms
Rooms	Guest Supplies	Swimsuit Bags for Use by Guests in Rooms
Rooms	Guest Supplies	Swizzle Sticks for Use by Guests in Rooms
Rooms	Guest Supplies	Tags, Baggage (Gratis)
Rooms	Guest Supplies	Tea Bags for Use by Guests in Rooms

Department/ Schedule	Account Name	Item Name
Rooms	Guest Supplies	Telephone Message Pads
Rooms	Guest Supplies	Thread for Use by Guests in Rooms
Rooms	Guest Supplies	Tissue for Use by Guests in Rooms
Rooms	Guest Supplies	Toilet Seat Covers
Rooms	Guest Supplies	Toilet Tissue
Rooms	Guest Supplies	Toothbrush for Use by Guests in Rooms
Rooms	Guest Supplies	Toothpaste for Use by Guests in Rooms
Rooms	Guest Supplies	Toothpicks for Use by Guests in Rooms
Rooms	Guest Supplies	Towelettes for Use by Guests in Rooms
Rooms	Guest Supplies	Tweezers for Use by Guests in Rooms
Rooms	Guest Transportation	Airport Van Maintenance
Rooms	Guest Transportation	Car Washing (Rooms Vans, Carts, Limos)
Rooms	Guest Transportation	Fuel Costs, Auto/Cart (Guest Transport)
Rooms	Guest Transportation	Guest Transportation Service Contracts
Rooms	Guest Transportation	Limousine Services, Guest (No Charge)
Rooms	Linen	Bath Towels (All Sizes)
Rooms	Linen	Bathmats
Rooms	Linen	Bathroom Throw Rugs
Rooms	Linen	Bed Pads
Rooms	Linen	Bed Ruffles
Rooms	Linen	Bed Skirts
Rooms	Linen	Bedspreads
Rooms	Linen	Blanket Covers
Rooms	Linen	Blankets, Guestroom
Rooms	Linen	Bumpers, Bed
Rooms	Linen	Bumpers, Crib
Rooms	Linen	Bunting
Rooms	Linen	Comforters
Rooms	Linen	Duvet Covers
Rooms	Linen	Duvets
Rooms	Linen	Hand Towels
Rooms	Linen	Mattress Cover
Rooms	Linen	Mattress Pad
Rooms	Linen	Pillow Cases
Rooms	Linen	Pillow Shams
Rooms	Linen	Pillows—Decorative, Down, Foam, Neck, Polyester, Throw
Rooms	Linen	Quilt
Rooms	Linen	Robes
Rooms	Linen	Rubber Sheets

Department/ Schedule	Account Name	Item Name
Rooms	Linen	Rugs, Bathroom
Rooms	Linen	Shams
Rooms	Linen	Sheets, Fitted / Flat
Rooms	Linen	Towels—Bath (All Sizes), Guestroom Bar, Hand
Rooms	Linen	Wash Cloths
Rooms	Operating Supplies	Afghans, Guestroom
Rooms	Operating Supplies	Amenity Baskets / Containers (Reusable)
Rooms	Operating Supplies	Aquarium Supplies, Guestroom or Lobby
Rooms	Operating Supplies	Aquarium, Guestroom or Lobby
Rooms	Operating Supplies	Bags, Beverage Glass Covers, Guestroom
Rooms	Operating Supplies	Baskets, Amenity
Rooms	Operating Supplies	Bathroom Scale
Rooms	Operating Supplies	Bathtub Safety Mats
Rooms	Operating Supplies	Bathtub Safety Strips
Rooms	Operating Supplies	Blackout Drapes
Rooms	Operating Supplies	Books, In-Room Guest Reading
Rooms	Operating Supplies	Bottle Openers, Guestroom
Rooms	Operating Supplies	Bottle Warmers
Rooms	Operating Supplies	Braille Signs
Rooms	Operating Supplies	Can Openers
Rooms	Operating Supplies	Candy Dishes, Guestroom (Gratis Candy for Customers)
Rooms	Operating Supplies	Canopies, Bed
Rooms	Operating Supplies	Cappuccino Machines
Rooms	Operating Supplies	Carafes, Guestroom
Rooms	Operating Supplies	Carts, Laundry
Rooms	Operating Supplies	Carts, Housekeeper
Rooms	Operating Supplies	China, Guestroom
Rooms	Operating Supplies	Clock Radios, Guestroom
Rooms	Operating Supplies	Clock/DVD Players, Guestroom
Rooms	Operating Supplies	Clocks, Guestroom
Rooms	Operating Supplies	Closet Rod
Rooms	Operating Supplies	Closet Sachets
Rooms	Operating Supplies	Clothes Brushes
Rooms	Operating Supplies	Coasters
Rooms	Operating Supplies	Coffee Mugs
Rooms	Operating Supplies	Coffee Pots
Rooms	Operating Supplies	Computer Monitors, Guestrooms
Rooms	Operating Supplies	Containers, Amenity
Rooms	Operating Supplies	Cords

Department/ Schedule	Account Name	Item Name
Rooms	Operating Supplies	Cords, Drapery
Rooms	Operating Supplies	Corkscrews
Rooms	Operating Supplies	Cots
Rooms	Operating Supplies	Cotton Balls
Rooms	Operating Supplies	Covers, Toilet Seat
Rooms	Operating Supplies	Crib Bumper Pads
Rooms	Operating Supplies	Crib Covers
Rooms	Operating Supplies	Crib Mattresses
Rooms	Operating Supplies	Cribs
Rooms	Operating Supplies	Cups, China (Guestroom)
Rooms	Operating Supplies	Dish Drainer, Guestroom
Rooms	Operating Supplies	Dishcloth, Guestroom
Rooms	Operating Supplies	Dishes for Use by Guests in Rooms
Rooms	Operating Supplies	Dispensers, Bath Tissue
Rooms	Operating Supplies	Dispensers, Lotion/Soap
Rooms	Operating Supplies	Do Not Disturb Cards
Rooms	Operating Supplies	Doilies, Guestroom
Rooms	Operating Supplies	Door Viewer
Rooms	Operating Supplies	Doormats
Rooms	Operating Supplies	Doorstop
Rooms	Operating Supplies	Dryers, Hair
Rooms	Operating Supplies	DVD Players, Guestrooms
Rooms	Operating Supplies	Emergency Exit Instruction Card
Rooms	Operating Supplies	Espresso Maker, Guestroom
Rooms	Operating Supplies	Facial Tissue Box Cover
Rooms	Operating Supplies	Flatware for Use by Guests in Rooms
Rooms	Operating Supplies	Gideon Bibles
Rooms	Operating Supplies	Glass Bags
Rooms	Operating Supplies	Glass Covers
Rooms	Operating Supplies	Glassware (All Types) for Use by Guests in Rooms
Rooms	Operating Supplies	Hair Dryers
Rooms	Operating Supplies	Hangers—Padded, Pant, Skirt, Suit
Rooms	Operating Supplies	Housekeeper Carts
Rooms	Operating Supplies	Humidifier
Rooms	Operating Supplies	Ice Bucket Liners
Rooms	Operating Supplies	Ice Buckets
Rooms	Operating Supplies	Ice Tongs
Rooms	Operating Supplies	Inflatable Beds
Rooms	Operating Supplies	Innkeepers Liability Card Frames

Department/ Schedule	Account Name	Item Name
Rooms	Operating Supplies	Ironing Board
Rooms	Operating Supplies	Ironing Board Cover
Rooms	Operating Supplies	Ironing Board Holder
Rooms	Operating Supplies	Irons
Rooms	Operating Supplies	Key Cards
Rooms	Operating Supplies	Keys, Safe Deposit Box
Rooms	Operating Supplies	Laundry Bags (Cloth) for Use by Guests in Rooms
Rooms	Operating Supplies	Luggage Racks
Rooms	Operating Supplies	Make-Up Mirror
Rooms	Operating Supplies	Mattress, Crib
Rooms	Operating Supplies	Mattress Protectors
Rooms	Operating Supplies	Microwave, Guestroom
Rooms	Operating Supplies	Mouse Traps
Rooms	Operating Supplies	Mugs, Coffee, for Use by Guests in Rooms
Rooms	Operating Supplies	Napkins (Paper/Cloth) for Use by Guests in Rooms
Rooms	Operating Supplies	Night Lights
Rooms	Operating Supplies	Paper Towel Holder, Guestroom
Rooms	Operating Supplies	Paper Towels, Guestroom
Rooms	Operating Supplies	Paper Tray Liners, Guestroom
Rooms	Operating Supplies	Phone Books, Guestroom
Rooms	Operating Supplies	Pitchers, Guestrooms
Rooms	Operating Supplies	Placemats, Guestrooms
Rooms	Operating Supplies	Playpens
Rooms	Operating Supplies	Plungers, Toilet
Rooms	Operating Supplies	Potholder Mitt, Guestroom
Rooms	Operating Supplies	Potholder, Guestroom
Rooms	Operating Supplies	Presto Logs, Guestroom
Rooms	Operating Supplies	Quilt Rack
Rooms	Operating Supplies	Radios, Guestroom
Rooms	Operating Supplies	Rollaway Beds
Rooms	Operating Supplies	Rubber Tub Mat
Rooms	Operating Supplies	Safety Deposit Box Keys
Rooms	Operating Supplies	Shaving Mirror, Guestroom
Rooms	Operating Supplies	Sheers
Rooms	Operating Supplies	Shower Curtain
Rooms	Operating Supplies	Shower Curtain Liners
Rooms	Operating Supplies	Shower Curtain Rings
Rooms	Operating Supplies	Shower Slippers

Department/ Schedule	Account Name	Item Name
Rooms	Operating Supplies	Slippers for Use by Guests in Rooms
Rooms	Operating Supplies	Speakers, Guestroom
Rooms	Operating Supplies	Spoons for Use by Guests in Rooms
Rooms	Operating Supplies	Stationery Portfolio
Rooms	Operating Supplies	Strainers, Guestroom
Rooms	Operating Supplies	Sugar Caddy, Guestroom
Rooms	Operating Supplies	Table Pads, Guestroom
Rooms	Operating Supplies	Table Protectors, Guestroom
Rooms	Operating Supplies	Table Tent Cards, Guestroom
Rooms	Operating Supplies	Tablecloths, Guestroom
Rooms	Operating Supplies	Teapots, Guestroom
Rooms	Operating Supplies	Telephone Directories, Guestroom
Rooms	Operating Supplies	Television Remote
Rooms	Operating Supplies	Throw, Guestroom
Rooms	Operating Supplies	Tissue Box Covers, Guestroom
Rooms	Operating Supplies	Toothbrush Holders, Guestroom
Rooms	Operating Supplies	Toys for Use by Guests in Rooms
Rooms	Operating Supplies	Trays, Guestroom
Rooms	Operating Supplies	Tumblers, Guestroom
Rooms	Operating Supplies	TV Guides, Guestroom
Rooms	Operating Supplies	Water Pitchers, Guestroom
Rooms	Printing & Stationery ...	Cable Guide Cover
Rooms	Printing & Stationery ...	Check-In Folders
Rooms	Printing & Stationery ...	Check-Out Folders
Rooms	Printing & Stationery ...	Check-Out Notices
Rooms	Printing & Stationery ...	Folios
Rooms	Printing & Stationery ...	Guest Guide
Rooms	Printing & Stationery ...	Hotel Maps
Rooms	Printing & Stationery ...	Housekeeping Reports
Rooms	Printing & Stationery ...	Innkeepers Liability Cards
Rooms	Printing & Stationery ...	Maps
Rooms	Printing & Stationery ...	Room Attendant Reports
Rooms	Printing & Stationery ...	Room Directories
Rooms	Printing & Stationery ...	Room Directory Binders
Rooms	Printing & Stationery ...	Room Rack Forms
Rooms	Printing & Stationery ...	Room Service Breakfast Card
Rooms	Printing & Stationery ...	Safe Deposit Record Cards
Rooms	Printing & Stationery ...	Telephone Message Cards
Rooms	Printing & Stationery ...	Water Conservation Cards
Rooms	Reservations	Internet Web Page Reservations
Rooms	Reservations	Reservation Fees (Chain Assessment)

Department/ Schedule	Account Name	Item Name
Rooms	Reservations	Reservation Fees (GDS)
Rooms	Reservations	Reservation Telephone Expense
Rooms	Reservations	Reservation Web Site Building and Maintenance
Rooms	Reservations	Stamps, Reservations
Sales/Marketing	Agency fees	Advertising Agency Fees
Sales/Marketing	Collateral Material	Collateral Selling
Sales/Marketing	Contract Services	Clipping Services
Sales/Marketing	Contract Services	Meeting Planner Surveys (Outside Service)
Sales/Marketing	Contract Services	Representation Firms, Convention
Sales/Marketing	Corp. Office Reimb.	Corporate Sales/Marketing Support
Sales/Marketing	Direct Mail	Address List Maintenance/Purchase/Rental
Sales/Marketing	Direct Mail	Database Marketing Expense
Sales/Marketing	Direct Mail	Mailing Lists
Sales/Marketing	Direct Mail	Newsletters
Sales/Marketing	Direct Mail	Postage for Promotional Mailings
Sales/Marketing	Dues & Subscriptions	Association Dues—Marketing Employees
Sales/Marketing	Dues & Subscriptions	Convention Bureau
Sales/Marketing	Dues & Subscriptions	Dues, Hotel Associations (Marketing)
Sales/Marketing	Dues & Subscriptions	Dues, Professional Associations (Marketing)
Sales/Marketing	Dues & Subscriptions	Hotel Association Dues (Marketing)
Sales/Marketing	Dues & Subscriptions	Hotel Sales and Marketing Association Dues
Sales/Marketing	Dues & Subscriptions	Magazines, Trade (Marketing)
Sales/Marketing	Dues & Subscriptions	Membership Dues, Associations (Marketing)
Sales/Marketing	Dues & Subscriptions	Professional Dues (Marketing)
Sales/Marketing	Dues & Subscriptions	Subscriptions, Trade (Marketing)
Sales/Marketing	Dues & Subscriptions	Trade Publication Subscriptions (Marketing)
Sales/Marketing	E-Commerce	Web Site Development
Sales/Marketing	Fam Trips	Familiarization (FAM) Tour Expenses
Sales/Marketing	Franch./Aff. Advertising	Cooperative Marketing Costs, National/Regional
Sales/Marketing	Franchise Fees	Franchise Fee (Chain Royalty)
Sales/Marketing	In-House Graphics	POS Promotional Materials
Sales/Marketing	Loyalty Progs./Aff. Fees	Frequent Flyer Programs
Sales/Marketing	Loyalty Progs./Aff. Fees	Frequent Guest Programs
Sales/Marketing	Loyalty Progs./Aff. Fees	Guest Loyalty Programs
Sales/Marketing	Loyalty Progs./Aff. Fees	Referral Programs
Sales/Marketing	Media	Advertising—Direct Mail
Sales/Marketing	Media	Advertising—Directories
Sales/Marketing	Media	Advertising—Internet
Sales/Marketing	Media	Advertising—Magazines
Sales/Marketing	Media	Advertising—Newspapers
Sales/Marketing	Media	Advertising—Publications

Department/ Schedule	Account Name	Item Name
Sales/Marketing .	Media	Advertising—Radio and TV
Sales/Marketing .	Media	Barter/Contra Agreement
Sales/Marketing .	Media	Brochures, Sales/Marketing
Sales/Marketing .	Media	Directory Advertising
Sales/Marketing .	Media	In-House Video—Welcome Channel
Sales/Marketing .	Media	Internet Advertising
Sales/Marketing .	Media	Magazine Advertising
Sales/Marketing .	Media	Media—Magazines
Sales/Marketing .	Media	Media—Newspapers
Sales/Marketing .	Media	Media—Other
Sales/Marketing .	Media	Media—TV
Sales/Marketing .	Media	Production—Magazines
Sales/Marketing .	Media	Production—Newspapers
Sales/Marketing .	Media	Production—Other
Sales/Marketing .	Media	Production—TV
Sales/Marketing .	Media	Telephone Directory Advertising
Sales/Marketing .	Operating Supplies	Telephone Directories for Departmental Use
Sales/Marketing .	Outdoor	Advertising—Outdoor
Sales/Marketing .	Outdoor	Billboards
Sales/Marketing .	Outdoor	Outdoor Advertising
Sales/Marketing .	Outside Sales Rep.	Marketing Service Fees
Sales/Marketing .	Outside Sales Rep.	Public Relations Service Fees
Sales/Marketing .	Outside Sales Rep.	Service Bureau Maintenance
Sales/Marketing .	Outside Services	Consultant Fees, Market Research
Sales/Marketing .	Outside Services	Customer Research/Survey—Outside Service
Sales/Marketing .	Outside Services	Direct Mail Expenses—Outside Service
Sales/Marketing .	P&ODC	Overnight Delivery (Marketing)
Sales/Marketing .	P&ODC	Freight Charges (Marketing)
Sales/Marketing .	P&ODC	Postage (Marketing)
Sales/Marketing .	P&ODC	Postage Meter Rentals (Marketing)
Sales/Marketing .	Promotion	Promotional Vouchers
Sales/Marketing .	Telecommunications	Registered Cable/Telex Address
Sales/Marketing .	Trade Shows	Booths at Trade Shows
Sales/Marketing .	Trade Shows	Trade Show Booth Construction
Sales/Marketing .	Trade Shows	Trade Show Promotional Items
Sales/Marketing .	Travel—Meals & Enter. . .	Meals—Entertainment
Telecom.	Contract Services	Music on Hold Service
Telecom.	Contract Services	Switchboard Repairs
Telecom.	Cost of Local Calls	Local Call Usage Expense
Telecom.	Cost of Local Calls	Telephone Local Trunk Costs
Telecom.	Cost of Long Dist. Calls .	Long Distance Call Usage Expense

Department/ Schedule	Account Name	Item Name
Telecom.	Cost of Long Dist. Calls .	Telephone Long Distance Trunk Costs
Telecom.	Costs of Internet Service .	Internet Access Costs
Telecom.	Operating Supplies	Telephone Cords
Telecom.	Operating Supplies	Telephone Face Plate
Telecom.	Operating Supplies	Telephone Headsets
Utilities	Electricity	Electricity
Utilities	Gas	Gas (for Utility Use)
Utilities	Oil	Oil (for Utility Use)
Utilities	Other Fuels	Geothermal Power
Utilities	Other Fuels	Propane (for Utility Use)
Utilities	Other Fuels	Solar Power
Utilities	Other Fuels	Wind Power
Utilities	Sewer	Sewer
Utilities	Sewer	Wastewater Surcharge
Utilities	Steam	Steam (for Utility Use)
Utilities	Utility Taxes	Taxes on Utilities (All Utilities)
Utilities	Water	Cogeneration of Water
Utilities	Water	Desalinization of Water
Utilities	Water	Water